- Lit Urells.

"Catching the Drift"

"Catching the Drift"

Authority, Gender, and Narrative

Strategy in Fiction | LAURA TRACY

Rutgers University Press | New Brunswick and London

Library of Congress Cataloging-in-Publication Data

Tracy, Laura, 1947–
"Catching the drift": authority, gender, and narrative strategy in fiction /
Laura Tracy.
p.   cm.
Bibliography: p.
Includes index.
ISBN 0-8135-1319-7
1. Psychoanalysis and literature.   2. English fiction—History and
criticism.   3. American fiction—History and criticism.   4. Transference
(Psychology) in literature.   5. Authors and readers.   6. Authority in
literature.   7. Feminist criticism.   I. Title.

PR830.P74T7 1988
823'.009'353—dc19   87-33698

British Cataloging-in-Publication information available

For Jessie and Aaron

Contents

Acknowledgments

I would like to express my gratitude and general indebtedness to all of my friends and colleagues who provided both emotional and intellectual support for this project; in particular to Barry Chabot, Lorna Irvine, Stanley Olinick, Michele Orwin, Jeanne Addison Roberts, and my editor Leslie Mitchner, without whose critical readings the final version would not exist.

"Catching the Drift"

"Catching the Drift"

Experience soon showed that the attitude which the analytic physician could most advantageously adopt was to surrender himself to his own unconscious mental activity in a state of evenly suspended attention, to avoid so far as possible reflection and the construction of conscious expectations, not to try to fix anything that he heard particularly in his memory, and by these means to catch the drift of the patient's unconscious with his own unconscious.

    —Sigmund Freud, "Two Encyclopedia Articles"

In this simple way the life long past is invented, which, as we know, thickens the present and gives all kinds of advice to the future.

    —Grace Paley, "Ruthy and Edie"

Transference Theory in Literature

S IGMUND FREUD stumbled upon the transference phenomenon during his treatment of Dora K. in December 1900. After three months with Freud, Dora precipitately broke off her analysis, rejecting Freud's interpretation that her chronic breathlessness and coughing spells were symbols demonstrating her erotic attachment to her father's mistress. Freud understood that her flight was not a direct response to the shocking content of his interpretation. It was less what he had said than his failure to consider how she heard it; it was, in fact, his unwitting separation of the message from the message bearer which provoked Dora's anger. As he reported when he published the case history five years after the event, the experience of treating Dora "obliged" him to speak of transference, for "within the theory of analytic technique . . . transference is an inevitable necessity."

According to Freud, transference occurs when "the patient is not satisfied with regarding the analyst in the light of reality as a helper and adviser. . . . On the contrary, the patient sees in him the return, the reincarnation, of some important figure out of his childhood or past, and consequently transfers onto him feelings and reactions which undoubtedly applied to his prototype . . . the patient produces before us with plastic clarity an important part of his life-story. . . . He acts it before us, as it were, instead of reporting it to us."[1] The patient fictionalizes the present, in words and deeds, creating a narrative composed by memories of past relationships.

Although Freud first identified transference as a therapeutic phenomenon, the concept also has profound implications for human relations outside the analytic situation. Extended to include a person's habitual and generally unconscious response to others in his or her environment, transference defines the attitudes that guide and, to some extent, even control perception of others. In theory and practice, transference functions as the ground of interpersonal relations of every type: parent and child, teacher and student, husband and wife, friendship, even writer and reader.

The transference phenomenon and narrative theory coincide at the point of the story. Analysts interpret transference response by making coherent the narrative their patients deliver to them piecemeal. Transference attitudes in fact become visible to the analyst precisely at moments of narrative disruption, when the pressure of repressed material creates an undeniable fissure in the fictional integrity the patient seeks in composing a life story for the analyst. The story the patient delivers verbally is, moreover, only a portion of the narrative the analyst interprets. Equally important are physical gestures; tones of voice; selection and placement of incidents and details; qualities of irony, humor, and pathos, all of which comprise a shadow narrative, the music accompanying the words of the patient's song. Attending to both the words and the music, the analyst's interpretations intend to effect a similar integration for the patient. In a sense, the analyst offers the patient a recomposed narrative, more coherent, more fluid, and more possible to live through than the one the patient has painfully discovered to be flawed in daily life.

Thinking of the transference phenomenon as a species of narrative calls into question the conventionally opposed concepts of truth and fiction. Trained as a scientist, Freud of course understood that his theoretical discoveries illuminated an underlying truth he connected to nature, beyond history and culture. Thus, for him, narrative was epistemologically unitary—if not divine, certainly undeniable, revelation. Contemporary social historians, literary theorists, and psychoanalysts have broadened that understanding. More recently, truth and fiction, connected to nature and culture, are recognized as themselves conceived in and directed by transference of ideological systems. A patient's narrative, therefore, while certainly informed by issues developed in the cauldron of early-childhood family relationships, is also affected by larger authority systems organizing the wider culture. As Freud correctly, and revolutionarily, discerned, positions of authority and power, submission and subordination, are reactions learned in response to real relationships; what he did not see is that these reactions are not necessarily inevitable and immutable. Systems of authority encoded as narrative structures "are like working apparatuses of ideology, factories for the 'natural' and 'fantastic' meanings by which we live. . . . Indeed, narrative may function on a small scale the way ideology functions on a large scale—as a 'system of representations by which we imagine the world as it is.' To compose a work is to negotiate with these questions: What stories can be told? How can plots be resolved? What is felt to be narratable by both literary and social conventions?"[2] Feminist theorists, like Rachel Blau DuPlessis, whose thinking I have just quoted, are concerned with the presence of multiple fictions in life, with comprehending "truth" as the ideological interpretation of a particular cultural and historical moment.

The question of narrative thus also encompasses the question of the speaker's authority. As Freud's case history of Dora K. makes clear, it is the writer whose authority over and within the text establishes the "truth" of the particular narrative fiction. That Freud was at least subliminally anxious about the power of the narrative act is lent credence by the five-year gap between the conclusion of Dora's analysis and his composition and publication of the case history. Ironically, it may have been his own unconscious transference to Dora and to his narrative which disrupted the certainty he proposed in the case history; it may have been his ambivalence which is symbolically represented in the silence preceding publication.[3] Dora's refusal to continue the "talking cure," an ironic reflection of the reader's power to reject textual authority, suggests that transference is as potent an issue for the reader as it is for the writer.

In this book I examine the effect of psychoanalytic transference in fiction, using the concept as a reading tool. I view the phenomenon from a dual perspective, that of the reader both consciously and unconsciously addressed by the writer, and that of the real reader's response to the text—in psychoanalytic terms, the reader's countertransference.

3

This sort of interpretation, of course, entails accepting the act of writing as a form of communication, although not necessarily understanding the text as a message-bearing document. Instead I consider the text a conversation with the writer. As with any conversation, the text needs to be understood through the written analogues to a speaker's physical gestures, facial expressions, mode of dress, and so forth. These are the symbolic details which convey the speaker's personality and enable the listener to place the speaker in a context larger than the particular verbal communication. Without such a context, as work done by J. L. Austin makes clear, communication is impossible.[4] Thus I direct critical concern toward a textual interpretation that includes the writer's conscious and unconscious imagination of the audience before whom the "speech act" is presented. The real reader joins a conversation in progress, just as the analyst joins a dialogue initially opened between the patient and the figures who inhabited his or her early childhood.

Like the notion of a personal unconscious, the concept of a literary unconscious is problematic and complex. As employed by literary critics, it frequently refers to images or subjects barred rather than removed from the writer's conscious expression.[5] To indict a writer on the grounds of unconscious failure to control technique, for example, is to imply that she would if she could. In contrast, here, I use the idea of the literary unconscious in the psychoanalytic sense. In his *Introductory Lectures on Psychoanalysis,* Freud defined as " 'unconscious' any mental process the existence of which we are obliged to assume—because, for instance, we infer it in some way from its effects—but of which we are not directly aware."[6] Freud alludes to affects appearing in the analytic situation, and in life, that are neurotic symptoms indicating the presence of material incompletely repressed from the patient's conscious mind. In daily life such failures of repression are visible as slips of the tongue, forgotten appointments, stammering, all the "psychopathology of everyday life." Philip Rieff points out that "memory, for Freud, is not a passive receiver whose performance can be measured quantitatively; it embodies a moral choice, a sequence of acceptances and rejections. . . . Since neurosis arises through the partial leakage of painful memories, the job of the analyst is to decipher entirely the palimpsest of the patient's mind, to illuminate all, not merely part of the obscure script."[7]

Like the analyst, the literary critic also is presented with a textual palimpsest in which unconscious material appears as the anomalies or distortions that disrupt narrative coherence. Such distortions, which can be detected in the confusion they engender in the real reader, represent the writer's unconscious separation of idea from word and are as obscure to the writer as they are to the reader. In a response analogous to that of the analyst, who often discerns the patient's transference by first becoming aware of and then interpreting his or her own countertransference to the patient, the real reader can piece together the writer's imagined reader by first working out his or her experience of the text.

In recent years examination of countertransference in analytic therapy accompanies an increasing self-scrutiny among members of the analytic community. Comtemporary analysts define countertransference as "the effects of the analyst's own unconscious needs and conflicts on his understanding or technique. In such cases the patient represents for the analyst an object of the past onto whom past feelings and wishes are projected . . . all expressions of the analyst's using the patient for acting-out purposes. We speak of acting out whenever the activity of analysing has an unconscious meaning for the analyst."[8] Failure to bring countertransference responses to conscious awareness results in a distorted analysis, sometimes leading to the patient's outright rejection of the analyst, as Dora K. rejected Freud.

Countertransference involves a complex and interesting paradox: it is both a violation of analysis and a certification that the analysis is proceeding correctly. The analyst strives for anonymity in his or her encounter with the patient, is generally seated behind the patient, keeps the office relatively devoid of characteristically personal details, and maintains neutrality in tone and gesture. He or she seeks, that is, to become the mirror in which the patient may see an authentic reflection. But "the act of understanding the patient's productions in analysis and the ability to respond to them skillfully is not based solely on logical conclusion. Frequently the analyst can observe that insight into the material come suddenly as if from somewhere within his own mind . . . the tool for understanding is the analyst's own unconscious."[9] As Freud realized, the analyst seems to "catch the drift" of the patient's unconscious mind with his or her own unconscious, bypassing intellectual examination, and locates his or her interpretations of the patient "by noting parallel reflections within himself."[10] Despite an impersonal facade, then, the analyst must achieve an intimacy with the patient characteristic of deeply personal relationships. This sort of intense empathy is easily analogized to the theoretical school of literary phenomenology, particularly as practiced by Georges Poulet. According to Poulet's work the "good" reader suspends distinguishing marks of external personality during the act of reading so that reader and textual voice may merge. Textual interpretation is grounded in this act of merger, which is shattered when the reader's attention is withdrawn from the text. Poulet predicates the act of understanding the text correctly on an initial act of identification by the reader, who will later exercise his or her critical faculty in order to articulate a textual interpretation.

Unfortunately, in a discussion of how to train students in his method, Poulet himself admitted that the evaluation of such a reading is as subjective as the reading itself. "What would Poulet do with a bad student of Poulet? . . . I would try to identify with my bad student, and I would not be able to do it; I would fail in this effort of identification. The sole criterion that I would have that Poulet's student was a bad student of Poulet would consist in the fact that Poulet could not identify with his student."[11] A good reading can be distinguished from a bad reading, therefore, only through the aegis of the reader's subjective consciousness, who, as every teacher of literature realizes, could be reading a self-created text rather than the one composed by the writer. Countertransference presents the analyst with similar dangers. Because the analyst understands the patient through the response of his or her own unconscious needs and conflicts, he or she must at some point gain awareness of these in order to disengage his or her own narrative from that told by the patient.

Analysts working on countertransference discern two movements within the phenomenon. The first develops from Freud's dictate that the analyst must listen to the patient with "an evenly suspended attention"[12] pervaded by what contemporary analysts call empathy, defined as "the process by which the analyst temporarily shares the quality, though not the quantity, of the patient feelings."[13] "The subjective experience of empathy is one of direct, nonmediated knowing. . . . For the most, one may be caught up with the patient's wishes and feelings, in a way not dissimilar to our suspension of disbelief in the presence of vividly realistic action on the screen or stage."[14] Considered psychoanalytically, empathy is a regression permitted by the analyst's conscious mind in the service of his or her work. Just as Poulet's "good"readings depend on the reader's disavowal of his or her own personality for the duration of the reading experience, so the analyst, during a portion of the analytic hour, suspends intellectual analytic abilities in order to apprehend the patient by experiencing the transference narrative at a nonmediated emotional level. Of course for the analyst to convey the knowledge thus garnered, this suspension must be temporary, limited by the analyst's self-awareness that permits recollection of the distance between the analyst's emotional processes and those of the patient. Equally, when the book is concluded, Poulet again becomes Poulet.

In addition to the empathic response, however, the analyst is subject to a response defined as identification. It occurs when the patient, attempting mastery of infantile issues, transfers responses to these issues onto the analyst. As the patient reenacts previously felt powerlessness, the analyst may feel the same sort of emotional frustration the powerless child experienced or may be placed in the role of the child's authority figures. In response the analyst may identify himself or herself with those remembered parental figures.[15] This dynamic is characteristic of a very young child's initial identification with the relationship system in the nuclear family. "There seems to exist an inborn tendency to identify, expressed first in relation to the nourishing person, the mother, then to other individuals."[16]

Similarly, it is a common enough occurrence for readers to "identify" with books—with a particular character, with the plot, with the thematic fantasy, or with some other element. Such identification often results in a mistaken, although stubbornly defended, reading of the text. Imitating the analyst's countertransference, this sort of reading results not merely in suspended disbelief but in identification with the writer to a degree that the emotional conflicts the writer possesses and unconsciously defends against are completely absorbed. The reader, of necessity, maintains the writer's system of defenses against conflicts now his or her own, blinded to real insight into the writer's use of methods and strategies in the text.

Analysts often discern the presence of "eccentric" countertransference responses—those motivated primarily by identification—by monitoring their somatic and emotional reactions during the analytic session. The analyst becomes bored or sleepy, fantasizes or daydreams; readers have similar experiences. Like analysts, readers need to be aware of idiosyncratic responses to certain themes, motifs, characters, situations, and styles. A reader alert to such emotional and physical responses can use them as clues to a perceptive interpretation of the text. For example, a reader who experiences Jane Austen's didactic narrator as overly intrusive, perhaps even browbeating, should consider his or her general response to that type of authority figure but at the same time use this now conscious sense of beleaguerment as material in constructing a reading of Austen's novels.

Identification and empathy are issues of equal importance for the writer as he or she addresses an imagined reader. Stephen Black argues that "the author, while writing, functions, as if he were engaged in a dynamic object relationship not only with his reader but also with his material,"[17] creating a transference relationship much like the one established by the patient to the analyst. The writer unconsciously expects of his imaginary reader the same sort of gratifications and frustrations he experienced in childhood, modified, of course, by later emotional and psychological development. Strategies and techniques he uses in the text are designed, consciously and unconsciously, to place his imagined reader in the position of authoritative parent, powerless child, or some mixture of the two, just as the patient transfers similar desires and conflicts onto the analyst. The real reader, then, may agree with Sartre that there are no bad books, only books whose reader one does not wish to become.[18]

In a successful analysis the patient's ego "splits" or dissociates into observing and experiencing segments; "introspection, attention, memory, judgment, evaluation, etc. [are] functions of the observing ego, while the experiencing functions are composed of the patient's emotional transference responses."[19] The analyst also accomplishes a split between the portion of his or her ego regressing in the service of the patient and the part retaining intellectual analytic capability. Real readers experience an analogous split, albeit ideally in sequential order rather than simultaneously. When the reader concludes the book, he or she should reactivate critical faculties and direct them toward understanding both the reading experience—the countertransference—and the text, paying particular attention to distinguishing subjective identifications from empathic and more distanced responses.

A successful text, like a successful analysis or critical interpretation, also depends on a split between the writer's experiencing and observing sensibilities during the creative process, particularly in delineating the structural position for the imagined reader. The writer will incorporate a greater proportion of subjective and unconscious material into the text when the identification response is primary and will exercise a greater degree of aesthetic and technical control when the empathic response is dominant. For example, writers of highly prescriptive genre literature such as melodramatic romance novels ironically are able to eradicate identification responses to their imagined readers because marketplace exigencies enable them to integrate their real with their imagined audiences. The writer who participates in an emphatic relationship with the imagined reader will be able to move from a temporary loss of intellectual and emotional distance toward a critical and evaluative posture in relation to the material as the result of consciously understanding the self and that the imagined reader does not coincide with the self.

This dynamic is similar to the patient's narrative, which becomes fragmented as unconsciously repressed material emerges. In the text, a writer's identification with the imagined reader produces a proportional quantity of anomalies and distortions that disrupt narrative coherence, so that intended strategies may be subliminally subverted. This sort of subversion is *unconscious* to the writer, for the process of identification is by definition fueled by unconscious needs, desires, and conflicts. There are writers, however, who consciously embed subversive narratives in their texts because they have imagined a reader who is subversive to the cultural period in which they write. Such a book might include a subtext of the sort examined by Sandra Gilbert and Susan Gubar, whose work demonstrates that nineteenth-century female writers covertly inscribed a female biography within an apparently conventional patriarchal narrative.[20] A good example of such conscious subversion occurs in Charlotte Brontë's *Jane Eyre*, particularly during the "happy ending" reconciling Rochester and Jane. To make the conclusion "happy," Brontë made certain to blind and cripple Rochester, ensuring an authentic marriage of "equals." This final scene, moreover, includes dialogue lending Jane the language of the male victor while Rochester sounds like the traditionally timid maiden.[21] Connecting these particular anomalies with the subtext narrating Jane's search for a mother figure, a search culminating in the affirmation of her ability to mother herself, reveals a concealed but nevertheless unified and coherent subtextual narrative. For critical interpretation, then, the concepts of transference and countertransference are most useful for illuminating anomalous texts that cannot be made coherent through subtextual readings. It is the relationship systems of these texts which such a reading can examine.

To summarize briefly, the writer's transference imago appears in the text as the relationship established with the imagined reader, a structural position then discerned by the real reader. In transferring both conscious and unconscious needs, desires, and conflicts onto the imagined reader, the writer places that reader in the relationship system he or she experienced as a child. Because familial systems of authority replicate cultural patterns, the position offered the imagined reader makes visible both personal and cultural necessity. The writer's unconscious identification with the imagined reader results in a text fragmented and disrupted; the writer's empathy with the imagined reader, on the other hand, may result in a subtext written in contradistinction to the overt narrative, which is nonetheless coherent and unified.

The real reader's countertransference is similarly responsive to identification and empathy through the aegis of the imagined reader. If the real reader strongly identifies with the position offered the imagined reader, the likelihood of a distorted or erroneous reading is high. In contrast, the reader who brings an empathic response to the imagined reader—initially merging with, later separating from—is able both to examine the reading experience—discerning the characteristics of the imagined reader—and to interpret the text objectively. The real reader here comprehends the imagined reader as a palimpsest. Using psychoanalytic interpretation as a model, the real reader produces textual meaning, not by removing layers to reveal a hidden core, but by understanding meaning to reside in the layers themselves.

Using psychoanalytic transference as a tool for reading necessarily calls into question the concept of authorial intention. This question, a relatively new one in the history of literary criticism, was introduced by the school of New Critics, who, in their justifiable effort to reform the anecdotal interpretation typical of nineteenth-century critical practice, came to consider the text as autonomous from its author. The famous 1946 essay "The Intentional Fallacy," written by W. K. Wimsatt and Monroe Beardsley,[22] Served to dispel the notion that the author's stated intentions concerning a text are relevant to its interpretation.

Post-New Criticism literary theorist E. D. Hirsch, Jr., has addressed the question in his larger discussion defining validity in the act of interpretation. Hirsch begins with his well-known distinction between textual meaning and significance: "Meaning is that which is represented by a text; it is what the author meant by his use of a particular sign sequence; it is what the signs represent. Significance, on the other hand, names a relationship between that meaning and a person, or a conception, or a situation, or indeed anything imaginable."[23] To Hirsch, authorial intention is directly connected with textual meaning, whereas significance involves the use made of the text by subsequent readers. Hirsch adds, however, that "the only question that can be relevantly at issue is whether the *verbal* meaning which the author intends is accessible to the interpreter of his text. . . . That a man may not be conscious of all that he means is no more remarkable than that he may not be conscious of all that he does."[24] In other words, Hirsch limits the question of the author's intended meaning to the structure and patterns of the words on the page, although he is careful to stress that "meaning is an affair of consciousness," and "consciousness is, in turn, an affair of persons . . . the meanings that are actualized by the reader are either shared with the author or belong to the reader alone."[25]

The concept of textual meaning actualized by the reader connects Hirsch's work to theorists in the school of reader-response theory. For these theorists, to varying degrees, textual meaning is allied to the reading process itself and resides in the transaction between the text and the reader. Unlike Hirsch, for example, Wolfgang Iser concentrates on the textual meaning located within the "gaps" or blank spaces of the text.[26] Such gaps invite the reader's participation to the extent that the reader becomes "co-creator of the work by supplying that portion of it which is not written but only implied."[27] Iser does admit, however, that the reader's imaginative activity is limited by the text, although he does not clearly describe how such circumscription takes place. Iser understands the writer's textual intentions to guide the reader's understanding, so he extends textual interpretation to meanings implied as well as those explicitly verbalized.

Further along the reader-response continuum is the work done from a psychological perspective by Norman Holland and David Bleich. Holland's central idea concerns the presence in each person of an "identity theme," defined as an individually characteristic style of coping with real experience. The reader brings this identity theme to bear upon the text, producing an interpretation as the result of transferring onto the text his or her characteristic patterns of defense and fantasy. Although Holland understands meaning to reside primarily in the reader, he does admit the idea of a somewhat autonomous text.[28] Bleich, on the other hand, in his "subjective criticism," locates textual meaning entirely in the mind of the reader and believes interpretation to be in no way constrained by an independent text.[29] These latter theorists, then, admit the question of authorial intention into their argument only insofar as its guides or matches the reader's perceptions of the text during the act of reading.

Between Hirsch on the one hand and Iser, Holland et al. on the other, a mediate position brings up the question of authorial intention when the writer is his or her own reader, or more precisely, the reader imagined by the writer. Because the imagined reader is addressed both consciously and unconsciously by the writer, the text, although it certainly bears marks of the writer's intentions in its verbal strategies, also may bear traces of the writer's unconscious conflicts in what seem to be counterintended responses produced in the real reader. For example, an authorially designated fairy tale is read as a novel because it includes a wealth of realistic incident; a melodramatic plot is coupled with philosophic intrusions from the narrative voice; a first-person narrator whom the reader is taught to trust disparages his own point of view. Such textual anomalies "may fit together," as David Gordon writes, "into a counter-intended meaning if we presume the agency of a specific unconscious process of distortion."[30] Examining the text from the perspective of psychoanalytic transference indicates that both what the writer says (the text's verbal patterns) and what the writer does not say (the text's blank spaces) are equally important in determining both the writer's intentions as to the effect the text has on an imagined reader and the effect actually produced on a real reader.

Subsumed under the question of authorial intention is yet another question: What is the text for? J. L. Austin's categories of language use, derived from his work on speech-act theory, are helpful in this regard. Consciously, the writer may intend the text to be "performative," or aimed at getting something done; "illocutionary," or doing something in the saying; or "perlocutionary," bringing about an effect by the performance.[31] When loosely translated into terms of consciousness and unconsciousness, however, Austin's categories collapse into each other. A writer might consciously intend the book to be performative, and while it may fulfill that intention to get something done, it may also be an unconscious illocutionary act, doing something *in* the saying, on the way to getting something else done. For example as I discuss further in chapter 2, the narrator of Ford Madox Ford's *The Good Soldier* intends to perform an act of retrospection, recreating nine years in his immediate past in order to separate historical reality from appearance. Yet, during his retrospective performance, he also unconsciously attempts to deny his participation in the sad affair he insists he only witnessed. Much of his narrative in fact functions to justify himself as a historian rather than a participant. In creating that narrator, did Ford intend his reader to respond to his narrator's innocence, the illocutionary position; to the narrator's guilt, the performative position; or to an assessment of the narrator as both guilty and innocent, the perlocutionary position?

Substituting, then, the concept of interpersonal transference for the categories of speech-act theory, it emerges that writers write to do something to someone—the consciously imagined reader; but in the performance, they create effects that have to do with the performance itself and with all the layers existing in the relationship established with that imagined reader. The question of to whom the text is directed also necessarily questions what the work consciously and unconsciously is intended to do to its imagined audience, or what the work is for. Just as psychoanalytic theory understands the individual as the culture writ small, so the question of textual intention asked in terms of the imagined reader is the contracted version of a larger question addressed to the text's cultural intentions and effects.

A clear example of this sort of double intention is the autobiographical text. The writer may intend to establish a historically accurate record but, at the same time, in the act of writing, create a fictive persona. Ironically, performing the autobiographical act certifies for the writer the existence of his or her historical persona, just as behind a conversation seemingly conducted to convey information lies the speaker's need to establish his or her "fictional" authority to do so.

Literary theorists' interest in the genre of autobiography has enormously increased during the past decade; it is an interest that also generated debate about generic definition. According to William Stengeman, "On the one side are those critics who continue to insist that autobiography must employ biographical—which is to say historical rather than fictional—materials. On the other side, there are those who assert the right of autobiographers to present themselves in whatever form they may find appropriate and necessary."[32] The continuum lies between the poles of fidelity to historical accuracy on the one hand and to the imaginative conception of one's life on the other.

The argument was initially engaged by Roy Pascal, in *Design and Truth in Autobiography*.[33] Pascal questioned the act of autobiography itself, for in its performance the autobiographer, by virtue of a self-conception determined after the fact, imposes a design where none is necessarily present. Pascal wondered whether it was perhaps more accurate to consider autobiography a combining of record and impression to produce a truth inaccessible from a straightforward adherence to facts and dates. Emphasizing autobiography as the *imaginative* truth of the writer's life renders its performance a creative act, a position also examined by James Olney in his distinction between the "bios" of biography and the "autos" of autobiography. He points out that critical work on biography antedates that done on autobiography, and this inconsistency is the result of a naive three-fold assumption about the writing of an autobiography: first, that the bios of autobiography could only signify "the course of a lifetime" or at least a significant portion of a lifetime; second, that the autobiographer could narrate his life in a manner at least approaching an objective historical account and make of that internal subject a text existing in the external world; and third, that there was nothing problematical about the autos, no agonizing questions of identity, self-definition, self-existence, or self-deception.[34]

Autobiography only aroused critical interest once the autos was recognized as problematic. The bios of autobiography then came to be considered the record of a life and the record of its perception. Obviously, as an autobiography is written while its subject lives, the record can be only partial. Autobiography so viewed becomes the portrait of the autobiographer at the time and in the act of writing, alone with the self-conceived history of the life itself. As Olney emphasizes, "It is through that act that the self and the life, complexly intertwined and entangled, take on a certain form, assume a particular shape and image, and endlessly reflect that image back and forth between themselves as between two mirrors."[35] From this perspective, not only does the autobiographer review the patterns of his or her life, but the very perceptions form the perceiving self.

It is at this point that the autobiographer's interpersonal transference onto the external world and in the text become important. Why, for example, would an autobiographer create one sort of persona rather than another? What is the effect, on a reader, of a victimized, suffering child-woman, to use the example of the English writer Jean Rhys, that the personality of an independent, assertive woman does not exercise? What sort of reader is this persona directed toward, and how does the imaginative conception of this reader affect the tone, style, language, and strategies used consciously and unconsciously in the text? Particularly interesting is a comparison between the fictional and autobiographical canons of a single writer. Does each genre address the same or a distinctly different imagined reader? Does this imaginary reader vary over time? Does the writer's imagined "autos" reader modify the figure of the imagined fictional reader? The autobiographer is subject to a transference response toward an imagined reader similar to that experienced by the fiction writer, equally susceptible to unconscious identification on the one hand and to conscious control through empathy on the other. The autobiographer's persona finds its mirror image in the narrator of the fictional text; each participates in the writer's imagined world in ways the writer unconsciously and consciously desires to behave in the real world.

Trained readers are taught to view with suspicion a naive reading that substitutes the narrator's voice for that of the writer, assuming one speaks for the other; and in fact, writers frequently use the distance between author and narrator as a central, text-motivating ambiguity. When we consider the writer in terms of psychoanalytic transference to an unconsciously imagined reader, however, the relationship between writer and narrator is significant in just the conflated terms it appears to a naive reader. Although the narrator often may not speak for the writer, the manner in which the narrator is involved in the textual world functions, from a psychoanalytic perspective, as a model of the writer's explicit and implicit relationship with the reader. The writer creates the narrator to act in an imagined world in much the same way he or she projects, or transfers, unconsciously held needs and desires onto the real-world among whom he or she lives. Ambiguities existing between a narrator and a textual world are analogous to ambiguities existing between the writer and the imagined reader. Transference as a reading tool, then, would be particularly useful as a method of illuminating texts containing highly ambiguous narrators.

Similarly, the autobiographer creates a persona to act in a reconstructed historical world, a world made fictional by virtue of the act of perceiving it. Critical work might begin with either position; that is, by defining the narrator's position in regard to the textual world and generating from it the writer's conscious and unconscious positioning of the imagined reader; or by defining the writer's position in regard to the real others in his or her life and focusing on the discrepancies between autobiographical data and the writer's conception of his or her relationship with the imagined reader. Although New Critics sought with reason to banish biographical material from critical interpretation, biographical research *is* a necessary adjunct to literary scholarship, for it serves the subsidiary but invaluable function of providing a larger context for the discrete text. Although biographical criticism certainly can degenerate into the unfortunate equating of the text with the events of the life, it also can regain for the text its vital element, reestablishing it as a dynamic encounter between personalities, engaging the real reader as once the writer engaged his or her imagined and historical readers.

The narrative unity sought by both the autobiographer and the creative writer resembles, of course, the personal coherence desired by the analysand. The latter is aided by the analyst, whose interpretations clarify the distinctions between transference and real-world responses. The real reader also seeks coherence, but his or her desire does not include a therapeutic motive. Rather, the unity the real reader seeks is like D. W. Winnicott's understanding of human creativity, defined by him as "a colouring of the whole attitude to external reality. . . . [C]ontrasted with this is a relationship to external reality which is one of compliance, the world and its details being recognized but only as something to be fitted in with or demanding adaptation."[36] For Winnicott, creativity is not solely involved in aesthetic production but also in providing the ground for the perception that life is valuable and worthwhile. Winnicott emphasizes that personal growth depends on learning to use real objects creatively, on developing an appreciation of the world as it is and yet retaining a sense of subjective authority. The real reader is creative in just this manner in the process and the aftermath of reading.

In the course of reading, the real reader makes two movements. First, he or she identifies with the imagined reader; later, he or she empathizes with the voice of the writer in the text. The transition from identification to empathy ideally permits the reader to experience the reality of the text first through a distorted subjective perception, later with an apprehension of the self meeting with and adapting the other for its own use. Creativity lies in this last position. Winnicott describes the sequential development of the self in relation to others in this way:

1. Subject relates to object.
2. Object is in process of being found instead of placed by the subject in the world.
3. Subject destroys object.
4. Object survives destruction.
5. Subject can use object.[37]

Loosely paraphrased, Winnicott believes that one must learn to recognize fundamental otherness in order to achieve a sense of subjective autonomy and authority. A person existing either in relation to or isolation from others is uncertain about boundaries and identity. In terms of Winnicott's developmental sequence as applied to the nature of the reading experience, the reader, first mistaking the text for him or herself, then discovers its autonomy and separateness, recuperating self-autonomy in the movement from identification to temporary empathic merger with the text, and finally uses the text to enrich and expand the real world to which he or she returns.

Issues of power and authority, of course, inevitably inform any relationship between self and other in the world. Within the connection between writer and reader such issues are crucially important because the creative act also is an authoritative act. The four writers examined in this book I selected both for the particular problems presented in their texts and because those texts display a loose schematic development from those marked by a predominantly unconscious and authoritative address to their imagined reader toward those employing a narrative address that invites collaboration in the creative process. I believe this progression involves the distinction between creating a lie and constructing a fiction. The former involves the reader (real and imagined) in a fundamentally destructive relationship; the latter uses the writer's conscious awareness of the conflicts transferred onto the imagined reader as the means of making fiction a dialogue between self and other. Therefore, in beginning with Jean

Rhys's work, moving through fiction written by Ford Madox Ford and Nathaniel Hawthorne, and concluding with Jane Austen's canon, and a brief look at short stories written by Grace Paley and Alice Munro I offer an affirmatively ascending argument for the personal and cultural use of literature.

Meredith Skura, analyzing the literary use of the psychoanalytic process, notes that the question of literature as therapy is "closer to moral than to aesthetic criticism" in the sense that Freud's "whole intellectual development can be seen as a series of increasingly complex answers to the single and essentially moral question of how we can cope with our uncivilized instincts."[38] As Skura reminds us, creative writers, as well as literary theorists, have been concerned with the use of literature. Iris Murdoch, according to Skura, "defines the good novel as 'therapy which resists the all-too-easy, life of consolation and fantasy'; bad novels, [Murdoch suggests] merely work out an author's 'personal conflicts in a tightly conceived myth' with no respect for things as they are rather than as the author might wish them to be."[39]

In constructing the chronology from Rhys to Austen, I extend Murdoch's proposition to argue that good literature is fantasy constrained by the reality of relationship systems and that as such, it intrinsically bears within it the potential for changing those systems. A writer who becomes aware of the screen of unconscious material through which she addresses her reader should enable the real reader also to become conscious of those distortions and, therefore, to know the other as other. In my continuum Austen emerges as a writer gradually comprehending the necessary distortions she transferred onto reality in order to live with it and recognizing those distortions as lies she created to permit desire and defense into social life. In discussing Austen's canon, I refer to work done by Nancy Chodorow on female psychodynamic development. Chodorow argues that because Western child-rearing practices require the female parent to provide primary nurturing during the period of infancy and early childhood, female children enter adulthood with fluid ego boundaries and so find their most comfortable relationships when connected to other people in their environment. At their best, these relationships become "good family" structures encouraging dissent and autonomy while maintaining a larger web of emotional connection.

Just as Chodorow understands that cultural child-rearing practices affect individual self-development, so it is possible to reverse her proposal, to perceive individual growth both as a model for, and as effecting cultural change. Literature traditionally makes cultural fantasies visible, both in terms of textual content and formal criteria. Chodorow's work indicates that female writers can offer a model, historically suppressed, for the conscious construction of relationships marked by the exchange of authority. Austen's canon displays a radical restructuring of her narrative address. She provides an example of how a writer's progressive consciousness about the reader she imagined for her work allows the real reader to enter the text as a collaborator in a relationship now based on mutual uncertainty, connected through compassion instead of domination.

In contrast, Jean Rhys is an example of a writer who encoded cultural unconsciousness in her address to her imagined reader, causing her work to be marred by an underlying hostility toward the individual reader as Rhys maintains an authority system which suppresses the female voice. Unconscious assimilation of that system meant, for Rhys, that her work was marked by a severe separation between form and content, between her unconscious desires and the articulation of her subject. I chose to begin with Rhys and to conclude with Austen to allow their work to act as framing devices for my larger proposal, which assumes that literature can produce both individual and cultural change. As "frame tales" Rhys and Austen become background for the cultural foreground made visible in the work of Ford Madox Ford and Nathaniel Hawthorne.

Although the work of both male writers serves to illuminate traditional patriarchal systems of authority, their work is contrasted, like that of Rhys and Austen, in terms of each one's address to his imagined reader. Ford, like Rhys, produced fiction based on a pervasive unconsciousness of the conflicts he transferred onto the reader he imagined for his work and, therefore, of the relationship he constructed with his real reader. As a male writer, Ford's work expresses issues raised by Chodorow—that if female children develop fluid ego boundaries requiring emotional connection, male children develop self-conceptions that define themselves as *not* female, not like their mothers. Boys, then, unlike girls, come to find comfortable those relationships marked by separation and hierarchy. Ford's work, in particular, takes as its subject sentimental romantic fantasies involving the cultural idealization of women yet at the same time subtly authorizes its male narrator, denying the implied mutuality of the romantic situation. In terms of the wider culture, Ford's work implicitly and ironically reinforces patriarchal use of the connection between knowledge and power as his narrators pretend to possess neither.

In this continuum, Nathaniel Hawthorne moves closer to Austen's reappraisal of cultural structures. Hawthorne, unlike Ford, diplays in his work a conscious apprehension of the system of authority inherent in the creative process: one which reflects cultural patterns of domination and submission. Hawthorne sought to ameliorate this hierarchy through an idealization of his imagined reader which, he hoped, would rebound onto his position as writer, lending to each an equality engendered in a mutual transcendence of the culture. Instead of embracing Ford's romantic mythos, Hawthorne took as his subject the struggle between men and women separated by cultural inequity. Ironically, therefore, Hawthorne's work, like Ford's, may lead present readers to a reassessment of Freud's oedipal theory. In its cultural implications, the oedipal theory suggests that the male child, abandoning his erotic desire for his mother, accepts instead his symbolic entrance into a culture that promises him his father's authority. Hawthorne's work indicates that although he consciously understood that male authority in the patriarchal system is sanctioned by degrading the female, yet he was unable to work through the idealization of the mother required by the oedipal resolution. Although his fiction contains several portraits of strong, independent women, his books ultimately validate the asexual feminine ideal that is the necessary ad-junct of the oedipal renunciation. It is this latter idealization which informs his unconscious address to his imagined reader. In the same way the oedipally idealized woman is denied public power, Haw-thorne addresses a reader he renders fundamentally powerless, fro-zen in the status of sacred icon.

Evelyn Keller, in her examination of the cultural connections among knowledge, power, and domination in the development of gender identity, says, "A dynamic conception of autonomy leaves unchal-lenged a 'potential space' between self and other—the 'neutral area of experience' that, as Winnicott (1971) describes it, allows the temporary suspension of boundaries between 'me' and 'not-me' required for all empathic experience—experience that allows for the creative leap be-tween knower and known. It acknowledges the ebb and flow between subject and object as the prerequisite for both love and knowledge."[40] I think the text is just such a "potential space," both for the writer and the real reader, where each can recognize the other through the under-standing of the transference phenomenon. In concluding, I offer brief readings of contemporary work by Grace Paley and Alice Munro in order to show how cultural change both is effected by and itself influ-ences literary structures. Finally, "catching the drift" of the individual writer means catching cultural drift and perhaps understanding that a tide, historically competitive, bears within it a cooperative depth.

CHAPTER 1

Jean Rhys: The Daughter's Revenge

> So as soon as I could I lost myself in the immense world of books, and tried to blot out the real world which was so puzzling to me. Even then I had a vague, persistent feeling that I'd always be lost in it, defeated.
> —Jean Rhys, *Smile, Please*

I N 1939, despite the publication of four books and several collections of short stories, Jean Rhys was lost in an obscurity so profound that those few readers who knew her work believed she was dead. It was not until 1955, after Rhys herself answered an advertisement placed by the BBC seeking information about her, that her novels attained any substantial public notice. Even so, until the 1966 publication of *Wide Sargasso Sea*, acknowledgment of Rhys's artistic merit was confined to a small, enthusiastic coterie.

Yet in the eighth decade of her life, Rhys earned the sort of fame almost designed to compensate for her earlier public failure. *Wide Sargasso Sea* won the prestigious W. H. Smith Literary Award in England, and Rhys was made a Fellow of the Royal Society of Literature. In 1978 she was given the CBE (Commander of the Order of the British Empire) for her service to literature. All of her pre–World War II novels were reissued. Her first novel, *Quartet*, was made into a film. Nevertheless, for Rhys fame and relative financial security came too late to bring with it a measure of peace—and perhaps the key to comprehending Rhys's novels is the understanding that fame would always have been too late to overcome the defeat she desired.

The discrepancy between Rhys's long obscurity and subsequent status raises several questions. Was her work inimical to the majority of readers between the wars when her books were first published because she focused on the alien and estranged female members of society, oppressed victims of a restrictive culture? Did her books, in their fierce concentration on such issues as female subjugation, poverty, and powerlessness, speak with a rage unacceptable to her historical matrix? Certainly Rhys's novels are focused on the existential anguish engendered in a female protagonist living at the margins of a patriarchal culture. But, using psychoanalytic transference as a reading tool to examine the relationships among the reader Rhys addresses, her narrator, her protagonist, and Rhys as author, this chapter indicates that Rhys's earlier books disappeared from public view as the consequence of her failure to raise cultural structures to the level of conscious scrutiny or to include or deal with the emotional and psychological continuities of her protagonists' lives. This failure emerges from Rhys's unconscious desire to replicate in her reader her sense of personal victimization and defeat, at the same time denying the reader her personal salvation, the creative art and authority of composition.

There exists a general consensus among critics that autobiographies written by women can be distinguished from those written by men. Mary G. Mason notes that "nowhere in women's autobiographies do we find the patterns established by the two prototypical male autobiographers, Augustine and Rousseau. . . . On the contrary . . . the self-discovery of female identity seems to acknowledge the real presence and recognition of another consciousness, and the disclosure of female self is linked to the identification of some 'other.' "[1] Although critics generally agree that the autobiographical project involves the writer in the effort to construct a coherent narrative, thereby shaping the random events of his or her life into a consciously or unconsciously imposed pattern, "Irregularity rather than orderliness informs the self-portraits by women. The narratives of their lives are often not chronological and progressive, but disconnected, fragmentary, or organized into self-sustained units rather than connecting chapters."[2]

Although every novel is not an autobiography, autobiographies and fiction are both acts of imagination behind which can be traced the residue of conscious and unconscious choices whose integration forms a personality. For Rhys, however, the boundary between autobiography and fiction was ambiguous. She wrote nothing at all until, at the age of twenty, she began a journal after the unhappy end of her first love affair. She herself has acknowledged that her work always was a therapeutic as well as an aesthetic act, her novels the vehicles into which she transferred emotional distress. In her autobiography, *Smile Please*, Rhys describes her initial journal-writing experience as impulsive and obsessed behavior; she felt as if "it wrote her." All her novels were written in the same manner, as she pursued the work under her hand by instinct, developing its shape and structure according to demands made by its internal coherence. This does not imply that Rhys was not an exceedingly careful stylist, perhaps even a perfectionist. According to her last editor, Diana Athill, Rhys would not permit publication of *Wide Sargasso Sea* until she had tinkered with the manuscript for a decade. Even after its publication she accused Athill of persuading her to publish an unfinished book. Rereading it, she had discovered two unnecessary words: "one was 'then,' the other 'quite.' "3 Nonetheless, her subjects were drawn from an emotional reservoir continually replenished by her real-life experiences. The early journals, for example, she later translated into *Voyage in the Dark,* her third novel. In fact, when she considered writing her formal autobiography, quite late in life, she realized that much of the material she defined as autobiographical had been consumed in her fiction.

Despite the compulsive quality of her composition, Rhys's translation of her life into fiction was not an attempt to bestow meaning and order on that life. If we agree that "the self . . . is largely defined by the choices one makes,"4 Rhy's novels emerge as a history of forfeiting choice, of avoiding self-definition with an almost conscious refusal to impose order or to find meaning. Rhys acted in consonance with Western cultural patterns linking objectivity with the masculine and therefore authoritative, while confusion is connected with subjectivity and therefore the feminine. Her career asks an implicit question about female writers in a patriarchal culture. To become speaking subjects, what are women required to give up? In a peculiar way, Rhys remained loyal to the civilization which attempted to silence her. Her novels are marked by a consistent failure to assert narrative authority, to explicitly empower either her narrator or her protagonist. Despite her compulsion to write, then, she does not seem to have identified herself as a writer. Instead, she remained "feminine," that is, passive, submissive, out of control, creative apparently despite herself.

Rhys's four early novels display a pattern familiar to female autobiography. Each is a fragment, an episode in a story composed of disjointed moments in time. Each defines its female protagonist by her response to a more powerful male other. Each is also dominated by a rage narratively identified as a general despairing fury at female life in the twentieth century, coupled with pervasive depression about the possibility of change. The emotional paralysis of each protagonist seems to obviate both a primary motive for autobiography—the "desire to synthesize, to see one's life as an organic whole, to look back for a pattern"[5]—and the desire to tell a story.

Rhys does not tell stories. The plots motivating her five novels are skeletal. They evoke the sense of an Ur-myth, outlines on which to hang primary emotions. The emotions, too, are carefully limited, restricted to depression and anger. Though Rhys's novels are about love affairs, affirmative, life-enhancing love does not exist in them. The challenge for a reader is to comprehend the source of the energy from which Rhys has drawn novels seemingly created out of a void so bleak that words and actions drift soundlessly, without meaning, change, or hope. The challenge for Rhys's reader, in the face of such willful hopelessness, is to understand the creative authority concealed behind the ethos of despair, to make sense of the critical acclaim epitomized by A. Alvarez, who identified Rhys, toward the end of her life, as "the best living English novelist."[6] Rhys's work cannot be dismissed as aesthetically flawed, nor can it be ignored as the misguided outpourings of a crippled personality. As Thomas Staley realized, "her fiction reflects a complex of values and an attitude toward life which both undercuts and opposes so many of the most cherished values, both public and private, of the bourgeois world.

There is an implicit challenge in all of her work to the entire fabric of social and moral order which governs so much of society."[7] But there is more to the challenge than a simple satire of the bourgeoisie; there is the paradox of the work itself: why did she write; whom did she imagine as her reader; where in the texts is located the ironic vision implicit in the juxtaposition through which she sacrifices her protagonist to despair while she invests herself with the power of the author?

It is impossible to understand Rhys's imagined reader, and therefore the relationship established between that reader and Rhys as author, without first examining her canon. The four early novels, set in twentieth-century Europe between World Wars I and II, concentrate on a figure consistent in her work. The first of these, *Quartet*, establishes Rhys's pattern with its protagonist, Marya Zelli, who is caught in a triangular relationship with a married couple after her own husband is arrested and imprisoned for smuggling contraband. Left destitute in Paris, Marya accepts Lois Heidler's invitation to share the Heidler apartment, although she intuits an underlying motive in the Heidler's apparent charity. The epigraph Rhys appended to the novel signals this awareness to the reader: "Beware the Good Samaritan—Walk to the right / or hide thee by the roadside out of sight / Or greet them with the smile that villains wear."[8] Marya's intuition is proved correct when Hugh Heidler makes his sexual desire for her explicit, and she realizes that his wife, trying to keep the marriage intact, has agreed to act as his procurer.

Quartet is autobiographical in a particular way. It documents the affair between Rhys and Ford Madox Ford when both were members of the expatriate artist community in 1924 Paris. *Quartet* and Rhys's second novel, *After Leaving Mr. Mackenzie*, focus on the affair and its aftermath, when Rhys considered herself abandoned by Ford. These two books, at least, seem to have been written with a very specific reader in Rhys's mind: Ford himself. They must be interpreted as attempts at revenge for what she considered Ford's emotional brutality. The anger pervading the novels therefore is both specific and general, at Ford as seducer and at the culture which condoned, with unarticulated sanctions against her, the subsequent abandonment.

But Rhys's epigraph also heralds a more concealed aspect of *Quartet*. The novel places Marya in the position of spiritual outlaw, the sort of antiheroic posture familiar in Western contemporary literature. Like her existential brothers, Marya is estranged from a culture unconscious of itself. She is an outlaw because to be in power implies the domination of someone or something more vulnerable. An outlaw, in contrast, is aware of a failing within the wider culture and defines him or herself as a figure foregrounded against that flaw. Because she stands against a delimited set of values, she implicitly asserts another set. But for Marya, that self-definition, and the self-confidence inherent within it, remain obscure. She recognizes herself solely a powerless victim. She thus dissipates her anger at the Heidlers in hysteria and transforms her outrage into passionate love for her seducer. She becomes another familiar figure, the woman scorned; the more deeply she loves, the more completely she is rejected. From a rebel posture, she gradually assumes the aspect of betrayed humanity.

This reversal from betrayer to betrayed, beloved to rejected lover, occurs in each novel. In each, also, the protagonist's transformation is inexplicable to her and yet constitutes the core event of her life. Julia Martin, for example, the heroine of *After Leaving Mr. Mackenzie*, conceives of her rejection as "the turning point of [my] life." "I was all right till I met that swine MacKenzie. But he sort of—I don't know—he sort of smashed me up. Before that I'd always been pretty sure that things would turn out all right for me, but afterwards I didn't believe in myself anymore. I only wanted to go away and hide."[9] Similarly, the eighteen-year-old Anna Morgan of *Voyage in the Dark* relegates herself to a life of demiprostitution after she is seduced by and falls in love with a much older, more sophisticated man. Although Anna survives her abortion, Rhys has stated elsewhere that her publisher forced her to recast those terminating paragraphs. As originally written, the ending implied that death is the inevitable conclusion of Anna's failed love affair. Much as

Charlotte Brontë at her father's suggestion altered the ending of *Villette* to permit the novel to close, if not happily, at least ambiguously, so Rhys, also heeding a male authority figure's advice, modified her bleak comprehension of Anna's life. That Rhys and Brontë should respond to similar pressures is not entirely coincidental; both identified themselves as minority members of a dominant culture. Yet where Brontë tries in her writing to entangle her protagonists' lives with the complexly depicted lives of her other characters in order to face the cultural forces promoting female submission, Rhys reduces the scope of her protagonists' lives to the confines of a single rented room. They exist on a continuum charted by Sasha Jansen in *Good Morning, Midnight*: "A room. A nice room. A beautiful room. A beautiful room with bath. A very beautiful room with bath. A bedroom and sitting-room with bath. Up to the dizzy heights of the suite. . . . Swing high. . . . Now, slowly, down. A beautiful room with bath. A room with bath. A nice room. A room. . . ."[10] The private estrangement Rhys's protagonists suffer is mirrored by an equally arid and isolated world. As Sasha finally realizes, "A room is a place where you hide from the wolves outside and that's all any room is."[10]

Sasha Jansen, in Rhys's fourth novel, is older than Julia Martin, Marya Zelli, and Anna Morgan. She is more clearly at the outer margins of a life lived for and through men. She is alone in Paris between the wars, where she has returned with money for some weeks on holiday, yet not enough to allay her omnipresent anxiety concerning her future poverty. Paris, for Sasha, is the emotional equivalent of a mine field, fraught with memories of separation and loss. She must avoid certain streets, certain bistros, certain times of day; she must avoid awakening the pain of her original years in the city, when she was beloved, loved, and betrayed. Thus Sasha is a more clearly delineated portrait of Marya, Julia, and Anna. Even when Rhys writes about these women after their affairs have ended, all three retain attachments to the men they loved. Sasha is adrift, her lover transformed into a pervasive emotional malaise of pain and despair. In this she is the prototypical figure of all Rhys's early protagonists, although all are in many ways interchangeable. An overview of Rhys's canon reveals each protagonist as an isolated, fragmentary personality, static in circumstance, cut off from the possibility of self-development, finally defeated by a passive acquiescence to forces she perceives as external to herself and too powerful to withstand.

Most important, all four women have transformed their anger into crippling depression. The rage fundamental to each personality emerges as hopeless impotence. Because no Rhys protagonist is permitted to realize herself as responsible for her own life, none possesses an understanding of the roots of her distress. Each instead is thrust by Rhys will-less into the world of the text. Each, lacking a sense of personal continuity, also perceives herself as the victim of an equally ahistorical and merciless culture.

Significantly, this pervasive anger, although not the paralyzing passivity, marked Rhys's writing practices. According to Diana Athill. "She wrote a novel . . . because she had no choice, she did it—or 'it happened to her'—for herself, not for others, in that it was at least partly therapeutic."[11] Spurring these bursts of compulsive composition was fury, the sort of rage accumulated through months and years of private brooding on public abuse. In her autobiography, Rhys remembers her first journals were written after she "accidentally" bought some brightly colored quill pens and a student's notebook to brighten her dismal boarding house room. Then, "My fingers tingled, and the palms of my hands. I pulled a chair up to the table, opened an exercise book, and wrote 'This is my Diary.' But it wasn't a diary. I remembered everything that had happened to me in the last year and a half [After her first devastating love affair.] I remembered what he'd said, what I'd felt, I wrote on until late into the night, till I was so tired that I couldn't go on, and I fell into bed and slept."[12] The next day her landlady remonstrated with her, saying her downstairs neighbor had complained about Rhys's equally loud laughter and crying in the writing process. Rhys, that is, wrote to achieve catharsis of long-simmering emotions, which emerged with a force indicative of the concomitant intensity of her long-suppressed aggression. Her books, although consciously written for herself, found an unconsciously imagined reader in the men who had abandoned her, whom she would expose, and for whose benefit she would now set the record straight.

Rhys's explicit denial of any desire for an audience is refuted by her overwhelming concern that her writing reflect "truth." As she defined the concept, truth implied honesty, or realistic representation, a desire to deny the distortion of individual perception. Writing her autobiography, therefore, was particularly problematic because although "a novel, once it had possessed her, would dictate its own shape and atmosphere, and she could rely on her infallible instinct to tell her what her people would say and do within its framework, . . . in a factual account she would have to rely on memory, not instinct, and this alarmed her. Her honesty was uncommonly strict, so she felt that the only dialogue she could use in such a book would be that which she was perfectly sure she remembered exactly."[13] Yet her autobiography is as carefully constructed as are any of her novels. In fact, her general overscrupulosity in the aesthetic structuring of all her books refutes the compulsive condition she claimed impelled her to write. Her novels and her autobiography are too well made, too carefully constructed, to be the products of an obsessed writer overwhelmed by her material. Spareness and clarity of prose buttressed by an intricacy of structure relentlessly drive her protagonists toward defeat and degradation. At best, it is possible to credit Rhys's claim only for her first draft; her finished manuscripts are the products of painstaking revision. The fury behind her novel writing is a controlled emotion, employed, perhaps unconsciously, as an aesthetic device to structure and shape.

The analysand's transference responses, crucial to analytic interpretation, appear to the analyst at moments when the patient's story is at variance with the manner of delivery. Reflecting the analytic situation, transference in a literary work can become apparent through anomalies between the narrative structure and the content—between, for example, Rhys's extraordinary attention to design and language, indicating her extreme perfectionism and concomitant active assertion of creative authority over the text, coupled with exceptionally passive content or story. This discrepancy is visible in both the novels and autobiography. Her initial three-volume journal can in fact be viewed as the template she continually redeveloped in her fiction, achieving its final rewritten form in *Smile Please*, the autobiography.

At a first reading, the autobiography seems to be a series of anecdotes, beads strung together on the metaphorical chain of Rhys's memory. Her intent, according to Diana Athill, "was that she would not attempt a continuous narrative but would catch the past here and there, at points where it happened to crystallize into vignettes."[14] In this, the autobiography, in its overt structure, closely resembles the novels. Neither moves along a linear plot design, focusing instead on achronological time shifts exposing the protagonist's interior experience at moments of particularly relevant emotion. Fracture, fragmentation, halts, and pauses, all establish a sense of stasis in movement, illumination accompanied by great pain. Rhys, of course, tutored by Ford and writing at the time and in the tradition of Joyce and Eliot, was a modernist. She displayed their affinity for, as Staley writes, "a conscious artistry, a predilection for the formal properties and organic elements of art, a deep commitment to the allusive, the mythic, and a subordination of the traditional narrative concerns of the realistic novel such as plot, event, and resolution of the characters' circumstances."[15]

Yet the style and precepts of modern art served, much as for Ford, to conceal an integrated structure underlying the apparent fracture of her overt style, a structure necessarily hidden because of its distinct variance with narrative content. Rhys's autobiography tells the story of defeat, of continual victimization. The overt structure of her memories emphasizes this content, encapsulating each new anecdote as a fresh, unconnected chapter, reflecting discontinuity and isolation. Each vignette concludes with a statement of despair, although she expressly does not make a pattern through which she could define and therefore control her life. Instead, she describes herself as the victim of her mother's cold reserve, her father's benign neglect, her nurse's active malevolence, her culture's racism and sexism. Although Rhys was a white woman in a country (Dominica) with a majority black population only two generations removed from slavery, she herself had absorbed a personal sense of colonialism marked by her extreme sensitivity to oppression. Modernism, emphasizing authenticity, alienation, isolation, and estrangement, served as the objective correlative of her interior despair.

Using the effaced narrative posture, developed first by Flaubert and later in the work of the British modernists, allowed Rhys to create a work which explicitly denied interference from the writer's prejudices. Her autobiography is permeated by the flat, unemotional tone of the historical chronicle. Describing one of many humiliating experiences during her school years, Rhys writes, "I borrowed a needle and strong cotton, went into the room where we left our hats and sewed a large tuck in each garter. Now, though not so smooth as some of the others', my stockings were passable. But as soon as I got home my mother noticed the change and objected so strongly to my wearing anything tight round my knees that I had to take the tucks out. Again my black stockings drooped." Rhys offers no analysis of the relationship between mother and daughter. Inevitably, it seems, the mother *would* object, the daughter *would* suffer. Rhys's anger at the suppression of dialogue between them is itself suppressed, transformed into a passive submission in the face of an inexorable authority. Later in the autobiography she is explicit about her understanding of that authority: "I dreaded growing up. I dreaded the time when I would have to worry about how many proposals I had, what if I didn't have a proposal? This was never told me but it was in every book I read, in people's faces and the way they talked."[16] She experienced authority as pervasive, an inescapable domination so general it must be real. That it was, in part, her own response which stifled her life was never, even in writing her autobiography, a concept she consciously examined. The tone of the work implies that even an autobiography, by definition a work based on the distortions of memory and skewed by individual perception, is no more than an accurate record of reality. The fragmented structure and the passively defeated content combine to create a portrait of the writer compelled to stammer out memories of continually recurring victimization and abuse unrelated to the writer's perspective on the world.

Instead Rhys's "reality" is a careful construction designed to persuade her reader that the active perfectionism and relentless creative drive were actually a passive acquiescence to an external compulsion. Rhys's memories all emphasize loss: her "first clear connected memory" at the age of six, when her birthday party marked the last family gathering in the beautiful villa before its sale was followed by the dispersal by her brothers and sisters; her memory of Meta, the nursemaid, who "had shown me a world of fear and distrust, and I am still in that world"; her memory of her mother, who "drifted away from me and when I tried to interest her, she was indifferent."[17] Her vignettes, apparently random though poignant samples of her early life, are in fact carefully selected, each memorializing a moment of personal humiliation she never forgot.

Rhys's feigned passive acquiescence to memory masks her deliberate choice to describe life in a series of static exterior views. Her use of an estranged narrator gives Rhys the distance of a witness, so that she need not participate even here, in the memories of her own life. For example, Rhys describes her decision to remain in England, where she went at seventeen to become an actress: "During a vacation from the academy I went to Harrogate to visit an uncle. It was there I heard of my father's death. My mother wrote that she could not afford to keep me at the academy and that I must return to Dominica. I was determined not to do that, and in any case I was sure that they didn't want me back. My aunt and I met in London to buy hot-climate clothes, and when she was doing her own shopping I went to a theatrical agent in the Strand, called Blackmore, and got a job in the chorus of a musical comedy called Our Miss Gibbs." Here she focuses on a string of events she has constructed in a cause-and-effect sequence. While tacitly admitting she disobeyed her mother's request and used a certain amount of ingenuity to do so, she omits any sense of autonomy or excitement she might have felt. Acts indicating she had taken control of her own life are thus described without any reference to the relationship systems against which she rebelled. Rhys demonstrates the same loose concept of determinism again, when she first has an opportunity to publish some of her short stories: "As soon as I was outside the flat I started feeling reluctant to let anyone see what I had written. I did take the notebooks round to the house the next day, but instead of going up to Mrs. Adam's flat on the second floor I left them with the concierge. I thought that Mrs. Adam probably got a lot of manuscripts and letters, and if mine was forgotten, well, that would be fate and have nothing to do with me."[18]

Having disengaged herself, Rhys places the characters of her narrative—her fictional protagonists and in her autobiography those with whom she lived—in the foreground. By emphasizing details of their personalities and circumstances, she invites the reader to identify with them. Ironically, although the technique is identical in both genres, the conquences for the reader are not, for in the autobiography, the reader's identification with the foreground characters, whom Rhys describes victimizing her, puts the reader in a class with the villains.

Rather than functioning as a catharsis through which she could dissipate emotions in a self-made world, Rhys's writing recreates the hierarchy of power and authority she experienced but ironically allows her surreptitiously to exercise the domination she believed she suffered in reality. Whereas readers often comment that her novels are emotionally "devasting" or "depressing," for Rhys, creating them was her salvation, as she expressly states in her autobiography. In none of her novels is her protagonist an artist in any medium, with the possible exception of Anna Morgan, who acts in the chorus of a traveling theater troupe. The creativity Rhys discovered as her own solution to a life of confused despair, she nowhere offers to her protagonists or, by extension, to the reader she encourages to identify with those protagonists. Creativity, in the form of narrative manipulation, is reserved for her narrator, the text's internal extension of Rhys as author.

The unremitting cruelty the narrator displays toward the protagonists in the early novels is demonstrated in each book's conclusion.
Feminist literary theorists have realized that conclusions represent
repressions of alternate versions as well as resolutions in narrative.
Rhys's conclusions go further, repressing, suppressing, and oppressing her protagonists. For Marya Zelli, in *Quartet*, the end comes
when, still desperately in love with her husband, she nevertheless
"began to laugh insultingly. Suddenly he had become the symbol of
everything that all her life had baffled and tortured her. Her only idea
was to find words that would hurt him—vile words to scream at
him. . . . He caught her by the shoulders and swung her sideways
with all his force. As she fell, she struck her forehead against the edge
of the table, crumpled up and lay still."[19] Julia Martin, finally degraded by accepting money from Mr. Mackenzie, an act signaling and
sealing her debasement by him, is reduced to life as one animal
among other voracious beasts: "The street was cool and full of gray
shadows. Lights were beginning to come out in the cafes. It was the
hour between dog and wolf, as they say."[20] Although the original
ending Rhys wrote for Anna Morgan in *Voyage in the Dark* was modified in the direction of ambiguity, it remains clear that Anna's dream
"about starting all over again, all over again"[21] only can result in
continuing her life of hopeless despair, moving from one lover to the
next as she makes a cultural and emotional descent toward a social
abyss. This is a pit already inhabited by Sasha Jansen, who understands that the way she receives her final lover in the novel represents
her present life: "I lie very still, with my arm over my eyes, as still as if
I were dead."[22]

Rhys's work, like her protagonist, is marked by nostalgia, the yearning for an existence lived in fantasy. She falls into the gap created by
desire, the perpetually sentimental memory of an object absent by
virtue of an initial recognition of individual limitation, of the loss of
infantile omnipotence. Rhys's perfectionism is engendered by this
nostalgia, as she continually seeks the ideal book to recapture an
experience that is ideal precisely because her imagination made it so.

Her concern with form is a concern for self-presentation, a concern imitated by her protagonists as they continually look at their images reflected in mirrors. Rhys works to guard against being seen from any perspective she herself has not seen first, just as her protagonists carefully apply makeup before venturing into public view.

In psychoanalytic terms, nostalgia and desire are the residue of the reality principle, when the infant understands that it is not omnipotent but dependent upon an outside agency for its physical and emotional survival. This recognition causes the infant to split the image of the mother, usually the primary nurturing parent in Western culture, into a bad and a good imago, internalizing the bad imago in order to exert some control over its nightmare aspect and externalizing the good imago, projecting it onto the real mother, who is idealized in order to construct an external protection against the internal bad object. Transference finds its configurations in the nostalgic yearnings for the good object and the defenses erected against the bad object. Issues of dominance and submission, power and authority, and in Rhys's case, sadism and masochism, therefore motivate the attitudes with which the individual meets reality; point of view becomes the necessary distortion of individual needs and defenses brought to bear on reality.

In spite of her use of the effaced third-person narrator, Rhys's novels achieve the effect of a first-person narrative because of their extensive interior monologues. All her protagonists ruminate about their condition, apparently searching for some final cause to explain their misery. This mode of narration, coupled with the fact that these meditations begin and end in despair and are intensely involved with the details of female life (makeup, clothing, sexuality, romantic love), has persuaded many of Rhys's readers and critics to assume that "collectively they form a stark portrait of the feminine condition in the modern world."[23] But Rhys has not created an Ur-myth of female life in the twentieth century; she has used the third-person omniscient voice to conceal the particularities unique to a first-person narrative, disguising the distortions inherent in the first-person voice by giving it secondary status within the text. For example, in a representative passage from *Quartet*, Rhys's narrator tells the reader: "Marya, hastening after him, began to feel as though she were playing some intricate game of which she did not understand the rules." Using a third-person perspective here, to describe Marya's general sense of confusion, disguises the understanding that Marya's confusion is her own, a state of mind not shared by the narrator, who is well aware of the rules. Later, when Marya is living with the Heidlers, the reader is told: "Marya always brought the cup and the sugar, for he was very majestic and paternal in a dressing-gown, and it seemed natural that she should wait on him. He would thank her without looking at her and disappear behind the newspaper. He had abruptly become the remote impersonal male of the establishment."[24] After reading this passage, the question for a more distanced reader must be Who is speaking? If these are Marya's perceptions of Hugh Heidler, then she *does* know the rules of the game. If they are delivered by the narrator, why is an impersonal voice structuring the plot so as to deny Marya the autonomy of action engendered by the perception of power? The reader must assume that Marya both does and does not "know," or that she unconsciously resists a coherent appreciation of what she experiences in order to deny some measure of responsibility for her own victimization. A less distanced reader, identifying with Marya, is left with Marya's own sense of confusion and necessary paralysis; and Rhys ensures that her readers will identify with her protagonists because their voices, insistently self-exposing, provide the only incidental details. In all other respects such as place, time, weather conditions, political events, the novels are as faceless as the third-person narrator. Although the books are located in Paris and London, each city is merely a backdrop. Even the men who betray and abandon are featureless representatives of the anonymous crowd relentlessly victimizing the protagonist.

Rhys's position on the feminist movement presents another difficulty for considering her work representative of female life. In writing her autobiography, and therefore reassessing her ideas and opinions, she said, "I'm not at all for women's lib. I don't dislike women exactly, but I don't trust them. You can never tell them what you really think, because if they know what you think they'll do you down. I'm not, I've never been intimate with them. It's not worth it. Sometimes I think I'm not like other women, that I lack feminine qualities." As David Plante, to whom she made this statement, understood, "she never asked why her main female characters acted as they did: they just did, as she did. There is about them a great dark space in which they do not ask themselves, removing themselves from themselves to see themselves in the world in which they live: Why do I suffer?"[25] A woman who distrusts other women makes an unlikely witness for them; yet ironically, when that distrust is understood as the particular mistrust of a particular person, Rhys's protagonists become portraits of a psychological type familiar in Western culture: the female masochist.

According to psychoanalyst and psychiatrist Natalie Shainness, the psychological origins of masochism are established in the first days of life, when the child's "first experience in the inequity of power comes in its relationship with its mother, or the primary mothering person."[26] Masochism, she says, is the result of a particular distortion in the personality resulting from a variety of behaviors on the part of the mother, including inattention, active cruelty, and overconcern. The adult masochist has failed to establish what Erik Erikson has defined as "basic trust"[27] and instead develops an exaggerated sense of powerlessness and vulnerability. In inviting her reader to identify with her protagonist, Rhys offers the reader a masochistic position in regard to the world of text. Likewise Rhys, according to the material in her autobiography, identified herself as vulnerable and powerless, a woman whose central memories focus on loss and humiliation and whose response was the furious paralysis leading her to exclaim: "People! I hate people! I hate everyone. I think they're all enemies."[28]

Replicated in Rhys's protagonists are behavior patterns peculiar to masochism as described in Shainness's clinical research. Masochists pay particular attention to the facial expressions and tones of voice of the people surrounding them in order to avoid the abuse they assume is sure to occur. Sasha Jansen, for example, reliving the humiliation she experienced during a stint as a receptionist in a Parisian dress salon, remembers that she immediately "placed" the new English owner: "He arrives. Bowler-hat, majestic trousers, oh-my-God expression, ha-ha eyes—I know him at once,"[29] Even though this recognition perhaps is correct, because it originates in Sasha's terror at her own vulnerability it serves to exacerbate her incompetence when faced with authority. Her subsequent dismissal is the result of a bleakly comedic scene during which she displays an almost moronic stupidity of which she is fully aware and yet unable to control. Although Rhys implies that Sasha loses her job because the cruelty extant in the world is brought to bear especially on its more sensitive inhabitants, nothing in Sasha's character, not even the bitter irony she uses to assess her own failings, convinces a more distanced reader that Sasha is worth saving. She has been a self-willed victim, masochistically ensuring that the worst she can imagine will occur.

"The submission to authority that underlies all masochistic communication is perhaps most evident in the messages that turn on the mechanism of capitulation. Here the masochist exhibits her inability to hold her own, her tendency to collapse in the face of opposition, the failure to counterattack when such a maneuver is called for. The abandonment of autonomy is displayed with painful clarity." Inevitably, the effect of universal capitulation both conceals and breeds enormous fury, usually transformed by the masochist into paralyzing depression. Rhys also uses this anger in her protagonists to fuel a typical masochistic defense. Her protagonists are bitterly self-ironic, offering the reader scathing assessments of their own failures. This irony which masquerades as a species of self-knowledge is actually congruent with the masochistic personality. It is used to disarm the antagonist, deflecting expected negative evaluations by voicing them first. Still, "the docile, yielding accommodator can, every so often, lash out in a hostile fashion."[30] So Julia Martin, six months after her love affair has concluded, enters a restaurant in which her former lover is seated *now* to slap his face, and Sasha Jansen assumes the aggressor's position in response to a young gigolo who has mistaken her for a wealthy woman on whom he can prey. Each act by each protagonist—from Marya Zelli's decision to live with the Heidlers through Sasha Jansen's decision to return to Paris—is conceived statically, as an impulsive reaction to another's desire or simply to what she perceives as her fate. Julia Martin, hesitating about making a trip to England to borrow money from an early lover, thinks, "If a taxi hoots before I count three, I'll go to London. If not, I won't."[31]

Within the analytic situation, transference response is not limited to an imitation of the analysand's position vis à vis authority experienced in reality. Instead, transference recreates the position with which the patient has identified. Thus the patient who has identified with the powerful parent will approach the analyst from the parent's position, in turn attempting to place the analyst in a subordinate one. In literature also, because of the nature of the authority invested in the author by virtue of the creative process, the issue of power in regard to the reader imagined for the work is of primary importance. The lines along which power is displaced may be unconscious to the writer, appearing through the form and style of the work, particularly in the narrating position the writer selects and the relationships established between narrator and protagonist, author and narrator, author and imagined reader, and narrator and imagined reader.

In Rhys's work, several of these relationships are conflated, so that Rhys the writer and her unnamed narrator are merged in the authority they exert over the textual world, while her protagonists and her imagined reader are merged in the textual position they occupy. Rhys denies both the imagined reader and the protagonist power to change the course of the novel. While author and narrator are omniscient and authoritative, protagonist and reader are limited, vulnerable, and submissive. As Staley realized, Rhys distances her narrator from her protagonist. Although Staley sees in this a "style [which] penetrates surface situations to probe deeply into the underlying relationships and conditions of the characters,"[32] the relationship between narrator and protagonist can also be comprehended as a sadomasochistic partnership, in which the mutually destructive attachment is maintained because the great fear is loss of attachment. So, for example, although Sasha Jansen, who assumes the protagonist's final form, claims she wants nothing more than to be left alone, she fantasizes the gigolo she has humiliated will return to debase her, and she clings desparately to the man in the next room, who represents her conclusive degradation.

Similarly, Rhys's narrator, distanced from and unemotional toward the protagonist, telling the story in fragments, also seems to desire solitude. But the narrator's authority is derived from an insistent return to the protagonist during moments of her humiliation. The narrator's authority, that is, depends on the protagonist's abasement. This motif is visible in all four of Rhys's early novels. In *Quartet* the reader is told: "And there Marya was; haggard, tortured by jealousy, burnt up by longing."[33] In *After Leaving Mr. Mackenzie*, "Julia had abandoned herself. She was kneeling and sobbing and wishing she had brought another handerchief. She was crying now because she remembered that her life had been a long succession of humiliations and mistakes and pains and ridiculous efforts."[34] *Voyage in the Dark*, the novel Rhys wrote first but that was her third publication, offers an interesting version of the protagonist's abasement by the narrator. Here Anna Morgan, only eighteen years old and supporting herself by working as a chorus girl, gradually discovers that she is living as a prostitute. Although much of this book is delivered to the reader through Anna's interior monologue, Rhys precludes the reader's identification with Anna by depicting her as thoroughly confused and helpless. The reader must depend on the effaced narrator, visible in the book's structure and strategies, for a coherent picture of Anna's condition. Anna's own refrain is insistently powerless: "Of course, you get used to things, you get used to anything. It was as if I had always lived like that" and "Of course, as soon as a thing has happened it isn't fantastic any longer, it's inevitable. The inevitable is what you're doing or have done. The fantastic is simply what you didn't do."[35] Anna's story, concluding with an abortion she barely survives, must be pieced together like a jigsaw puzzle because Anna herself is unable to comprehend her life in any context larger than the fleeting impressions of immediate sensory experience. Were the protagonist herself more assertive, the narrator's decision to tell the story in fragments would be, in turn, more suspect. Why fracture a story of success? Fracture belongs, quite properly, to failure. Rhys's narrative structure, apparently constructed in the service of modernism, functions as well to imprison the protagonist in a world lacking all connection. According to the subtext implicit in the narrative structure, the protagonist is memorable only when reacting to a situation controlled by another.

That the distance Rhys establishes between narrator and protagonist places each in a relatively rigid relationship of dominance and submission is particularly clear in her fourth novel, *Good Morning, Midnight*. Through the humiliation of Sasha Jansen, she describes the inevitable defeat of the masochist, who, ironically, actively engages in her own destruction. Sasha has returned to Paris from England, where she had gone to recover from a failed suicide attempt. Told in a series of flashbacks and present-time narratives, Sasha's story is almost entirely contained within her mind. Here Rhys attempts to give her protagonist the power of speech and, with it, the authority of self-scrutiny. Sasha discovers that she must not walk down certain streets, or enter certain cafés, because of the memories these awaken. Yet simply returning to Paris induces her to reexperience "spots of time" encapsulating her steady deterioration. All her memories involve painful humiliation. She remembers her brief employment in the dress salons where she acted as receptionist, terminating in her complete rout by the new English owner. She remembers her marriage, initially so promising, quickly dwindling into a sordid and continuous search for money, marked by her husband's frequent mysterious absences and by the other women he insisted she entertain; she remembers the death from neglect of her infant son and her husband's final desertion. These events are drawn from Rhys's own life, during the period of her first marriage to the Dutch writer Jean Lenglet, and all are recalled by Sasha with scathing self-irony. Hating the world, Sasha

44

also hates herself because the world has, she claims, failed to leave her "one rag of illusion to clothe [herself] in."

But beneath the apparent self-loathing lurks a steady sense of her unique qualities coupled with the sort of romantic fantasies which impel women to accept masochistic relationships. Sasha implies by her very act of self-examination that she is more sensitive, more loyal, more honest than those who degrade her. But the examined life she pretends to lead strangely lacks self-consciousness. As Plante realized about Rhys, Sasha's self-scrutiny is a groping in the dark, more of an effort not to know than an attempt to illuminate her active participation in the circumstances victimizing her. Her self-excoriation functions to keep at bay the real self-consciousness which would signify emotional death—the knowledge that she had an alternative, that the life she led was not inevitable.

Good Morning, Midnight is particularly interesting among Rhys's early novels because in it Rhys brings almost to conscious expression the understanding that the position from which anyone experiences life can be reversed. The masochist can become the sadist, the victim the victimizer, as in Sasha's meeting with a young gigolo. Her fur coat, a present from a former lover, is all the property she retains from a life lived in almost the same way the gigolo obtains his income. Mistaking former riches for present affluence, the gigolo marks her as a target. She, in contrast, quickly recognizes him and decides to play out the "comedy." She thinks, "But after all . . . this is where I might be able to get some of my own back. You talk to them, you pretend to sympathize; then, just at the moment when they are not expecting it, you say: 'Go to hell.' "[36] Initially, then, Sasha enters the relationship to exact revenge on all her earlier abusers; she will, she thinks, quite literally take their place. Because Sasha is a female rather than a male gigolo, however, her profession has always been implicit. She has considered herself not a prostitute but an outlaw; financial gain was only the tangential result of a relationship based on love. This attitude demonstrates her fundamental sense of powerlessness. Rather than acknowledge her life to be self-willed, she believes she merely aims at a counterconventional honesty constantly betrayed by the men who take advantage of her. She misconstrues the demimonde she inhabits for a place of romance and authenticity, a mistake also made by Emma Bovary. But where Flaubert understood the nature of the oxymoron coupling romance with authenticity, Rhys, by virtue of her failure to achieve genuine self- or cultural consciousness for her protagonists, comprehends Sasha as an antihero. She believes Sasha's corruption is a form of innocence existing in a world decayed at its very core. Gradually Sasha loses sight of her desire to humiliate the gigolo, although she does so during their lovemaking scene when she tells him he need not complete the physical act but can go straight to where she has hidden her money. When at last he leaves her, driven away by her callous cynicism, Sasha reverts to a romantic fantasy of his return, completing her final degradation when she submits sexually to another man who has menaced her throughout her stay in Paris.

Staley writes, "Ultimately . . . the novel upholds Beckett's view that memory is useless, which the images emanating from Sasha's consciousness bear out."[37] Staley believes Sasha's interior meditations, reviewing her past history, were designed to unravel the tangled web which has led to her present condition, were intended to lead Sasha toward the possibility of an active assertion of will in the world. Memory was to guide and teach, to illuminate the pattern concealed in the random movements of an apparently chaotic life. Although it would be easy to understand Sasha as waiting for a Godot who never arrives, Rhys's unconscious manipulation of her transference relationship with her imagined reader renders Sasha's memory useless. Structurally, Sasha becomes both narrator and protagonist, victim and victimizer, for the novel is nearly a complete interior monologue; it traps the reader within Sasha's pretense of self-consciousness. Her memories of past humiliations are reenacted in present degradations, creating a vicious circle of despair and defeat from which Rhys, disguising her creative power as helplessness, give the reader no exit.

The sense of a malignant fate hanging over Sasha—derived from the role reversal between Sasha and the gigolo, which is revealed as yet another turn of the same screw—is emphasized by the concluding "dialogue" between Sasha and what should be her observing consciousness. The question Rhys appears to be asking is which voice is the genuine Sasha and which the world-corrupted Sasha. The separation between the two voices is the traditional patriarchal split between romance and sexuality; the romantic voice dwells on memories of "being young, and about being made love to and making love, about pain and dancing and not being afraid of death, about all the music I've ever loved, and every time I've been happy," whereas the sexual voice focuses on present-time reassessment, insisting, "I mustn't sing anymore—there you are. Finie la chanson. The song is ended. Finished."[38] It is the same dialogue which exists eternally between Didi and Gogo as they wait, beneath the tree nearly bare of leaves, for Godot, continually seesawing between faithless hope and faithful despair. Nostalgia keeps them waiting, yearning for an invisible ideal savior, just as nostalgia masquerades as the bitter irony pervading Sasha's observing consciousness.

It is in fact the observing voice, corrosive in its defeat, which is the "real" Sasha. It is the voice of cynical hatred, the inevitable other note of naive sentimentality, which ensures her present paralysis because to find another mode of life, to make memory useful, she would first have to give up the cynicism Rhys regards as wisdom. Finally, Sasha's answer is in a section of Rhys's autobiography also cast as a trial between consciousness and its interior judge: "Pride, anger, lust, drunkenness??, despair, presumption (hubris), sloth, selfishness, vanity, there's no end to them, coolness of heart. But I'm not guilty of the last. All the others."[39] The final sin, of which Rhys absolves herself, is the sin which would interfere with relationships; the sins to which she confesses are consequences of already failed relationships. Once again, the emphasis falls on an abusive other.

Two images concluding *Good Morning, Midnight* grant the same absolution to Sasha: the "dialogue" between self and soul is accomplished after she has "turn[ed] over on my side and huddle[d] up, making myself as small as possible, my knees almost touching my chin"; before her final submission to the man from the next room, she says, "I look straight into his eyes and despise another poor devil of a human being for the last time. For the last time. . . . Then I put my arms round him and pull him down on to the bed saying: 'Yes—yes—yes. . . .' "[40] Returning to the fetal position, regaining an infant innocence, she allows herself a final rebirth in sexual passion, at last willfully participating in her own abasement, transforming her defeat into a final, bitter affirmation of the pathos of human community. Although her concluding "yes—yes—yes" is, of course, Rhys's ironic recapitulation of Molly Bloom's triumphant affirmation concluding Joyce's *Ulysses*, it is at the same time the bitter irony Rhys defines throughout her canon as experiential wisdom. Unable to conceive of self-directed action, of action which is not distorted passivity, she cannot imagine an alternative for Sasha which integrates innocence and irony, which understands the self as the choices it makes.

In addition, by giving her imagined reader a specious form of self-observation through the self-conscious dialogues incorporated in the novel and autobiography, Rhys implicitly denies the reader's experience of her authorial power. The imagined reader is neither self nor other in the dialogue but a pawn of the relationship between the two. Snaring the reader between innocence and sexuality, Rhys exercises over the reader the same sort of authority she herself experienced as a small child caught between naive vulnerability and the half-understood mysteries of adult life. Implicit in her novels and in her autobiography is the subtext that the only escape from her dilemma lies in destroying herself before she can be destroyed by the other. The reader, then, is offered only the questionable salvation of self-destruction, a motif made explicit when Rhys's final protagonist, Antoinette Rochester, succeeds in committing suicide.

Natalie Shainness believes, together with psychiatrists working in the school of family systems therapy, that "people generally marry a surrogate for the more powerful parent, the parent whose behavior has had the greatest impact on them. The sex of that parent is irrelevant. Masochists tend to marry surrogates for the more dangerous, hurtful parent. . . . Meeting a man who evokes the repetition compulsion, the masochistic woman deludes herself into thinking he is strong. She knows herself to be weak, she admires strength, and she believes she has found it in him. What she sees as strength is most likely the same kind of coldness or cruelty that existed in her damaging parent."[41] Furthermore, because the historical and cultural structures predisposing women toward masochism are reflected in marriage as an institution, women making masochistic marriages frequently confuse an apprehension of cultural oppression for personal defeat. Because Rhys does not allow any protagonist to realize herself as in some way choosing her relationships, each also can possess no understanding of the unconscious motivation leading her to replicate her victimization. Instead, each perceives herself adrift in time and space, the pawn of external authority. Although *Wide Sargasso Sea*, Rhys's final novel, also has a protagonist who is a pawn in a sadistic marriage, Rhys attempts to place her in historical context. Yet, ironically, the effort reveals that Rhys has mistaken the institution for the individual.

The success of *Wide Sargasso Sea*, both in craft and critical acclaim, is due to a real distinction in the structure of Rhys's final protagonist. For the first time in her canon she placed her protagonist in a cultural and psychological context and, in doing so, changed the nature of the relationships among herself as author, her narrator, and her imagined reader. The answer to the question of why Rhys failed to give any of her protagonists the conditions of her own salvation—the creative ability to translate actively her passive aggression—may be that the authority embodied in the creative process frightened Rhys because she unconsciously identified such power as "unfeminine." Despite her own experience (no matter how submissively she behaved she was still rejected), she linked authoritative behavior with abandonment. In general, of course, Rhys had correctly assessed the punishment meted out to an "assertive" woman in Western culture. Nevertheless, in selecting Antoinette Cosway Rochester as her last protagonist,

Rhys symbolized her attraction to art as both a method of transformation and a means of salvation. Bertha Rochester is the fictional wife
imprisoned by her husband in the attic of Thornfield Hall in Charlotte
Brontë's *Jane Eyre*. In that novel Brontë indicates, through the book's
thematic design, that when Bertha sets fire to the house and then
leaps to her death from its battlements, she is making a final gesture
of rebellion against Rochester. Transforming Bertha into Antoinette,
Rhys extends and illuminates Brontë's depiction. In Rhys's version
Antoinette is more clearly Rochester's victim; her suicidal leap more
clearly represents the cultural dis-ease women suffer in patriarchal
society. Antoinette/Bertha reflects Rhys's own rebellious stance.
While Rhys's novels do not destroy the patriarchal literary house,
they do delineate the bleak and devastated lives of women considered
marginal or useless within patriarchal structures. In Brontë Rhys recognized another very angry woman outlining cultural pathology. Like
Brontë, for Rhys the way out was writing. Transforming Bertha into
Antoinette, Rhys transforms herself through the creative act from
passive victim to active witness, using her aesthetic power to salvage
the remnant of self Sasha Jensen has become at the conclusion of *Good
Morning, Midnight*.

Although Rhys's Antoinette Rochester possesses all the character
traits of her fictional sisters, unlike them she lives in the nineteenth
century and her life is destroyed by relationships other than of male
and female lovers. Antoinette is sister, friend, mistress, wife, and
daughter; she lives in a wider world than Rhys's earlier protagonists.
Just as Sasha Jansen carefully circumscribed her memories to limit her
pain, so Rhys attempted to avoid her own anger, an emotion she
believed was generated by her perception of female powerlessness,
by locating her early protagonists solely in the immediate present.
Only with her final novel, written in her early seventies, was Rhys
able to recognize and move beyond the sort of anger which functions
to protect the self from an anguish so extreme as to make passivity an
acceptable alternative. Only in *Wide Sargasso Sea* was Rhys able to

complete the life story of a woman imprisoned by her willed helplessness yet enraged by her prison.

In an examination of *Wide Sargasso Sea*, the question of Rhys's interest in the Brontë book is, of course, inevitable, particularly because *Wide Sargasso Sea* functions as a repressed version of *Jane Eyre*,[42] much as Bertha Rochester represents aspects of personality Jane had to suppress to succeed in the historical context of early Victorian England. The Rhys novel reverses the question implicit in the Brontë novel. Instead of Brontë's definition of Rochester as the victim of a malign fate in his marriage to a lunatic, Rhys seeks to discover the personal and cultural contingencies which would impel a woman to marry the sort of a man who finally both repudiates and imprisons her. But Brontë also recognized the power Rochester wielded and found it necessary both to blind and cripple him before she would allow Jane to contract a marriage of "equals." Rhys implies that Antoinette was less fortunate and instead found herself ensnared because she fell in love, then indicted by her husband for her failure to efface her personality before his. Although points of comparison between the two novels are many and varied, centrally important is Rhys's effort to make Antoinette's life coherent in the same way Brontë allowed her reader to follow Jane from child to adulthood.

Jane Eyre is a fictional autobiography, and I believe that in addition to the obvious idea of a woman imprisoned by her husband, the metaphorical condition of Rhys's earlier unmarried protagonists, it was also the concept of autobiography which drew Rhys's attention. Until *Wide Sargasso Sea*, Rhys herself had been writing and rewriting her own autobiography in fictional form. Although the apparent isolation of each protagonist, as well as the fragmented novelistic structure, seems to deny Rhys's desire to discern a coherent pattern, it was finally in her own nonfictional autobiography that she was able to duplicate the actual relationship she experienced with authority figures in life.

In her fiction, Rhys unconsciously identified and merged with the oppressing narrator, placing the protagonist and reader in the power-less position she experienced in life. In her autobiography, in contrast, she identified with the protagonist—herself—so that although she wrote the book, she experienced the authority of her creative act as fragmented and impulsive and her memories as so painful that she could identify and reexperience herself as victim. Autobiography, therefore, was a congenial form through which she could satisfy the pain of nostalgia through the renewed pain of self-flagellation. Hers could be the hand wielding the leather thongs scarring her own back. Even more important, the autobiographical project allowed Rhys to admit to her fictive impulses the most powerful other in her life, for whom the man acted as a screen and whose early presence made the later painful love affairs inevitable. For Rhys, behind the man was concealed a woman. As Evelyn Keller has recognized. "rigid separation between the psychological and emotional modes of dominance and submission, designed to suppress the power of the infantile mother imago, functions in precisely reverse fashion—the internalized power of the mother, and therefore of conflicts about personal autonomy and self definition, endure."[43]

In *Wide Sargasso Sea*, alone among Rhys's novels, Antoinette Rochester is the daughter of an intricately depicted mother. In solving the riddle of Antoinette's marriage Rhys found it necessary to unlock her own psychological history and discovered in Brontë's book one model of a coherently structured female life. Furthermore, in Brontë's protagonist Rhys could recognize another very angry woman writing an autobiographical fiction. Through Brontë's narrative Jane Eyre shapes her life, discerns its pattern, and discovers its lineaments involve an absent biologic mother followed by a series of surrogate mother figure. As a novel, then, *Jane Eyre* functioned for Rhys as a double mirror in which she could see a pattern completed both for her protagonist and for herself.

That Rhys should come to a resolution about mothers and daughters so late in her life is not surprising in light of recent psychological work indicating that emotional separation of daughters from their mothers may not occur until the fourth decade of life.[44] Quite possibly, until she had lived most of her life, Rhys was not able to distinguish emotions she owned from those generated in response to her mother. According to Nancy Chodorow, whose work addresses the dialectical connection between individual selves and social structures, female children experience a greater difficulty in developing ego boundaries which adequately define them as different from their mothers and, concomitantly, experience themselves as more continuous with others in their environment. Chodorow proposes that a woman retains a lifelong primary attachment to her mother as the earliest object of needs and desires.[45]

In concert with Chodorow, theorists working in the school of object relations psychotherapy argue that the child's pesonality and psychological development is determined, to a large degree, by the social world into which the infant is born. The self is a product of its social context and displays its form in its consistent pattern of reactions and responses to other objects, or people. In its ontological identity the self is relational even though it may perceive itself, like Rhys's early protagonists, as defined by an absense of relationships. Rhys's pre–World War II novels solidly demonstrate modernist concern about the estrangement of the individual burdened by self-consciousness in an industrial society. Rhys implies that relationships, in their very structure, are fraught with danger; that two selves cannot survive within a relationship; and that the structure of society, monolithic in practice, works always toward the extinction of the weaker self.

Ironically, it is just this perception of cultural juggernaught which dooms Rhys's early protagonists. Perceiving themselves as helpless victims renders their anger toothless and leads them to fall back on the ineffective and masochistic weapons of irony, cynicism, and depression. Chodorow comments,

If [people] feel ambivalent about or out of control of a relationship, they may internalize, or introject objects in relation to themselves or in relation to a part of their self, experiencing external relationships as internal and their feeling in relation to someone else as an internal sense of self. A very young child, for instance, may feel invulnerable and all-powerful because it has introjected, or taken as internal object, a nourishing and protecting maternal image, which is now experienced continuously whether or not its mother is actually there. Alternately, it may feel rejected and alone . . . because it has taken as an internal object an image of [its mother] as rejecting and denying gratification.[46]

In the case of the latter imago, the connection felt between mother and child is suffused with pain, and the child, paradoxically, will unconsciously seek the mother through the experience of emotional distress.

Yet although the child grown into an adult would perceive itself as a victim, anger at its victimization would be channeled, in the main, internally against a self perceived as powerless and loathsome, worthy of rejection. In this way, women internalize the misogyny inherent within a patriarchal structure. Rhy's early protagonists, translating their self-loathing into masochistic behavior patterns, exemplify this dynamic. Pain signals the closure of their relationship with men; because they are treated unlovingly, they feel loved. But because Rhys fails to explore the origins of their distress, the connection between their pain and their desire for it is never explicit. They are isolated in landscapes of a frozen present; with no emotional memory they are ensured no future.

As a writer, Rhys claimed she was not conscious of the shape, the structure, perhaps even the plot until a novel's internal coherence had impelled her toward a conclusion. Although she knew where she began a novel, she did not know where it would end or how she would traverse the ground between each pole. Unconsciously, she denied her experience of narrative control, a gesture also denying a consciously shaped address to some imagined reader. Her reader would have to seek her; she would not seek him. Edward Said has written, "Consciousness of a starting point, from the viewpoint of the continuity that succeeds it, is a consciousness of a direction in which it is humanly possible to move, as well as a trust in continuity."[47] For the first time, with Antoinette Rochester, Rhys worked with a protagonist whose conclusion she knew before she started writing; thus she both was assured of Antoinette's continuity and necessarily aware of the reader such a character would affect.

Brontë makes abundantly clear that rage has transformed Antoinette into the near-bestial monster locked away in Rochester's attic, a rage recognizable as an extreme version of the despair Rhys's early protagonists translated into depression. Antoinette is not in despair; she is active rather than passive, as Brontë made clear through Antoinette's last violent bid for freedom. Her death is a gesture of final independence; she can choose at least that much and, in the event, also choose to destroy her jailer. Antoinette ends not with a whimper, as Rhys's early protagonists surely must, but with enraged rebellion, her death a mark of contempt for the society which has imprisoned her. Selecting Antoinette as her protagonist forced Rhys to deal with the rage her previous protagonists turned against themselves. She also was forced to bring to nearly conscious expression, through the novel's imagery and narrative structure, the sadism through which she achieved the catharsis embedded for her in the creative process. Rhys personifies her narrator's sadism in Rochester's character and voice. Addressing Antoinette, he offers her this chilling challenge: "You hate me and I hate you. We'll see who hates best. But first, first I will destroy your hatred. . . . My hate is colder, stronger, and you'll have no hate to warm yourself. . . . I did it too. I saw the hate go out of her eyes. I forced it out. . . . She was only a ghost. . . . Nothing left but hopelessness."[48] The human shell to which Rochester reduces Antoinette is strikingly similar to the conclusive degradation Rhys designed for each of her earlier protagonists.

Because Rhys knew Antoinette's conclusion, her own novel necessarily begins with Antoinette's point of origin. Significantly, the starting point Rhys selects is the record of Antoinette's mother's alienation from both the white and black population of the West Indian island of Domenica where they live. The mother whose name is also Antoinette is ostracized for her extreme beauty, sensual in aspect; for her poverty; and because she is a literal as well as a figurative stranger in

Domenica. Rejected herself, then, for qualities Rhys considered essentially female—beauty, poverty, alien status—the mother responds to her female child only with hostility and dislike. Like Rhy's memories of her own mother, Antoinette's childhood memories are centered on rejection: "She pushed me away, not roughly but calmly, coldly, without a word, as if she had decided once and for all that I was useless to her. She wanted to sit with Pierre or walk where she pleased without being pestered. . . . I was old enough to look after myself." "My mother never asked me where I had been or what I had done." She might rest if I left her alone, she said. Once I would have gone back quietly to watch her asleep on the blue sofa—once I made excuses to be near he when she brushed her hair, a soft black cloak to cover me, hide me, keep me safe. But not any longer. Not any more."[49]

In contrast, Antoinette's mother emphatically dotes on her son, Pierre, born crippled and mentally impaired. In much the same way Brontë uses Rochester's physical maiming to symbolize his emotional weakness, Rhys metaphorically maims Antoinette's mother through the physical disability of her son. The mother's ambitions for power in the public sphere are directed through Pierre, too weak a vehicle to support her desires. Accordingly, Rhys suggests that the daughter, who is both physically strong and mentally alert, is rejected precisely because she *is* a daughter, mirroring and extending her mother's impotence.

Rhys also employs the mother's beauty, inherited by her daughter, to explicate female powerlessness. With bitter mordancy, she parodies the value of female beauty in her description of the mother's end. Still beautiful, though mad from grief since her son died, she is confined, attended by a sexually abusive caretaker. Unlike her daughter, she does not struggle against her confinement but instead submits to sexual molestation as the tribute paid to beauty, as had each of Rhys's apparently sane early protagonists. Her beauty, a coin she might trade for marriage, becomes the mark of her disgrace outside the socially sanctioned institution. Antoinette's mother provides her daughter with both an object of attachment and an object lesson. Her death concludes a life permeated by degradation. Antoinette's mother is the recapitulation of all of Rhys's early protagonists. In contrast, as Rhys well knew, Antoinette's death in *Jane Eyre* was a triumph of will; her leap from the parapet of Thornfield, an act of anarchy and revolution. How, then, did Rhys negotiate Antoinette's development from a woman who seeks pain as the affirmation of her primary sense of self into one who expresses anger with an outrage so passionate it destroys both her prison and herself? And does Rhys allow her imagined reader to participate in Antoinette's transformation?

Throughout Rhys's canon the persistent experience of her protagonist is loss, generally through abondonment or rejection by a male lover. Like Antoinette, Rhys's early protagonists court loss because of their earlier experience with a rejecting mother. Although only Julia Martin, in *After Leaving Mr. Mackenzie,* is explicitly displayed in a scene with her mother, a relationship clearly the precursor of the mother-daughter relationship in *Wide Sargasso Sea* and also modeled on memories of Rhys's own mother, each defines herself only as she exists in response to a dominant man. It is because the early books fail to make the connection between a protagonist's pain and her pervasive nostalgia that the protagonist perceives herself as defeated by a brutal impersonal environment and that the imagined reader experiences an equal sense of powerlessness at the hands of a faceless, colorless third-person narrator, an inexorable external authority. In contrast, although Antoinette's nineteenth-century world is no less brutal than the twentieth-century landscape inhabited by Rhys's earlier protagonists, in *Wide Sargasso Sea* Rhys was forced, by her knowledge of Antoinette's end, to make the connections, to discern a pattern.

Also unlike the earlier books, *Wide Sargasso Sea* is separated into several distinct first-person narratives, interspersing Antoinette's interior meditation on her life with an interior recapitulation by Rochester. The narrator's external domination is given, through Rochester, internal textual status. Furthermore, Rhys also allows Christophine, the black nurse and maid who acts as Antoinette's "good mother," to retell Antoinette's story. The several versions of the same story, like the flat, neutral tone Rhys used to narrate her autobiography and the third-person narrations in the earlier novels, ostensibly permits the reader to make an independent evaluation of the tale. The structure reflects Rhys's use of the "self and soul" monologue/dialogue in *Good Morning, Midnight* and the "trial" in the autobiography. The effect produced is of an effort toward an honest, impartial evaluation. But the apparent impartiality is refuted as the early protagonists end in what seems inevitable defeat and paralysis, and the reader experiences equal despair, cut off from the author by her rigid control of focus and detail, forced to identify with the powerless protagonist despite the apparent possibility of independent judgment. Denied the author's omniscience and creativity, the reader is as imprisoned in an attic of Rhys's creation as Antoinette by Rochester.

The split narrative structure making *Wide Sargasso Sea* functions in a similar fashion. Although Rochester is given his own voice, his sections are carefully contrived to include unconscious self-damnation. It is impossible, despite the familiarity of the first person voice, for the reader to identify with Rochester as he explains his own sense of victimization as a younger son "forced" to marry a mad heiress because of the laws of primogeniture; as he describes his young wife with a complete lack of compassion for her quite obvious vulnerability and misery. Rochester in fact conforms almost too precisely to the description of the sadist whose cruelty is stimulated by the perception of weakness. Antoinette's dress, slipping from her shoulders because of weight she has lost through the anxiety of their relationship, strikes him as sloppy; now the symbol of her sensuality, which once he has awakened it, he defines as repulsively indiscriminate lust; her physical gestures—the way she walks, the way she sits holding one limp wrist in the other hand—all awaken a contempt which he justifies by citing her unloving egotism. Despite his first-person narrative, then, the reader, who has been encouraged to identify with Antoinette because the initial section of the book is developed through her first-person reassessment of her childhood, is manipulated both to despise and to experience Rochester's cruelty.

Yet Rhys does not allow the reader's identification with Antoinette to endure throughout the novel. Through Antoinette's first-person narrative she herself is able to recover the forces which imprisoned her. The act of writing her "autobiography" forges the sense of continuity necessary for her to transform her self-defeating anger into outrage. This outrage is fueled by the fact that Antoinette, unlike Rhys's earlier protagonists, has been physically imprisoned. Her rage is thus justified; in burning Thornfield she commits not an insane act but one appropriate to her circumstances. Rochester clearly has breached the social contract between the man who protects and the woman who submits, a contract existing with merely rhetorical force for Rhys's twentieth-century protagonists.

Heretofore, Rhys's protagonists directed their anger against themselves as the source of difficulties they perceived as emanating from another too powerful to combat. Because her autobiographical project enabled Antoinette to remember her mother and therefore to reexperience the primary causes of her anger, and because Rhys knew that Antoinette's society literally, as well as symbolically, confined her, it became possible for Rhys to integrate, in this protagonist, the social structure and the individual personality. As Antoinette remembers her mother, she becomes conscious of the discrepancy between her own needs and desires and the outrages perpetrated by the social system; with this distinction, she is free to act. In this, Antoinette reflects male psychosexual development as described by Chodorow. Boys, in contrast to girls, respond to the mother/son relationship by early learning to define themselves as not female, and thus the scope of their personality encompasses traits excluded from the feminine self. A boy understands, because of obviously visible gender differences, that he is what or whom his mother is not. In a sense, just as Jane Eyre learned to mother herself, Rhys's Antoinette Rochester resolved her relationship with her mother by revenging herself—by transforming herself into the son her mother always wanted, one powerful enough to burn the house down.

Nevertheless, Antoinette's revenge is not offered to the reader. By the time Antoinette sets fire to Thornfield, the novel has made another assertion, now emphasizing Antoinette's insanity in quite conventional terms. Although Rhys ironically comments on social definitions of madness by highlighting Antoinette's degraded physical state, her wild hair and torn clothing, Antoinette's narrative voice in the final section is formed in the broken cadences of lunacy. Despite Rhys's seeming effort to portray Antoinette's shattered connection with reality as the natural consequence of her imprisoned isolation, the narrating voice she creates to move Antoinette toward her final denouement is a combination of hallucination and fantasy. While the reader may sympathize with Antoinette, identification is impossible. Antoinette's voice is that of the alien traditionally locked away on a "ship of fools" or confined in the back ward of an asylum. Although her suicide can be reinterpreted as "sanity" in the midst of an insane world, it is a world no longer inhabited by the reader.

Instead, the reader is first tempted to identify with Christophine, whose bitter assessment of Antoinette's victimization imitates the observing-ego segments of the "self and soul" dialogue in *Good Morning, Midnight*. Christophine is the "good mother" on whom Antoinette has projected the idealization designed to protect the ego from the ravages of the internalized "bad mother." In this case, however, Rhys selected a peculiar object for Antoinette's idealization. Christophine is a mysterious figure who practices voodoo, who may be, in fact, a witch. Thus, in Christophine, Antoinette idealizes a figure combining nurturing with magic, much like the traditional concept of the fairy godmother. But, at the same time, Rhys severely limits Christophine's power. Her magic fails. When she gives Antoinette a love potion for Rochester, it operates as a poison, making his latent brutality manifest; when she pleads Antoinette's case before Rochester, her explanation serves to cement his comprehension of Antoinette's evil personality. Even the "good mother," Rhys implies, is flawed and finally powerless in the face of male authority, so that Christophine's cynical evaluation of Rochester's malignity becomes another form of masochistic self-destruction. In addition, Christopine makes ironically visible the real cultural power exercised by the "witch." Even the nonsexual female is fundamentally powerless—she may preserve herself but cannot save her daughter.

The reader's position in *Wide Sargasso Sea* emerges, therefore, with painful clarity: "A zombie is a dead person who seems to be alive or a living person who is dead. . . . People here call them Mounes Mors (the Dead Ones)."[50] In her final novel Rhys made the implicit relationship between writer and reader explicit. In the four early books, the reader was invited to identify with the protagonist; reader and protagonist were merged in the protagonist's despair and paralysis, while the narrator was given the writer's omniscience and creative authority. The novels imply that the reader, like the writer, could understand but not assist the protagonist. Actually, the narrator's pretense of powerlessness, reinforced by the fragmented narrative structures and parallel to the writer's assertion of her own lack of control in the face of the writing process, was refuted by the narrator's sadistic connection with the protagonist. Unwilling rather than unable to conceive of a self-willed life, the narrator assumed a passive aggressivity toward the protagonist, mirroring the writer's passive aggression toward the imagined reader. In the details selected, the tone of flat neutrality, the frozen scenes of humiliation emphasizing the protagonist's victimization, the narrator insists the protagonist must suffer, at the same time denying any responsibility for the point of view ensuring her pain. The writer reflects this insistence as she carefully denies the reader the active creativity through which she transformed her own passive defeat. Nearly at the end of her life, Jean Rhys said, "I must write. If I stop writing my life will have been an abject failure. It is that already to other people. But it could be an abject failure to myself. I will not have earned death."[51]

The death Rhys finally earned, she denied to her reader. Despite the translation of her protagonist from a twentieth-century attempted suicide into a nineteenth-century success, Rhys never varied the place she offered her reader in her novels. The reader, in each of them, was one with the large corps of living dead whom Rhys hated and feared and against whom she wrote to revenge herself. Made explicit in *Wide Sargasso Sea*, Rhys's "zombie" reader is the alternate ego of her protagonist; where the latter is a "living person who is dead," the former is one of the "dead person[s] who seem to be alive." It is in this understanding of Rhys's appreciation of her reader that her transference imago emerges with the greatest force. Dead persons who remain alive do so in memory, specifically in the sort of memories out of which Rhys fashioned her fiction. Neither truth nor fantasy, Rhys's novels are memorializations, monuments to her refusal to exorcise the dead specters haunting her present reality. Creating her novels out of misery, she clung to the very despair which, she believed, impelled their creation. But because she misperceived the act of creation as an act beyond her control or conscious comprehension, in turn she denied its power to her reader, instead using her authority to abuse her reader, as she believed she herself had been abused. Finally, Rhys identified with the concealed sadism within the masochistic persona, with Julia Martin's understanding that "people are such beasts, such mean beasts . . . they'll let you die for want of a decent word, and then they'll lick the feet of anybody they can get anything out of. And do you think I'm going to cringe to a lot of mean, stupid animals? If all good, respectable people had one face, I'd spit in it."[52]

It is ironic that many of the readers who have responded most enthusiastically to Rhys's work are female. Natalie Shainness writes, "Masochistic women . . . daydream of overcoming their helplessness and passivity by meeting and attaching themselves to someone who possesses power." In devoting themselves to Rhy's novels, her female readers have done just that—attached themselves to someone who uses power insidiously—and experience with Shainness has defined as hypno-suggestibility. Limited in duration to the period of the encounter, "hypno-suggestibility causes the masochist to accept whatever the other person says as correct just as surely as if she had been hypnotized into believing it. Totally paralyzed by the power and the idea of the other person, she loses any ability to think for herself and allows the other's viewpoint to be imposed on her immediately and totally. Having accepted the premise of the other, the masochist will then rationalize why it is so as a means of justifying her acceptance."[53] Rhys's readers, in praising her novels as definitive statements of the female condition in the twentieth century, capitulate to brilliant aesthetic objects which serve to extend rather than illuminate the powerlessness and vulnerability experienced at all times by all oppressed people, readers as well as women.

CHAPTER 2

Ford Madox Ford's *The Good Soldier* and the Tietjens Tetralogy: Knowledge Is Power

That puts me in mind of. . . . These six flat monosyllables will be spoken at break of Judgment Day; they are the leisurely herald notes which signal that time has stopped, that human activity must suspend and every attention be bent toward discovering the other leisurely country words which follow. This is the power that beginnings have over us; we must find out what comes next and cannot pursue even the most urgent of our personal interest with any feeling of satisfaction until we do find out. *The Speaker of these words holds easy dominion* [emphasis added].
—Fred Chappell, "The Storytellers"

FORD MADOX FORD was a storyteller. Over some fifty years of writing, Ford managed to publish thirty-one novels, in genres ranging from realistic fiction to historical fantasies and fairy tales; to write numerous unpublished manuscripts; to compile a large body of critical essays on literature and the arts; to write memoirs and travel literature; and to compose twelve volumes of poetry. It is exactly this prolixity that stands as one of the central problems offered by his work. To write so much and write consistently well would be unusual, and there is a striking difference between what are thought to be Ford's best works and those justifiably eclipsed and obscured. *The Good Soldier*, considered by Ford to be the book into which he put "all I knew about writing,"[1] is generally considered one of the finest novels of the twentieth century. The Tietjens tetralogy, written between 1922 and 1929, is generally acclaimed as the best novel, in both aesthetic and thematic terms, to emerge from the chaos of World War I. Ford's historical trilogy fictionalizing the life of Katherine Howard as *The Fifth Queen* and his extraordinarily charming memoirs and cogent critical essays have also drawn critical praise.

When Ford wrote well, that is, he wrote as well as James, Pound, Eliot, Lawrence, and Conrad, all of whom Ford knew as members of the relatively small literary community in London during the first decade of the century. Like them, Ford was engaged in documenting in fiction the transformation of an entire world view. But unlike them, his fictionalizing often seemed compulsive. He insistently varied genre and generally changed narrative point of view from one work to the next. Each novel seems almost to be an experiment in perception, as if Ford continually put on a fresh persona to discover which most successfully could live in the new world. "In the course of his career he had thrown up clouds of ink around himself like a cuttlefish. He existed somewhere behind the extravagantly dramatized personalities of the last Pre-Raphaelite, the Tory English gentleman, the simple kitchen-gardener or the literary pundit, the benevolent, omniscient headmaster of a whole school of writers in Paris and New York."[2] Yet despite his genre variations, the effect of his tone is consistent. He attracts the reader with an attitude of openness and sincerity and a forthright address. In this, his tone is coincident with his prolixity. There simply is so much material, and so much of it using Ford in his own person as narrator (the autobiographical memoirs, travel literature, and criticism), that the reader must sense a real effort to offer a portrait of the writer vivid as life. Ford's memoirs engage exactly as a particularly delightful, anecdotally inclined dinner guest charms the company by selecting incidents and using language designed to enchant. It is not coincidental, therefore, that in his critical essays Ford explicitly considered the writer's connection to his reader, proposing that art could bridge the gap between individual human perceptions.

Ford's critical theories deal with this relationship both in textual strategies to attract and hold the reader's interest and in the tenets of literary Impressionism, a theory he developed in collaboration with Joseph Conrad. For Ford, Impressionism was "the frank expression of the writer's personality,"[3] so that the writer renders reality according to the impression on his or her sensibility. Such a connection both to French ideas and to painting was natural; Ford's grandfather, a dominant influence in his life, was Ford Madox Brown, attached to the Pre-Raphaelite group, which included Dante Gabriel Rossetti, Holman Hunt, and John Millais. Madox Brown spent most of his early life in France, his spiritual home, and spoke English all his life with a pronounced French accent. Ford inherited his francophilia both from his grandfather and from his own father, the music critic Francis Hueffer, who was well known for his scholarship on twelfth-century Provençal poetry. In their allegiance to France, Ford and his grandfather (although not his father) manifested a central tension informing their lives and their work: their sense of constant alienation in their homeland.

In his painting, Madox Brown sought to render the sensual reality of a scene through a concentration on an exactitude of detail, using sharply contrasting lights and shadows to attain a heightened form of realism particularly striking in the oversized canvases he favored (as Ford was later to find the multivolume novel congenial). The painter's eye, then, became the transmitting medium between a reality undistinguished by artistic perception and the sort of re-creation which would bring forward the order and beauty inherent in an apparent chaos. Madox Brown believed he was the instrument through which a natural aesthetic could be realized. Like his literary counterpart, Emile Zola, he found beauty in the most mundane scenes. These ideas Ford subsequently translated into the concepts of literary Impressionism. But as practiced by Ford, literary Impressionism was far less capable of or interested in rendering reality than in recording the nature of perception, perforce a portrait of the artist at work. As Ford well knew, "the school . . . recognizes, frankly, that all art must be the expression of an ego."[4]

As a technique, however, impressionism presented Ford with an inherent contradiction. The massiveness of his canon, as well as the explicit concern for his reader throughout his critical work, indicate that he found the relationship between writer and reader extremely important and complex. By his own account, he understood as early as his first manuscript, published when he was nineteen, how intense was his desire for an audience.[5] Ford wanted to create a social aesthetic, designed to intrigue, attract, ensnare, enrapture, and impress a distinctly realized audience. He was well aware that an undisguised focus on the writer's perceptions would weaken connection with the reader.

Furthermore, with his inherited sense of personal alienation strengthened by a childhood spend attempting to find a sense of self not obliterated by the great figures of Victorian literature and art who visited Madox Brown, Ford also knew that communication is at best a tenuous business, perhaps demanding as conduits such extreme states of emotion as great love or hostility. As Christopher Tietjens remarks in *Parade's End,* when he recognizes that he has indeed fallen in love with Valentine Wannop, "You seduce a young woman in order to be able to finish your talks with her. You could not live with her without seducing her; but that was the by-product. The point is that you can't otherwise talk. You can't finish talks at street corners; in museums; even in drawing-rooms. You mayn't be in the mood when she is in the mood—for the intimate conversation that means the final communion of your souls. You have to wait together—for a week, for a year, for a lifetime, before the final intimate conversation may be attained . . . and exhausted."[6]

Translating Christopher's comprehension of love as intimate conversation into literary terms expresses the points of Ford's own dilemma. On the one hand, he desired to establish a relationship with his reader through which both writer and reader would experience the sort of communion possible through the intimacy of mutual perception. Writer and reader would converse with each other. On the other hand, using Impressionist techniques meant attracting the reader's interest (and love) by what could be misconstrued as a display of egoistic self-aggrandizement. On a more fundamental level, Impressionism involved a self-publicity antithetical to Ford's personality.[7] A writer proposing to establish an intimacy with his reader similar to that of two lovers is really proposing to make a private affair public, to bring love into the marketplace. That Ford was well aware of, and disturbed by, this contradiction can be understood from his description of the writer, who "will, in short, employ all the devices of the prostitute."[8]

Ford's conflict lay in his simultaneous desires for anonymity and intimacy—for the security of the omniscient voice and the familiarity of the Impressionist first-person perspective. In cultural terms, he connected anonymity with taciturnity, behavior defining the masculine, whereas intimacy meant speech—or chatter—and the feminine. The enormous amount of material in his canon is one of the ironic consequences of his dilemma. Despite the variety of genres and narrating personas, Ford's address to his reader was consistent. He desired to engage the reader in a relationship intimate only to the reader. He sought to retain for himself the authority of silence, while ironically forcing his reader to identify with his feminized, powerless, chattering narrator. The final effect of the literary techniques Ford development, such as achronological time shifts and the *progression d'effet*, in which the reader is led through a sequence of gradual revelations functioning as disguises for a major shock, is confusion. The real reader often closes Ford's novels baffled about discrete plot events, character motivation, time sequences, even setting. Although Ford might argue that such confusion reflects the terms of real life, it also serves to protect the writer's authority within the text. The writer knows more and is in control of material only apparently accessible to the reader. This confusion necessarily interferes with a direct connection between writer and reader. Although Ford, through his tone and thematic concerns, openly invites the reader to participate in a relationship of forthright equality, the real reader must engage in a hunt for a writer always offering but never fulfilling a promise of intimacy which seems to recede infinitely like the image reflected in a hall of mirrors.

The question, then, is whether Ford was aware of this disjuncture.

Is the confusion the consequence of conscious desires he projected onto the reader he imagined for his work, or is it the result of unconscious needs and conflicts directing him to build an extensive body of writing and a theory of aesthetics on the quicksand of an unexamined personality? Moreover, because Ford's fictional subject was a constantly reiterated version of the traditional romantic love fantasy, which functions as the cultural articulation of Freud's oedipal nexus, his work brings out the subtle Western connection between the possession of knowledge and power.

Freud believed the most important psychic work of childhood was concentrated, for both genders, between the ages of two-and-a-half and six years, with the resolution of what he termed the Oedipus complex. According to psychoanalyst Charles Brenner, "Freud discovered rather early that there were regularly present in the unconscious mental lives of his neurotic patients fantasies of incest with the parent of the opposite sex, combined with jealousy and murderous rage against the parent of the same sex. Because of the analogy between such fantasies and the Greek legend of Oedipus, who unknowingly killed his father and married his mother, Freud called this constellation the Oedipus complex."[9] Freud quickly realized that this complex of fantasies was general to human development, that is, normal as well as neurotic. Freud also realized that resolution of this stage of development would necessarily be distinct for boys and girls. Boys, fearing retaliation from the father, learn to repress and repudiate both the murderous and incestuous wishes by transforming these, in large part, into identifications. The boy becomes like the father, instead of separate from him. Defining what he called the Electra complex, Freud theorized that girls translate erotic desire for union with the father into desire to bear the father's child. A little girl becomes *like* the mother *in her relation* to the father. Loosely translated through feminist psychoanalytic theory, the boy agrees to forfeit present erotic satisfaction, accepting instead the promise of power held out to him along with his father's name and cultural role. The girl, also forfeiting present satisfaction, accepts instead her mother's powerlessness, sanctioned by cultural definitions of femininity. In terms of behavior in the world, if the oedipal nexus is successfully resolved, the little boy learns to dominate and the little girl learns to submit.

I have, here, conflated the traditional psychoanalytic interpretation of the Oedipus complex with its radical revision. Although orthodox psychoanalysts understand that the individual superego, "the internalized images of the moral aspects of the parents," is formed as a consequence of successful oedipal resolution, they do not extend this understanding to cultural patterns determining the use of authority. Yet the individual superego is the internalized reflection of the culture, now functioning unconsciously as the moral sphere of the personality, which includes "the approval or disapproval of actions and wishes on the grounds of rectitude; critical self-observation; self punishment; the demand for reparation or repentance of wrongdoing; and self-praise or self-love as a reward for virtuous or desirable thoughts and actions."[10] If resolution of the oedipal nexus implies that the male child becomes like the father, such resolution also implies that the male child will locate self-approval and self-love in defining as virtuous those actions the father has earlier so defined. As Evelyn Keller says, his resolution brings with it a definition of autonomy secured by "assimilation of paternal (legitimate) power. . . . In place of the lure of maternal intimacy, the son is offered, through his identification with his father, the future prospect of dominion over the maternal."[11] Furthermore, the wider culture links assimilation of paternal power to objective knowledge, while it devalues feminine forms of knowing that rely on the subjective criteria of intuitive reasoning and sensual apperception.[12]

What happens, then, when the oedipal resolution is not quite successful? Because a successful resolution is an ideal theoretical construct, there remain for most of us conflicts that fragment the repression of the desire for erotic union with the mother. This failure, of course, results in the many and varied neurotic behaviors Freud's theories were originally designed to treat, failures traditional psychoanalysts understand as conflicts about individual autonomy, intimacy, separation, power, and love. Such conflicts determine, at the individual level, a separation between behavior and fantasy. Analogously, such conflicts emerge in writing as anomalies between form and subject. The writer, consciously attentive to aesthetic techniques guiding form, may nevertheless unconsciously incorporate childhood fantasies into his subject, distorting what should be the integration of form and content in the aesthetic object. Conversely, attending to subject material may leave open to unconscious derivation questions of form, particularly choice of narrating position. The narrator, or narrating position, can function as a key to unconscious conflict between form and content, because the narrator, in relation to the textual world, reflects the writer's conscious and unconscious relationship to the imagined audience he addresses. In addition to the narrator, form includes point of view, genre, language, style, tone, and structure, whereas subject material embraces the work's thematic and plot concerns. Meaning resides exclusively in neither the form nor the textual material, for it is an ever-spiraling, cohesive expression of all textual elements. In psychoanalytic transference terms, meaning is illuminated through an examination of how what is addressed to whom.

In the wider cultural context, the oedipal nexus reflects patterns of traditional patriarchal authority. Offered his father's social power, the male child learns to separate knowledge and love; for love, culturally defined as union, is experienced as the province of the mother. Ironically, to bridge the chasm between love and power, a gap untenable in real behavior, the culture offers a romantic fantasy suggesting that romantic love—love for an object always unattainable because it is directed toward someone modeled on the originally unattainable mother—will provide solace for the nostalgic yearning which is the sign of the cultural neurosis indicating a partially repressed oedipal desire. Strict adherence to the romantic fantasy of an ideal love union, therefore, indicates a culture unconsciously fearful of and conflicted about communal autonomy. At the individual level, such adherence, of course, reflects an equal conflict about personal autonomy, extending to questions of intimacy, domination, collusion, and submission.

Specifically, it is the textual incongruence of form and subject material resulting from such conflicts which reveals the pattern of the writer's transference. For some writers, like Ford, personal conflict reflects an experience of cultural conflict. For Ford in particular, that conflict centered on an idealization of cultural modes of authority coupled with an individual yearning for the sort of union precisely denied by the cultural definition of the masculine. Separating knowledge and power from love, Ford's work is marked by narrators who profess ignorance in order to garner their reader's love by denying personal authority while textual structures operate to confuse the reader, reserving to the narrator the power to order chaos. The same narrator who seems to know nothing is in fact the voice in Ford's novels whose denial is used to conceal his knowledge of the whole. Ford's insistent use of multiple narrative positions is especially relevant in these terms when we realize that he employed these varied personas to narrate what finally emerges as the same story endlessly retold. From his first manuscript, a fairy tale published in 1892, through his final novels and travel literature, Ford varied his genre but not his subject, consistently exploring the terrain of human relationships in a world apparently made despite personal desire. This thematic material is, of course, the romantic fantasy of unattainable union.

Ford's unconscious conflicts emerge both in the incoherent narratives which leave the real reader confused while Ford states his intention to enlighten and in the obsessive way (through eighty-seven volumes) he said what he seemed compelled to say. As Sondra Stang says, "Ford on the whole (though there is evidence of a good deal of rewriting) 'corrected' through a new version, a new novel."[13] As he wrote, Ford consciously sought his "ideal" novel; what he achieved, unconsciously, was a kaleidoscope of narrators fragmented from a whole whose coherence he desired less than its disunity. *The Good Soldier* and the Tietjens tetralogy indicate that Ford's experience of the modern world is one of profound fracture: with the past, with received tradition, and in all relationships. In confusion, using perspectives bestowed on multiple "personas," he could deny patriarchal authority and yet attain power indirectly, satisfying to some degree a conflict engendered by a culture that defined the masculine through a devaluation of the feminine.

Ford's dilemma, the desire for "feminine" union antithetical to the unconscious directives from his culture to define himself as masculine through separation, is reflected in both his life and his work. When Ford wrote *The Good Soldier* in 1913, he believed himself to be both a literal and an emotional outcast from the cultural and literary alliances that previously formed a significant part of his life. His ten-year collaboration with Conrad was over, ending a connection exceptionally important to Ford, who wrote after Conrad's death that they had worked "with absolute oneness of purpose and with absolute absence of rivalry."[14] Thinking of Conrad and echoing the thematic content of most of his own work, Ford quoted Novalis: "It is certain that my conviction gains immensely as soon as another soul can be found to share it."[15]

But as in his novels, here too an apparently romantic and naive statement is belied by the complex form of the relationship between the two men. Ford and Conrad met when Ford was twenty-five and Conrad forty. Although Ford certainly was the more published writer, Conrad clearly was the genius, and during the next ten years Ford acted as Conrad's nurse, scribe, and business manager and in general attempted to clear Conrad's path of any hindrances to composition. During their collaboration Conrad did complete most of his own major works and with Ford wrote three novels. Although Ford's own work languished to some degree, he later wrote, "If I know anything of how to write, almost the whole of that knowledge was acquired then . . . the pleasure derived from his society was inexhaustible; his love, his passion for his art did not, I believe, exceed mine, but his power of expressing that passion was delicious, winning, sweet, incredible . . . our friendship remained unbroken and only interrupted by the exigencies of time, space and public events."[16]

Yet their friendship was broken by 1913, severed over the scandal

Ford created when he left his wife to live with the novelist Violet Hunt. Thinking about the relationship between Ford and Conrad, and therefore the conditions of Ford's life just before he wrote *The Good Soldier*, as well as about attitudes he habitually incorporated into literature, we must take into account the discrepancy between what Ford reported and the realities of his life. That Conrad was very fond of Ford and depended almost completely upon him during the ten years of their association is undeniable. That during that time they engaged in intense and passionate conversation about literature, about literary theory, and therefore about human nature and the general conditions of human life is undoubtedly true. But that Conrad reciprocated Ford's spiritual kinship is doubtful. Conrad seems to have obtained from Ford the sort of collaboration he initially sought when he approached Ford in search of a working writer who could help him develop ease in English composition. As he was in fact a great artist, and as such, intensely responsive to the people and places in which he found himself, it is easy to understand that he would meet Ford's passion for intellectual conversation with equal fervor. But Conrad wrote his own books, while Ford, in a sense, worked on Conrad's. Their relationship seems to have been fundamentally asymmetric in authority; Conrad was always dominant in their intellectual and artistic activity, while Ford would almost subversively steal authority through the back-door, culturally feminine method of nurturing and supporting. That Ford could romanticize this asymmetry and define it as authentic mutuality illuminates his conflict between love and authority.

In a short story about another storyteller, Fred Chappell, a contemporary American writer, summarizes an approach toward fiction like Ford's: "What if Uncle Zeno's stories so thoroughly absorbed the characters he spoke of that they took leave of the everyday world and just went off to inhabit his narratives? Everything connected with them would disappear; they would leave no more sign among us than a hawk's shadow leaves in the snow he flies above."[17] Like Uncle Zeno, Ford used his fictions to absorb his life. In his imagination, at least, his reality was defined by his fantasies. After Conrad's death Ford noted, in reference to the "unbroken" quality of their friendship, "It is in the end better if the public will believe that version—for nearly ideal literary friendships are rare, and the literary world is ennobled by them."[18] The public would receive the portrait of their perfect friendship through Ford's words, specifically through the biography of Conrad he wrote two months after Conrad's death in 1924. Conrad's wife, and other contemporary readers, have defined the biography as fiction and, moreover, as a degrading portrait of Conrad.[19] In it, Ford repeated the technique he also used to create, in *The Good Soldier*, John Dowell's retrospective account of his relationship with Edward Ashburnham. Dowell loved Ashburnham in the way Ford loved Conrad, and with a similar asymmetry of authority between them. It would not be inconceivable for Dowell to write about Edward, as Ford wrote about Conrad: "And his delight was just as great if the trouvaille had been mine as if it had been his own. Indeed, the highwater mark of our discoveries was reached with a phrase of mine—'Excellency, a few goats!'—which so impressed him that twenty years later he was still chuckling over it. It was that generosity that atoned for, say, his abusive letters written about myself to his friends."[20]

Carefully examined, what emerges from the language of this memory is a sort of double vision. Ford clearly desires to praise Conrad, but in doing so, he inserts himself behind the narrative. That is, putting Conrad's generosity in the foreground, he nevertheless is "forced" to admit that the perfect phrase was his own creation and that, furthermore, Conrad's generosity allowed Ford to "overlook" Conrad's abuse. Ford even records Conrad's insulting letters in a phrase designed to appear accidental ("that atoned for, *say*, [italics mine] his abusive letters"), as if he, as narrator, just happened to select that memory when any other would equally well serve in the sentence.

In Ford's relationship with the reader he imagines for the anecdote, the grammatical structure subtly reverses the relationship of authority he experienced in life with Conrad. In reality, Conrad was authoritative and powerful, Ford the eternal subordinate. In cultural terms,

Conrad inhabited the patriarchal position, Ford the devalued feminine place. In the anecdote, Ford as narrator, while directing the reader to praise Conrad, also forces the reader to see, "to really see,"[21] not Ford's subordination but his forbearance, and through that forbearance, Ford is able to attain over the reader an authority he was forced to forfeit with Conrad. Ford's authority lies in his implication that his is the perceiving eye, his the authentic memory, his the real generosity; for Conrad's abuse, as well as his incorporation of Ford's own creative work into his novels, must have been a flaw of which Conrad was unaware. Conrad's "generosity" would have prevented him from such action had he been conscious of its significance. In the relationship Ford is forging with the reader, then, he implies that only he can, and will, tell the whole, the coherent truth. His double vision permits him, on the one hand, consciously to control the reader's vision through content, which confuses the reader by combining notions about Conrad's generosity *and* his abuse, and on the other hand, implicitly, perhaps unconsciously, to direct, through his sentence structure and tone—his form—the reader's comprehension of Conrad. The anecdote allows Ford, as narrator, simultaneously to create and dispel confusion in his reader by proclaiming his union with Conrad while at the same time insisting on their separation.

Although it would be an error of psychoanalytic criticism to conflate the writer's life with his work, in Ford's case his life often was his work. His massive canon was an attempt to re-create his life while he lived it; and his use of multiple genres, blurring the boundaries between autobiography and fiction, between criticism and fiction, between autobiography and criticism, contrasts with the consistency of the grammatical structures used by his many narrators. In most of his books, in all genres, there exists the same double vision, the sort of sentences constructed to allow the narrator to make statements in subordinate clauses which are subtly denied in the dominant clause, as in the Conrad anecdote.

Inevitably, issues of authority and submission are among the central residue of early attitudes transferred onto and patterning adult life. In text, grammatical construction is one aspect of form, the use of which is generally unconscious when the writer is focused on the content of his story. Although Ford was doubtless aware of his desire to praise Conrad, and also perhaps aware of his secondary need to assert his own importance, he probably was unaware of the method of assertion and the effect on his real reader. In Ford's imagination, his reader would respond to the passage about Conrad with admiration for Conrad and affection for himself as narrator; unconsciously, to win the reader's affection for his narrator, he also needed to exert the sort of authority over that reader he experienced with Conrad, perhaps because it was Conrad's authority that called forth Ford's own affection. In a sense, the passage offers an excellent portrait of the real connection between both writers during their collaboration; yet to reach this level of authentic description it is necessary to read "through" Ford, to scrutinize his narrative act in terms of the effect he imagined it would have, and to distinguish that effect from the real reader's response.

Issues indicating a conflict between dominance and submission, authority and love, are centrally important both to psychoanalytic transference and to Ford's work, in its thematic concerns and formal elements. To examine these issues in *The Good Soldier* we need an understanding of Ford's early life, for in a sense Ford's relationship with Conrad was the distillation of the one he experienced with both his grandfather and his father, the primary influences on his career. As Stang says, "Madox Brown was the undisputed hero of Ford's auto-biographical writings."[22] Ford reports that he looked like "the King of Hearts," "was the most benevolent of men, the most helpful and the kindest," and "was as a grandfather extravagantly indulgent."[23] Madox Brown was a figure of great romance both in his art and in his personal life, and to some degree, Ford's personal history was a re-creation of Madox Brown's life. Like his grandfather, Ford married at the age of nineteen, eloping, as did Madox Brown, with a girl in her teens. More important, both separated humanity into artists and "the stuff to fill graveyards,"[24] and both formed particularly strong bonds with other male artists—Madox Brown with William Morris, Rossetti, and other Pre-Raphaelites; Ford with Conrad and the many contemporary writers he admired and assisted—and finally, both espoused a form of romantic Toryism founded on the same sort of naive feudalism Ford lent to Edward Ashburnham and Christopher Tietjens. Most striking, Ford adopted the persona of an old man when he was still a very young one, habitually wearing the Inverness cape inherited by his grandfather from Rossetti, conversing with his own contemporaries in the manner of someone even older than Madox Brown. Olive Garnett, Ford's childhood friend, noted in her diary in 1893, when Ford was twenty, "It is true that Ford speaks to everybody as if he were their great-grandfather."[25] The same impression of Ford was echoed just a few years later by Stephen Crane, who predicted that Ford "will end up by patronizing God who will have to get used to it and they will be friends."[26] Ford, that is, idealized his grandfather, both before and after the older man's death, seeking through the icon he made of Madox Brown an identification strong enough to resist all the doubts and anxieties he held about self-autonomy.

Psychologically, identification is both a primitive and a universal response, occurring during the earliest stages of ego formation when the infant identifies itself as like the nurturing other, or more precisely, as like the parent figure. The still-immature ego soon becomes gradually aware that the nurturing agent is outside the self and thus outside the self's control. As a gesture of psychological self-protection, then, the very young child splits the mothering figure into a good and a bad object, first unconsciously internalizing the bad-object mother in the effort to control her. Yet according to W. D. Fairbairn, "Since she is not wholly bad, the unsatisfying mother, after internalization, is split into a good mother and a bad mother; and usually the good mother is projected back onto the real external mother who is then idealized so as to make real life relations as comfortable as possible."[27] Ford's striking exclusion of his mother from nearly all his memoirs lets him transfer his idealizing emotional response to a mother figure to Madox Brown.

Further evidence of this transfer is that almost nowhere in Ford's many written reminiscences about Madox Brown does he use the technique of double vision. Instead, in the attempt to draw a well-rounded, loving portrait of his grandfather and therefore to conscientiously admit any faults his grandfather may have possessed, Ford integrates subject and form by keeping his own narrative position in the foreground, as in "Nothing can prevent my mixing up names. I suppose I inherit the characteristic from my grandfather who had it to a dangerous degree."[28] This is markedly different from the passage describing Conrad, where Ford effaced his narrative position, limiting it to subordinate clauses which in form depend on, while in content deny, the subject of the dominant clause.

In describing his grandfather, identification permits him to place himself grammatically as his grandfather's coeval. The narrator is as important as the material narrated because the narrator draws his identity from the content of his story. In his address to the reader, Ford here has modified the position of authority he occupied in the Conrad anecdote. There, Ford as narrator implicitly assumed authority to direct and guide the reader's comprehension of Conrad. Conrad emerges as in fact less generous than the narrator, who demonstrates his own larger magnanimity by forgiving character flaws beyond Conrad's control. The reader is expected to attend to the tone of open-handed forbearance and to ignore the contradiction in content which renders the anecdote a sly, backhanded attack. By the very act of effacing himself as narrator, Ford expected to control the reader; it was a technique he later used with marked success to create the narrating position in *The Good Soldier*.

In contrast, when describing his grandfather, the foreground narrative position dictates that he address a reader of whose forbearance he is certain because, identifying with an idealized subject, he also possesses the subject's authority. Although the effect of the passage remains authoritative toward the reader, it is with the power of the grandfather, benevolent, humane, perhaps wise, eager to indulge the "child" reader and act as exemplar for him. Without the narrative effacement, the sly, underhanded quality also is lost, permitting the reader genuinely to admire an authentically admirable voice. In Ford's conflict between love and power, therefore, his identification with his grandfather represents a successful repression of oedipal desire, transformed by his assimilation of his grandfather's authority and, quite literally, his name, as Ford's name at birth was Ford Madox Hueffer. Although Ford claimed he changed his name to avoid the anti-German sentiment developing in England just before World War I, the new name was a reiteration of those words in his original name reflecting his grandfather. Naming, of course, as in the biblical Adam's act of naming, symbolically lends the namer control of the named, or in Ford's case, symbolic self-control. In renaming himself, Ford disclaimed the name he had inherited from his father, symbolically indicating a conflict between love and power unresolved despite his attempt to identify with his grandfather.

Ford's fictional canon also demonstrates this conflict. Most of it is in two genres, the historical and the realistic novel. The historical novels, among which I include the Tietjens tetralogy,[29] are pervaded with the effects and tones of Ford's fairy tales. Although the books are linked to historical reality, they contain the happy endings and the starkly contrasting good and evil characters of legends and fables. Moreover, they address the reader with the narrative inversion Ford initially used in his first fairy tale, *The Brown Owl.* There, although Ford pays a glancing respect to the "once upon a time" traditional form effacing the narrating voice in favor of the tale, his narrator, a contemporary teller of an ancient story, frequently intrudes on the narrative to connect legendary details with incidents external to the tale currently experienced by the audience. The narrator assumes the human wisdom of the "grandfather," who uses the plot matter of the tale as a didactic allegory to educate his young listeners about the world in which they live. Brenner remarks, "The problem of guilt over oedipal wishes has always to be dealt with in fairy stories. Since these stories are for little children, and for simple, childlike adults, simple devices suffice to set at rest the guilty consciences of the audience."[30] In contrast, Ford's realistic novels, including *The Good Soldier*, secure authority for the narrator through the technique of double vision: putting the subject in the foreground and ostensibly effacing the narrator. Realism, for Ford, appeared to mean unhappy resolutions, bleak justice, and confusion. The straightforward, uncomplicated relationship he imagined he shared with his grandfather is wholly absent. Instead, these novels depict relationships fraught with anxiety and ambiguity experienced by human beings uncertain often of both the nature and the exercise of personal authority, and they are marked overtly by a disjuncture of form and subject material in the text.

Ford, of course, experienced the two modes in his personal life. While his grandfather was legend, even though perhaps justifiably idealized, his father was "the Just Man!"[31] representing cultural conscience for Ford. His father was Francis Hueffer, music critic of the *London Times*, a German immigrant who had married Catherine Madox Brown, the younger daughter of Ford Madox Brown. Hueffer, like his son, was remarkably prolific during his much shorter career. Before his death at forty-three, when Ford was sixteen, Hueffer had edited the Wagner-Liszt correspondence and an extensive group of books called *The Great Musicians* and written *The Troubadours: A History of Provençal Life and Literature in the Middle Ages* in addition to his regular newspaper column.

Ford records two central memories of his father. In the first, he remembers that his father "habitually," called him "the patient but extremely stupid donkey,"[32] in contrast to his grandfather's firm belief that all his grandchildren were geniuses.[33] In the second, he remembers that his father's last words to him were, "Fordie, whatever you do, never write a book," in opposition to his grandfather's ambitions for his artistic career. Ford reports that his "fate" was settled for him when his grandfather threatened to "turn you straight out of my house if you go in for any kind of commercial life."[34] Whereas Madox Brown retained to the end of his life the vivid and romantic dress of the Pre-Raphaelite radical artist, Hueffer, a large man whom Ford resembled physically, thoroughly converted to stiffly proper English customs after his immigration.

But Francis Hueffer was much more, in character and accomplishments, than a simple antithesis to Madox Brown. His scholarship on the troubadours was both well known and extraordinarily well respected; he demonstrated his own brand of heroism in his voluntary decision to change countries, a move in no way dictated by financial circumstances; he was the embattled defender of Wagner's music in Victorian England. Ford reports, "In the seventies and eighties there were cries for the imprisonment alike of the critics who upheld and the artistes who performed the Music of the Future. The compositions of Wagner were denounced as being atheistic, sexually immoral, and tending to further Socialism and the throwing of bombs. . . . I really believe that my father, as the chief exponent of Wagner in these islands, did go in some personal danger."[35] Like Madox Brown, then, Hueffer was a figure of personal authority and conviction, whose life and work overshadowed and influenced that of his son.

Undoubtedly, it would have been easier for Ford had his father been in life the forbidding figure he necessarily became in Ford's psychological structures. Idealizing his grandfather, Ford relegated his father to the internalized bad-mother position, the child's nightmare image externally symbolizing internal anxiety, self-doubt ambivalence, and self-hatred. His father also represented the world, imposing the undeniable restrictions of the reality principle on the small child. Ford remembered, "He was enormous in stature, had a great red beard and rather a high voice. He comes back to me most frequently as standing back on his heels and visibly growing larger and larger."[36] Yet in his work on troubadour poetry, Hueffer provided Ford with the romantic theme later to permeate most of his work.

According to Hueffer's text, the constant theme of medieval Provençal poetry was "an aristocratic lady dissatisfied with her husband and openly calling for death to come and kill him soon in order that she may be reunited with her lover." But the text emphasized that "not all ladies were inexorable; not all troubadours contented with a purely ideal worship. Ardent wooings led to passionate attachments, and lovers' bliss was frequently followed by lovers' quarrels."[37] In other words, Hueffer left his son a legacy mixing medieval romantic fantasy with a vision of sexual reality, pleasure begetting pain, in contrast to Madox Brown's thoroughly naive romanticism.

The two men left Ford with a dichotomous experience of authority as well. His father combined German authoritarianism with Victorian cultural ideals. Hueffer, the literal alien, adopted to the letter English culture and became more at home in the strange country than in his homeland. Madox Brown, by birth an English citizen, retained his lifelong allegiance to French customs and philosophy, possessing as well the artist's disdain for bourgeois sensibilities. He associated with groups (William Morris's craft guild and the Pre-Raphaelite painters) antiauthoritarian in their fundamental tenets and emphasized individually determined rather than socially sanctioned ideals, while Hueffer insisted his son respond to a set of impersonal standards judgmentally enforced.

Ford's novels frequently contain plots and characters ironically commenting on a childhood caught between two powerful and opposed figures. His books, both the fairy tales and the realistic fiction, revolve on plots using a configuration of the troubadour situation. For example, *The Good Soldier* would attain a peculiar ironic humor if the story were told from the perspective of Florence Dowell. Florence, who is married to John Dowell, has a passionate love affair with Edward Ashburnham, coincident with her desire to inhabit Edward's ancestral manor, thus certifying her own aristocratic origin. Within the world of the novel, however, Florence is the central antagonist. Using her, Ford comments slyly on his father's infusion of reality into romance. Yes, he seems to say, the "ladies" may well be passionate, but are they ladies? Nancy Rufford, on the other hand, the novel's ingenue, who also falls in love with Edward, passes through a single episode of sexual passion, experienced as a fantasy after her first— and only—glass of wine: "She never touched alcohol again. Not once after that did she have such thoughts. They died out of her mind; they left only a feeling of shame so insupportable that her brain could not take it in and they vanished."[38] There, Ford implies, in contrast to Florence, is a genuine heroine, whose passion has been described by Denis de Rougemont: "Romance only comes into existence where love is fatal, frowned upon and doomed by life itself . . . passion means suffering."[39]

The plot of the Tietjens tetralogy is, from the narrow focus of the relationship between Christopher Tietjens and Valentine Wannop, similarly an extended, almost straightforward contradiction of Hueffer's understanding of the troubadours. Christopher and Valentine are lovers who avoid sexual consummation for three volumes because they are among the "some who do not," the few people left after the devastation of World War I who retain their belief in order and principled behavior. Sylvia Tietjens, an aristocrat married to Christopher, is in contrast early established as the great villain of the novels, and her sexual passion for Christopher therefore is colored with the taint of a morbid perversion.

Not surprisingly, Ford used the technique of double vision to memorialize his father. Like Conrad, his father was a figure too powerful for Ford to attack directly, so that his subversive bid for authority was necessarily couched in concealed forms. For example, he wrote, "Similarly with my father, who was a man of great rectitude and with strong ideals of discipline. Yet for a man of his date he must have been quite mild in his treatment of his children. . . . Nevertheless, what I remember of him most was that he called me 'the patient but extremely stupid donkey.' And so I went through life until just the other day with the conviction of extreme sinfulness and of extreme stupidity."[40] It is not simply that Ford begins the passage complimenting his father and concludes by castigating him, but also that his tone is one of calculated whimsy. Remembering his childhood, Ford intends to create the effect of a child writing, could a child possess the necessary language skills. In doing so, Ford places the reader in the child's position, identifying with the narrator. The reader should experience the sort of pathetic sympathy for the abused child which calls forth the vitiated resentment of the victim, rather than the will to do battle with an equally powerful antagonist. As Keller says, "Domination and submission are twin ploys—both substitutes for real differentiation and for dynamic autonomy. In both, the net result is curiously the same. For children of both sexes, and for most of us as adults as well, the mythical power of the mother endures."[41] Ford's father and grandfather represented to him antithetical conceptions of authority, and therefore of culture, creating a psychic conflict Ford attempted to resolve in his fiction by re-creating versions of each position together with his own felt powerlessness. In his fiction the conflict engendered by the male authority figures populating his memoirs is transferred onto his female characters, reasserting the "mythical power" of the mother, which Ford attempted to deny by excluding his mother from his autobiographical material.

The Good Soldier offers a particularly striking example of the conflict between form and subject indicating the presence of an imagined reader as transference imago. The novel's content focuses on a tale of adultery and betrayal among two couples, one English and one American, set in Edwardian England. Structurally, the tale is told retrospectively in four sections, of which the first three are flashbacks on the past relationships among the four principal characters and the fourth details the events after the adulterous liaison becomes known to the narrator. Sections two and three are each designed to illuminate and expand material in the preceding section. Here Ford developed the *progression d'effet*, through which the reader is gradually offered an increasing number of secondary details so that final clarification of the primary plot comes as a shocking surprise. The technique functions like the physical display of a magician, who conceals the mechanics of the trick behind a welter of diversionary movements. The reader is offered a narrative that appears open but in fact functions to conceal rather than reveal. The series of retellings from multiple perspectives, moreover, is often at variance with an underlying subtext, so that a simple story gains ambiguity despite the narrator's articulated intention to be clear.

The storytelling of many analysands displays the same ambiguity of a tale of several tellings, structured to reveal and to obscure, and representing a process at variance with underlying content. Transference shapes such narratives. The analysand develops a persona to narrate the story unconsciously, as the story itself is unconsciously directed to an imagined version of the analyst based on the analysand's transference needs. Within the analytic situation are at least four people: the patient, the patient's narrating persona, the analyst, and the imago of the analyst to whom the patient directs his or her narrative.

To narrate *The Good Soldier*, Ford chose the American, John Dowell, who is also the betrayed husband within the small group of four friends. Dowell is a curious choice of narrating personality. Naive, sentimental, fundamentally passive, not overly sensitive or intuitive, his personality is in almost direct contrast to the story of sexual violence, passion, and psychological mystery he relates. Furthermore, in his style of narration Dowell emphasizes his confusion and uncertainty. As Susan Lanser has recognized, "Insecurity, defensiveness, apology, and self-deprecation are all forms of reticence not conventionally expected of a narrator."[42] Thus through the form of his narration Dowell appears to speak to a reader more authoritative than he, perhaps one who can give him the absolution he seems to seek as he emphasizes his role as witness and historian rather than participant in the grim events of the story.

Ford personifies Dowell's audience, within the text: "So I shall just imagine myself for a fortnight or so at one side of the fireplace of a country cottage, with a sympathetic soul opposite me. And I shall go on talking, in a low voice while the sea sounds in the distance and overhead the great black flood of wind polishes the bright stars." This personification establishes an immediate pseudointimacy with the real reader, who now has been given a marked placed in the narrative. Together, Dowell and the reader will discover the truth of the "sad affair"[43] he has witnessed. Ford reinforces this pseudointimacy with another trick he frequently uses in his writing. Many of Dowell's sentences conclude with an ellipsis, a grammatical form implying a shared context of information, sensibility, or culture. To understand Dowell's elliptical sentence endings, the reader must develop an intuitive sympathy with both Dowell's mind and situation. In this fictive harmony, in the peaceful and conventionally soothing ambience of a fireside chat, Dowell and his listener/reader will leisurely investigate the previous nine years of Dowell's life.

Shockingly, then, through his retrospective first-person narration, Dowell discovers, along with the reader, that his wife and the English husband have been lovers for almost the entire period of the couples' acquaintance; that the English wife conspired with them to conceal the relationship from Dowell; that the English husband, Edward Ashburnham, is a habitual philanderer; that his apparently proper and rather coldly reserved wife, Leonora, seethes with both hatred and sexual passion for her husband; and that Dowell's own wife, Florence, was an accomplished liar who gulled and emasculated Dowell from the first moment of their meeting. Dowell's narration portrays him as the innocent and unknowing victim of a conspiracy contructed by the other three. In concert with Ford's aesthetic belief that a novel should be written in language echoing the cadences and style of colloquial speech,[44] Dowell's narrative presents him as frank and straightforward in his direct address to the reader/listener, whom he implies is as baffled and confused as he by the "dark" truth of what had appeared to be a tranquil and serene way of life.

Form and subject in this novel therefore contradict each other at the juncture of the narrating voice. The novel is about a tale of violent passion and betrayal; Dowell narrates it from the perspective of detached observer. "This is the saddest story I have ever heard,"[45] he begins, denying through the passivity of his style any responsibility for the sordid events. Ford invites the reader to sympathize with Dowell, whose appeal should lie in his innocent victimization and consistent confusion. Dowell's pretense is that his ignorance denies him authority. In effect, Ford, through Dowell, attempts to separate love from knowledge and power, a fracture which should place Dowell in the feminine position, along with the reader invited to become Dowell's confidante. Thus, the real reader's autonomous perspective on the tale is closely manipulated, despite what appears to be an open narrative told by a narrator who is ideally suited by his apparent disinterestedness to convey accurately the truth of events and who makes a great effort to retrace the sequence of their occurrence. The reader is manipulated to ignore Dowell's authority as narrator, to ignore the violence and confusion of the story he chooses to tell. Dowell emerges from the juxtaposition of form and subject as a self-identified victim complexly manipulating his status to victimize his reader.

Placing Dowell's narration in the context of a relationship with his reader permits the configuration of Ford's transference imago to become visible. Although Dowell seems to inhabit the feminine, submissive position, his narrative in fact directs the reader to place his identifiably female characters in that position. Dowell addresses a reader who is *like* him in two ways. First, this reader will identify, as Dowell identifies, with Edward Ashburnham. Second, this reader will disparage, as Dowell disparages, all the female characters. Dowell's reader is a man who feels as powerless as Dowell, but theirs is an ironic loss of power, one which certifies their self-worth. Like Ford's grandfather, Dowell implies that he and his reader are the sensitive members of a culture which degrades sensitivity. Like Edward Ashburnham, whose honor finally causes his death, Dowell pretends that his ignorance is an innocence shared with his reader, which denies them both the knowledge functioning as the sign of cultural authority.

Considered in the context of a dynamic relationship, Dowell's narrative appears to be an extended example of phatic communication, designed to soothe both himself and his listener, while also diverting the listener/reader from the narrative's main point. That main point is Dowell's own control of the violent events in which he denies participating yet from which he receives gratification. Dowell's insistently stated desire, to locate the truth, is literally misleading. His is not a search for meaning but a search for control, a search he fulfills passively. By pretending to desire nothing other than truth, he limits both his pain and his culpability; by emphasizing his status as witness, he gratifies himself vicariously. Ironically, Dowell's masked activity functions to render the reader passive. Dowell, thoroughly in control of the sequence and perspective from which the story is told, ensures, by making his narration as confusing as possible, that the reader must accept his authority. Covertly, then, Dowell accepts the cultural connection between knowledge and power as he explicitly voices his ignorance and powerlessness.

Not coincidentally, the question of Dowell's reliability has been central to criticism of *The Good Soldier*. Since Mark Schorer's seminal assessment of Dowell in 1951,[46] critics have aligned themselves on either side of the issue, on the one hand insisting with Schorer that Dowell is a masterpiece of comic irony, and on the other that Ford intended Dowell's narration to be tragically reliable.[47] From the perspective of psychoanalytic transference, Dowell is both. The question of Dowell's reliability is an assertion in literary terms of Ford's conflicted conscious and unconscious ideas about personal authority. Seen as a comically unreliable narrator, Dowell reveals the cultural prejudice which links authority with objectivity while relegating subjective impression to a position of passive submission. Understood as tragically reliable, Dowell's narration participates in the romantic fantasy that love (or union with the mother) produces, inevitably, sorrow and suffering.

Inescapable in either case, however, is the fact that Dowell, the innocent victim, is the character who obtains all his desires when the novel concludes. Dowell admits his success in typically indirect fashion:

So here I am very much where I started thirteen years ago. I am the attendent, not the husband, of a beautiful girl, who pays no attention to me. . . . Not one of us has got what he really wanted. Leonora wanted Edward, and she has got Rodney Bayham, a pleasant enough sort of sheep. Florence wanted Branshaw, and it is I who have bought it from Leonora. I didn't really want it; what I wanted mostly was to cease being a nurse-attendant. Well, I am a nurse-attendant. Edward wanted Nancy Rufford and I have got her. Only she is mad. . . . Why can't people have what they want? The things were all there to content everybody; yet everybody has the wrong thing . . . it is beyond me.[48]

Reading this statement through Ford's double vision implies that Dowell is sexually responsive and romantic, the sort of man Edward was, who could sweep a young, beautiful girl into a passionate love affair, and implies as well that his entire life has been a series of accidents. In contrast, Dowell now both has everything he always desired and in the way he desired it: Nancy Rufford, in the nonsexual, unilateral relationship in which he is most comfortable; his wife Florence dead and Dowell revenged without direct violence on her; Edward dead and memorialized in a way which allows Dowell to idealize openly Edward's heroic personality and yet retain the appearance of being free from envy or jealousy; and Edward's wife Leonora remarried to a man much like Dowell, as "rabbity" and probably as dominated by his wife as Dowell was, again Dowell's revenge on her for her humiliating assessment of him as a sexual invalid. In fact each character is punished according to Dowell's fantasies. Each achieves not what he or she wants but what he or she deserves according to his or her relationship with Dowell. Because Dowell seems passive, ignorant, and innocent, he can insist on the mystery of Providence while the world of the text actually operates on the strictest principles of self-serving justice. Dowell, like Ford's father, assumes the cultural position of the patriarch whose "objective" principles control the lives of all who inhabit his sphere.

Dowell's personified reader/listener, on the other hand, receives nothing from the narrative, not even genuine enlightenment, because Dowell apparently concludes the book as confused as he has begun: "I know nothing. I am very tired." Unlike the examples of Ford's autobiographical passages using double vision, here his real reader is not even given a narrator to admire. Although Dowell makes a bid for his reader/listener's respect through his final identification with the heroic Edward ("for I can't conceal from myself that I loved Edward Ashburnham—and that I love him because he was just myself. If I had had the courage and virility and possibly also the physique of Edward Ashburnham I should, I fancy, have done much what he did"), that effort is canceled for Ford's reader as Dowell describes the aftermath of Edward's suicide in the book's concluding paragraph. Even assuming that Ford's reader would not be repelled by the outrageous exaggeration of Dowell's fantasied similarity to Edward, Ford divests Dowell of all of a hero's dignity: "I didn't know what to say. I wanted to say: 'God bless you,' for I also am a sentimentalist. But I thought that perhaps that would not be quite English good form, so I trotted off with the telegram to Leonora. She was quite pleased with it."[49] The vision of Dowell "trotting off" perfectly describes his character; as Ford well knew, style is the man.

Even here, however, Ford has a dual purpose. While Dowell's phrase divests him of dignity, it also indicates he possesses the same wry irony about himself and his relationship with Edward that marked Ford's memoirs of his relationship with Conrad. Dowell is thus both more and less than he presents himself, perhaps even heroic in a manner impossible for Edward, who, as a sentimentalist, also was thoroughly lacking in humor or ironic self-deprecation. Ford's real reader, caught in Ford's double bind, receives nothing from the narrative other than an aesthetic experience—no education, no illumination, no comfort, no communication.

The real reader is given the implicit burden of Ford's conflict through the form of the novel, just as the real reader of his memoirs is given a similar burden as Ford makes statements for which he grammatically denies responsibility. Ford, through his narrator's passivity, denies the gratification both of the act of writing and of rendering the reader passive. Evidence attesting to Ford's ambivalence about similar conflicts in his personal relationships can be drawn both from his memoirs (1931, 1934) and from Arthur Mizener's outstanding biography, particularly those sections relating the dissolution of Ford's first marriage.

Although Ford's affair with the novelist Violet Hunt precipitated his separation from his wife, his memoirs suppress all mention of Hunt, focusing instead on his own sense of victimization. Ford depicts himself as the same sort of victim Dowell becomes, one whose suffering must be discerned by the astute observer because his "compassion" for the other prohibits him from making his plea for sympathetic understanding. According to Mizener's research, Ford subsequently adhered to the same pattern in relationships with several of the other important women in his life. Both Stella Bowen, the Australian painter with whom Ford lived between 1922 and 1929, and Jean Rhys, with whom he had an affair in 1924, draw portraits in their own work of Ford as a man who was "irresistible to women in his suffering."[50]

The striking inconsistency of form and subject in *The Good Soldier* ensnares the real reader, ensuring that she or he is both responsible for piecing the tale together and penalized for doing so. The form used by Ford—the transference imago—focuses and shapes the narration just as an analysand's transference shapes his account of himself, the narration of his story. The effect on the real reader is thereby parallel to that on an analyst, who must experience, but not react to the effect intended by the analysand, in order to comprehend the full range of the transference.

Perhaps this is nowhere more completely visible than in the dedication letter Ford appended to the novel ten years after its initial publication. Just as Dowell proposed an intimacy with his personified reader/listener denied by his style and covert manipulation of the textual world, so the loving letter dedicating *The Good Soldier* to Stella Bowen was written in the service of an extinct relationship, at a time when the emotional separation between Bowen and Ford was fast headed toward a formal break. The letter is filled with double vision, subtly comparing its narrator to the younger writers Ford believed had usurped his place in English letters, to their detriment. To fully apprehend the meaning of that letter, and to integrate it with the text of the novel, the real reader must defend against Ford's embedded self-portrait as the victim both of his contemporaries and of an emotion which overwhelms him. In fact, Ford's narrating persona in the letter and Dowell's voice in the novel are markedly similar. Both grope forward in a world beyond their comprehension, certainly not of their own making, facing a justice bleak and uncompromising in its blind severity. Yet both retain their desire for truth, for beauty, for love. The reader who mistakes this posture for genuine intimacy finds him or herself, like Stella Bowen, seduced and abandoned.

In using a passive narrator in *The Good Soldier*, Ford placed the observing voice inside the narrative and externalized the action. Through his style, Dowell describes a world beyond and around him, so his narration seems to be delivered to the reader from inside the core of his story, while all the events of the story occur outside his shell of confusion. In contrast, using an omniscient narrator combined with a passive protagonist in the Tietjens tetralogy allowed Ford to obtain the same effect on his reader but to write a fantasy rather than a "realistic" novel. Loosely, *The Good Soldier* satisfies his father's uncompromising standards while displaying their flaws. The Tietjens saga satisfies his grandfather's comprehension of the world as a place of romance and honor while at the same time admitting that the world's corruption makes of romance and honor a fantasy. Yet, in both books the narrator is subtly active while the real reader is rendered passive, made to experience a world out of his or her control, while the writer controls it all.

The four novels of the Tietjens saga focus on the disintegration of English culture during and after World War I by detailing the experience of Christopher Tietjens, younger son of an aristocratic family possessing vast properties in Northern England. Christopher is the same excellent feudal landlord connected to and concerned about all strata of his society whom Ford first created in Edward Ashburnham. Like Edward, Christopher is a "good soldier" in personal and public life; unlike Edward, Christopher experiences public, as well as private, life breaking apart around him. Thus Ford chose the conventional bildungsroman form, the story of a young man's self-development told through his adventures in the world, as the vehicle to analyze and document the fracture of the world itself. In contrast to the traditional bildungsroman hero, Christopher moves out into a world that is visibly disappearing. Immediately, then, what appears to be Ford's selection of a conventional form is disputed by his intended subject.

In fact, *Parade's End* is about modernism, "the great and irreversible change in human consciousness that took place when the shift from the civilization of the nineteenth century to that of the modern world as we know it occurred under the stress of World War I."[51] Although critical definitions of modernism are diverse, there is theoretical agreement that modernism implies a radical break with received tradition as manifested in aesthetic, political, religious, cultural, and psychological life. In developing his theory of the unconscious, Freud was essentially modernistic in his implication that human life found its motivations outside of conscious human agency. Ford, as well, was a premature modernist when he developed literary Impressionism in the first decade of the century. Acknowledging that "the Impressionist gives you, as a rule, the fruits of his own observations and the fruits of his own observations alone,"[52] he also admitted membership in an aesthetic movement fundamentally conceived as a mode of asking rather than answering questions. As individual perception is fundamental to modernism, so too is the understanding that the world is received distinctly by each individual, who must then attempt, with what can only be flawed success, to render private comprehension publicly accessible. The third-person omniscient form, implying the possibility of mutual vision and a central authority, was thus abandoned by writers such as Woolf, Proust, and Joyce, who realized the complex difficulties of attempting to describe fragmented interior life using forms inherited from the culturally integrated eighteenth and nineteenth centuries.

Ford's desires and conflicts ran counter to modernism. Although he was centrally concerned with private life, by it he meant privacy rather than psychological interiority. Critics have called him a great psychological novelist, but he was more concerned with concealing psychological reality, with the sort of privacy in life to which Christopher adheres as a cultural standard. Sylvia Tietjens finally proves her villainy not by her adultery but by her willingness to make a scandal in front of the servants. The modernist attempt to investigate the human psyche would have been anathema to Ford. In contrast, for example, to Woolf's *To the Lighthouse*, Ford used multiple perspectives less to establish difference of character than as a charade to conceal their lack of difference. Sylvia Tietjens and Valentine Wannop, the novels's respective female antagonist and protagonist, are nearly complementary figures, different only in that each completes the other. Sylvia, extremely tall and beautiful, the personification of evil sexuality, balances Valentine, extremely short and nearly plain, a complete ingenue whose post-Victorian scruples keep her virginal for nearly all four volumes. Sylvia, like Valentine and like Christopher, comes to make a cult of chastity, as does Edith Ethel Duchemin, whose love affair with Christopher's friend Vincent Macmaster underscores the principles which keep Christopher and Valentine apart. Both Christopher and Sylvia learn to retreat from present reality through daydreams so powerful they function almost like hallucinations. Most significant, Christopher, Sylvia, and Edith Ethel all, at various moments, use the same phrase, "napoo finny." Although the phrase was contemporary slang, and therefore could reasonably be expected to have been in general use, character differentiation is accomplished most powerfully through particularity of language. The dialogue selected for a character indicates personality, and in *Parade's End* all the characters sound remarkably alike, although the content of their speech differs. For example, throughout the novels Ford made wide use of exclamation points to conclude sentences, a device indicating a rather ingenuous character. Yet Valentine's characterologically viable exclamations are no more frequent than Christopher's or Sylvia's.

The characters achieve distinction only through narrative direction, with the exception of Sylvia and perhaps Leonie Tietjens, who is the French wife of Christopher's older brother Mark and a version of Jane Austen's Miss Bates. Sylvia's voice seems to attain an independence of personality almost beyond Ford's aesthetic control. Critics have realized that one of the major problems offered by the novels is Sylvia's character.[53] The real fascination and depth of her dialogue continually pushes her beyond the confines of the villain of the piece, the role Ford marked out for her. Similarly, Leonora Ashburnham in *The Good Soldier* frequently threatens, by the intricacy of her character, to escape her designated role. Both characters seem to meet the reader directly, unmediated by narrative direction, by virtue of the real power they exercise on the other characters in the novel and through their psychological complexity. In both novels, Sylvia and Leonora are the characters most actively in control of the plot; both are given creative power nearly equal to that of the narrator. In Keller's cogent formulation, because Ford's conflict about personal authority forces him to a rigid separation of those who dominate from those who submit, Leonora and Sylvia represent the enduring power of the mother whom Ford's narrators both fear and long to suppress.

Rather than a genuine attempt at psychological exposure culminating in unresolvable ambiguity, Ford's effort was toward psychological concealment, concluding in the fairy tale style of happy ending. *Parade's End*, often cited as a "war novel," as "more about our world than his,"[54] is inescapably a fantasy depicting a simpler world where good and evil are easily recognizable and distinct, where after much travail good triumphs, where "oracles" speak and magic is accepted as mundane.[55] As a fairy tale, *Parade's End* exists on a continuum of Ford's creative development begun with the composition of *The Brown Owl* in 1892, and its narrative voice resembles as well the narrative style in Ford's memories of Madox Brown. In those memoirs the narrator and central character are almost collaborators in the pleasure derived from the memory, and the imagined reader also is invited to collaborate with the narrator and central character, joining them to memorialize a character whose memory enhances them all.

But if we use the concept of psychoanalytic transference to examine Ford's imagined reader in *Parade's End*, Ford's address to his reader is less benign than in his memories of Madox Brown, for the pivotal point of the four novels is the perspective lent to Sylvia Tietjens, the central antagonist. Recall that in *The Good Soldier* Ford employed a passive first-person narrator to tell a story of sexual passion and violence. The narrator was internalized in the novel's structure; Dowell looked outward at the world around and in the first person re-created that world ordered according to his own desires. Dowell, then, determined the priority and significance of each event and character, and he therefore can be defined as the novel's point of disjuncture between narrative design and subject. In theoretical terms, Dowell represents the culturally repressed feminine. *Parade's End* reverses that structure. Narrated by an omniscient narrator, the books nevertheless bear the pretense of first-person narrations because of Ford's extensive use of first-person interior monologues. Yet these voices, with the exception of Sylvia's, all tend to merge into one another so that the final effect remains that of an integrated omniscient narration. The world surrounding the characters is torn by war and a disintegrating social system, and this public violence is reflected in the chaos and sexual warfare afflicting their personal lives. Ford's aesthetic problem, therefore, was to find a way to tell a story about chaos and still satisfy his psychological desire to establish order; to tell a story using techniques of psychological exposure and yet satisfy his desire for personal concealment; to tell a story using techniques meant to provide the reader with an experience of cultural disintegration, but satisfy his desire to educate the reader in the standards of cultural harmony. Solving those problems meant constructing a novel whose activity was, in a way, external to the world of the text. Unlike Dowell, who functioned as the actual active center of *The Good Soldier*, *Parade's End* contains a genuinely passive center in the character of Christopher and locates activity covertly in the character of Sylvia Tietjens. Sylvia, then, becomes Dowell's reversed figure—the feminine externalized, expressed traditionally as the witch.

Christopher is the consciously personified figure of the omniscient narrator in *Parade's End* in the same way Madox Brown was the personified or coeval narrator of Ford's earlier memoirs. With this integration between narrator and protagonist Ford satisfies Dowell's desire to *be* Edward Ashburnham, a desire impossible to fulfill given the realistic structure of *The Good Soldier*. Moreover, the integration of the narrator and Christopher allows Ford to render the narrator passive, and therefore guiltless, in the face of the general cultural disintegration. The narrator is no more responsible for creating portraits of violence than Christopher is for the awful destruction marking the battles in which he participates as a member of the British army. Christopher does not act, he resists. Any actions he finally commits are failures of resistance. On the one hand, Christopher, like Valentine, "can touch pitch and not be defiled."[56] On the other hand, all action in the novels is evaluated according to its effect on Christopher. Where, in *The Good Soldier*, knowledge was linked with power and authority, in *Parade's End*, power is connected to action. As in *The Good Soldier*, however, in the later books Ford also subtly undermines the patriarchal culture as a result of his conflicted attitudes about authority and love.

On the surface, the integration between Christopher and the narrator should absolve the imagined reader of war guilt as well, for the reader has been directed to identify with Christoper. But what seems to be a community built despite general corruption is actually a hierarchy of authority with the real reader at its lowest point. Although the real reader is invited by narrative direction to identify with Christopher, in the last volume Ford creates a personified reader in the character of Mark Tietjens, Christopher's brother. While Christopher's passivity functions to keep him out of action but in control, Mark's final passivity places him under the control of the general omniscient narrator, who allows Mark's wife Leonie, the particular narrator of *The Last Post*, to act as surrogate narrator.

Mark has been the indispensable head of a large government department. But by the final volume, Mark lies in a thatched shed, incapable of speech or movement, the victim of a mysterious paralysis. He is nursed by Leonie, whose incessant conversation functions to reveal plot information while concealing behind its torrential barrage the psychological states of the other characters. Leonie knows everything superficial and nothing in depth, all appearance and little reality. Christopher virtually disappears as an active presence from *The Last Post*, leaving the reader, accustomed to understanding the world through Christopher, to learn of him secondhand; like Mark, the reader is deprived of speech and action, made dependent on a voluble, good natured nurse whose intuitive penetration is adequate to distinguish good from evil but fails at psychological complexity.

Mark's illness is also deliberately ambiguous. Mark believes his paralytic state is his voluntary protest against the armistice agreement prohibiting England from invading Germany. If the illness is feigned, the reader's power is akin to what Mark imagines his own to be: temporarily suspended in favor of higher principles. The reader's passivity thereby is subtly rewarded by Ford, who through Mark defines it as honorable behavior. But if the illness is authentic, as Mark's doctors believe and Ford hints, then the reader also has been paralyzed because he inhabits Mark's position as the passive observer. Only one character—Sylvia—and the omniscient narrator remain active.

Sylvia's activity is the crux of the disjuncture between form and subject. She represents the enduring power of the mother which the cultural separation of love and power is designed to defeat. Like the omniscient narrator, she has the power to control plot events. Most of Christopher's difficulties occur because she has "pulled the strings of shower baths," that is, she has destructively meddled in Christopher's life in order to assert her own importance. Ford might as well have suggested Sylvia pulled puppet strings, for at various moments she manipulates all the characters: "She never spoke to another woman [or man] but to make her a lady's maid or a cat's paw" (731). Just as Christopher is the text's consciously personified narrator, a figure Ford could admire himself for becoming, Sylvia is Ford's unconsciously personified narrator, the character made to bear the burden of the narrator's creatively malign manipulation of the plot, the other characters, and the imagined reader.

Because Sylvia also is a character within the text, Ford can use her to achieve the same double vision as in his memories of Conrad and his father. Sylvia's direct comments on the culture surrounding her, and her visible action as the nightmare representative of that culture, allow Ford to disengage himself from contemporary social mores while ensnaring the reader. "The game she plays is to torment him [Christopher] to provoke him into intimacy" (718); the same game Dowell plays with his personified reader/listener; the same game Ford, through Sylvia, plays with the imagined reader of *Parade's End*. Sylvia is the fairy tale's witch, disputing in the absolute evil of her character the realistic content of the tetralogy. To integrate Sylvia's character into the text, Ford is forced to make almost explicit its quality of fairy tale, and in fact the whole tetralogy bears a passing resemblance to the Hansel and Gretel tale. Despite the overlay of war and battlefield scenes, the sense of Christopher and Valentine, two innocents wandering hand in hand through a greenwood to be trapped by a child-eating witch, is pervasive.

Just as Sylvia as a character is the key to the disjuncture between narrative structure and subject, the crucial scene through which Ford intended to save his imagined reader's interest is the final denouement between Mark and Sylvia, just after she has invaded the grounds of the house in which Christopher and Valentine now live. In concert with her general cleverness, Sylvia first sends her son and an American woman, who has rented the Tietjens estate, down the hill to annoy Mark, who lies in his open-air shed paralyzed but alert. Sylvia herself approaches last, a figure of mystery and evil, recognized clearly only by Mark.

Had this scene been constructed in accordance with Sylvia's established character, it should have concluded with the general rout of the household, a unit Ford indicates is so tenuous that Christopher and Valentine derive their income from Christopher's sale of antiques: their house is their showplace, and their furnishings and their permanence are continually sold out from under them. But in a fairy tale what seems evanescent is often most solid, and so when Sylvia reaches Mark, it is the latter who is the victor, despite his paralysis. Sylvia's explicit excuse is that her principles prohibit her from endangering a pregnant woman (Valentine is carrying Christopher's child), but her defeat is also necessary to save the reader's commitment to the novel. Because the reader has been herded into a tighter and tighter box with Mark, his sudden victory is magical, the nearly inexplicable working of a benign Providence. Even Sylvia is aware that larger forces are at work: "It had been obvious to her for a long time that God would one day step in and intervene for the protection of Christopher. . . . It is, in the end, she reluctantly admitted, the function of God and the invisible Powers to see that a good man shall eventually be permitted to settle down to a stuffy domestic life" (794).

But *Parade's End* is less a Christian than a patriarchal mystery. Sylvia's suspicion of the existence of a higher power is echoed by Mark. In a peculiar fashion, he connects himself with that power. Deciding that his illness is a matter of willed action, he realizes that "he must have spent quite a disproportionate amount of his time in thinking about the motives of Sylvia" and that "his sister-in-law Sylvia represented for him unceasing, unsleeping activities of a fantastic kind" (724). Realizing that Sylvia, when she approaches him lying in his shed, is weeping, he also realizes that her defeat has been accomplished and that "his, Mark's, occupation was gone. He would no longer have to go on willing against her; she would drop into the sea in the wake of their family vessel and be lost to view" (830). Mark, that is, has ceased all physical activity but has retained the illusion that it has been the power of his mind bent against Sylvia which saved Christopher, much as the audience of a melodrama wills the villain to defeat. In that movement, Ford lends the imagined reader, through Mark, both the magical power of childhood thought, in which wishing is believed to be as potent as action, and the cultural power of the father to protect his child.

Mark has, in fact, returned to a second childhood, also a second chance, during which he meditates on the events leading to his father's suicide. Long assuming that he indirectly caused his father's death by passing on to the older man rumors about Christopher and Valentine, he comes to realize that his father was not the sort of man to commit suicide; he therefore absolves himself of patricide. The plot events accompanying Mark's realization are so tangled (involving suspected incest and adultery) that the effect is one of "wishing makes it so." Mark wishes, and Ford wishes with him, to reestablish innocence in the greenwood. This solution implies that to Ford, the resolution of his conflict between love and power could only be achieved magically. In cultural terms, Ford has accepted the patriarchal structure by literally banishing the sexual mother, inserting instead pregnant but eternally virginal "Valentine."

With this resolution Ford, Mark, and the imagined reader achieve complete integration. By portraying Mark as personified reader of *The Last Post*, Ford has directed his imagined reader to identify with a mind at work without its body. All the ambiguities of physical existence have fallen away. Despite his paralysis, Mark is the hero of the last volume so that the imagined reader, who has retreated before Sylvia's progress for three volumes, finds himself miraculously saved precisely by virtue of former defeat. Using a version of his double vision technique, Ford connects his own creative power with Mark; both exercise an authority dependent on passivity. On the one hand, the reader, with Mark, can rejoice at the fairy tale's happy ending, good triumphant over evil. On the other hand, Ford, who also is responsible for Sylvia's creation, can, like Mark, maintain that he resisted rather than created her.

Ford's work, like that of Jean Rhys, presents an example of a writer absorbed by unconscious cultural patterns. Where Rhys, as a woman, consciously identified herself as the oppressed victim of patriarchal authority, Ford, although male, suffered the same felt oppression by defining himself as an artist. Like Rhys, he apprehended the cultural distinction between love and power, and like Rhys as well, he desired love, although choosing love meant submission. But although Rhys almost seemed to revel in submission, her work is marked by a narrative structure which reflects patriarchal hierarchy, so that her narrator comes to dominate her protagonist—while Rhys dominates her reader—unconsciously resolving her conflict between love and authority along traditional lines. Rhys, a female writer, addresses her unconsciously imagined reader as if she possessed male authority. Unfortunately, because Ford *was* male, such reversal was more difficult. Addressing his reader through the culturally designated feminine position caused him sufficient unconscious discomfort to force him to seek authority indirectly, through passivity. Ironically, the suffocating mass of Ford's eighty-seven volumes can be understood as the same type of behavior displayed by women who "resolve" their oedipal nexus. Rendered impotent, they attempt, unconsciously, to regain power by becoming possessive and intrusive. Finally, Ford's intrusion into every possible genre exposes an unconscious and unresolvable conflict between submission and domination in the context of a culture that mistakes sensitivity for submission, and instead defines dominant men as heroes and dominant women as witches.

CHAPTER 3

Nathaniel Hawthorne's *The Blithedale Romance:* Narrative and Interpretation

> . . . The real personage—may be said to have been created mainly by ourselves!
> —Nathaniel Hawthorne, *The Blithedale Romance*

T HE LITERARY CRITIC Frank Kermode writes that "the capacity of narrative to submit to the desires of this or that mind without giving up secret potential may be crudely represented as a dialogue between story and interpretation." This dialogue "begins when the author puts pen to paper and it continues through every reading that is not merely submissive."[1] Kermode is suggesting that interpretation, when it is not dialogue, is a mode of domination—and failure to interpret, conversely, is "submission" to the text. He extends this idea to the social sphere and, like George Orwell in *1984*, alludes to a central irony inherent in a dynamic that is intended to illuminate and clarify but that becomes instead an instrument of control when those in power interpret others according to their own needs and desires.

Evelyn Keller, reflecting on the connection between gender and power, believes "it is a persistent fact of our culture that men tend to be especially preoccupied with questions of their autonomy and are considerably more likely than women to seek to support that autonomy through the pursuit of mastery and domination. This fact reflects not simply the greater access that men have to power, but, more deeply, our very definition of what it means to be masculine. It is a reflection of the psychosocial construction of man."[2] Interpretation, then, as a method of domination can be a response to fears of loss of autonomy, and in Western culture it plays a role in resolution of the oedipal nexus as the male child moves to enter culture as masculine by gaining autonomy from his mother. At the individual level, resolution for little boys presumes the repression of erotic desire for the mother in return for a self-definition manifested by dominating behaviors intended to devalue the power of the female. In the larger culture, interpretation and domination merge in the endless objectification of the female in literature and art, in representations of the female form and psyche as objects whose unconscious power is displaced and diluted through the continual interpretation which appears to authorize their existence. Thus Kermode's understanding that the nature of narrative links story and interpretation in continuous dialogue places the text in the culturally female position and the reader in the position of masculine interpreter.

What is the place of the male writer in this dialogue? Although the act of creation is implicitly an act of authority over the text, also implicit is the writer's understanding that his "product" must "submit" to its many readers. Ironically, for the male writer, the desire for an audience may be fraught with cultural conflicts not experienced by the female writer, whose more fluid sense of self involves a continual interchange of authority between self and other. Traditionally in the West, male writers have been considered "effete," and even "effeminate," in part because their activity is private, not public like the identifiably masculine activities, but perhaps also because within the act of writing inheres an act of submission. Therefore, to regain the masculine position, the male writer may, like Ford Madox Ford, deny responsibility for his creation by connecting the act of narration with the act of observation and witnessing, or like Nathaniel Hawthorne, he may usurp the reader's position, complexly intertwining the act of narration with the act of interpretation.

Hawthorne was explicitly concerned with the interpretation his work would receive. Each of his novels and short story collections is introduced with preface material subtly directing his readers how to receive his texts. In fact, in the preface to his last novel, *The Marble Faun*, Hawthorne extends his direction to include a description of the reader's persona: "He meant it for that one congenial friend—more comprehensive of his purposes, more appreciating of his success, more indulgent of his shortcomings, and, in all respects, closer and kinder than a brother,—that all-sympathizing critic, in short, whom an author never actually meets, but to whom he implicitly makes his appeal whenever he is conscious of having done his best."

Hawthorne's interpretative method is of course shared by psycho-analysis in theory and practice, for the analyst's interpretations are designed to enable the patient to reach a self-definition by reconstruct-ing the narrative of his or her past history. Hawthorne's major subject, like that of psychoanalysis, was interpreting the past to discern its secrets and therefore understand its influence and effect on present and future behavior. It is ironic, then, that whereas in analytic practice interpretation is used, theoretically, to dispel the patient's transfer-ence, in Hawthorne's work, interpretation certifies his transference to, and reveals the configurations of, his unconsciously imagined reader, whose position in the text he hoped to inhabit. For Hawthorne, inter-pretation merged with transference when he used analysis to dominate and conceal unconscious fear and desire. He idealized his reader only to effect a spurious merger designed to displace and dilute the reader's authority, just as Western women discover that a similar cultural ideal-ization only authorizes their powerlessness.

Hawthorne's address to his imagined reader, therefore, illuminates a traditional model of authority, covert in operation, which masquer-ades as the displacement of authority while assuming power through the effect of interpretation. Moreover, Hawthorne's secondary subject was the romantic fantasy which is the conscious articulation of re-pressed oedipal desire, experienced as the nostalgic love for an object necessarily unattainable. Throughout Hawthorne's canon, his work valorizes the asexual idealized female figure inevitably the adjunct of oedipal renunciation. Thus interpretation in his work is a means of retaining power in the face of obscure forces almost too powerful to be withstood, forces constrained by using the myth of female purity to deny female sexuality, interpreting female power as powerlessness. Both modes—the usurpation of the reader's interpretive authority over the text and the romantic fantasy sanctioning female powerlessness—are particularly evident in *The Blithedale Romance.*

The Blithedale Romance is the most explicitly autobiographical of Hawthorne's novels, for it focuses on characters Hawthorne encountered and events he experienced during his year at the Transcendentalist commune of Brook Farm. Many passages are taken almost unrevised from his Brook Farm notebooks, for example, the memorably grisly aftermath of Zenobia's suicide, which suggests that in composing the novel Hawthorne was less interested in events than in his perception of them. With a title which indicates it will penetrate the surface of reality to the allegorical and allusive significance below, like Hawthorne's other romances, the *Blithedale Romance* actually is a work of secrecy, concerned with maintaining rather than revealing distortion. The narrator Hawthorne created to tell the tale even extends this motif of secrecy and suppression through a narration which, while claiming interpretation, is informed by duplicity and evasion.

As many critics have realized, Miles Coverdale, a minor writer whose name reveals his constant attempt to mystify and distort, is a badly disguised portrait of Hawthorne.[3] Coverdale does not act, he interprets. For example, arriving at Blithedale during a late winter storm, it is his misfortune to contract a heavy cold which sends him to bed for the first week of the new community's life. His misfortune, as Hawthorne gradually makes clear, is also his desire, as from his bed he can observe and analyze without subjecting himself to return scrutiny.

Briefly summarized, what Coverdale observes are the relationships among the four dominant characters of the novel: Hollingsworth, a social reformer obsessed by his vision of prison reform; Zenobia, a dramatically beautiful, sensual, and wealthy young woman in love with Hollingsworth; Priscilla, a very young, slight, timid maiden who appears at Blithedale possessing no known past but who is gradually revealed to be Zenobia's half-sister and successful rival for Hollingsworth's affections; and Westervelt, a mysterious, evil figure who has over both women some compelling hold complexly entangled with his mesmeric talent. These, together with Moodie, who is revealed to be father of both Zenobia and Priscilla, form the cast of characters for Coverdale's quite conventional nineteenth-century melodrama.

Coverdale's narration, much like that of the analysand, is fraught with anomaly and inconsistency. As Frederick Crews states, "No narrator ever had worse luck than Coverdale in learning the most essential facts about the figures whose story we are supposed to enjoy."[4] Most of the scenes he describes are observed literally through a "glass darkly": from the branches of a tree under which pass and repass Zenobia and Westervelt engaged in conversation caught by Coverdale only in snatches, forcing him to imply or creatively reconstruct the rest; or through the back window of his hotel, which "coincidentally" looks into the windows of the rooms occupied by Zenobia and Priscilla, at a scene with Westervelt which Coverdale can barely perceive what with window shades, glass, and distance. Two of his most important revelations are actually creative interpretations, in which he first reconstructs a narrative originally told by Zenobia and later relates the autobiography of old Moodie; for the most crucial encounter of the plot, the meeting between Zenobia, Hollingsworth, and Priscilla, he arrives "half an hour late."[5]

Coverdale's narrative is also punctuated by inexplicable gaps in coherence. He fails to tell his reader, for example, how he knew that Zenobia would take rooms in the hotel next to his own, or that Priscilla is the veiled lady compelled by Westervelt to act as sibyl on a Boston stage, or most important, how he came to find Zenobia's handkerchief and understand it as evidence of her suicide. As Crews observes,

Coverdale not only takes poetic liberties with the events he is narrating; he represents himself as having known how they would turn out before they occurred. His dreams and fantasies at Blithedale, if they had been recorded, 'would have anticipated several of the chief incidents of this narrative, including a dim shadow of its catastrophe.' It is impossible to say whether Coverdale has really had foreknowledge or has seriously altered the facts in recounting them; the only certain point is that we are meant to see some degree of correspondence between his tale and the secret inclination of his mind.[6]

Certainly Crews correctly assesses the tale as the mirror of Coverdale's secret, perhaps unconscious, desires. If we look more closely, however, at the way Coverdale represents Hawthorne's conscious and unconscious relationship with the world of Blithedale, in order to discern the reader Hawthorne rather than Coverdale imagined for the book, Coverdale occupies a somewhat altered position. Voyeur of course, Coverdale becomes less the narrator of the text than its reader/interpreter. The community of Blithedale, as he interprets it, functions as the objective correlative of his interior world. He is an isolate surprised by community, while the community itself is a utopian ideal transcending its own time, place, and inhabitants. Blithedale is so attractive to Coverdale because it represents for him objectified desire, nostalgia made concrete but always receding before its complete realization.

Kermode writes, "We may like to think, for our purposes, of narrative as the product of two intertwined processes, the presentation of a fable and its progressive interpretation (which of course alters it). The first process tends toward clarity and propriety ('refined common sense'), the second toward secrecy, toward distortions which cover secrets";[7] and I would add, toward authority. As interpreter of the text of Blithedale, Coverdale asserts authority over his desire by forcing the text to conform to his conscious transference imago—his palpable yearning. Within this model, although Coverdale is interpreter, he is also analysand, while the "analyst"—the personified reader to whom he delivers information—becomes his creature by virtue of his interpretation. His distortions, then, are not mysterious gaps in his narrative but form the content of the narrative itself. Coverdale is an interpreter whose act of interpretation is an effort to dominate text and reader with the appearance of elucidation while covertly distorting and mystifying it.

The issue is to be explored in this novel is the act of narration—the assertion of authority through re-presentation. Coverdale is the analysand who places the analyst in the position he experienced himself when he was a powerless child, when his life was controlled and created by the narrative structures of the powerful others whose "reality" he was forced to observe. Coverdale remains an observer, but now his act of observation grants him the power of narrative authority, the ability to enter and control another's life by reconstituting narrative sequence.

So, although Coverdale can be understood as wavering between literature and human affection—between control and the loss of it— his verbal gestures toward humility are mendacious. He may warn his reader that as soon as one places a friend under observation, "we insulate him from many of his true relations, magnify his peculiarities, inevitably tear him into parts, and, of course, patch him very clumsily together again. What wonder, then, should we be frightened by the aspect of a monster, which, after all—though we can point to every feature of his deformity in the real personage—may be said to have been created mainly by ourselves!" (64)—but the crucial element in his warning is his underlying pride in what Mary Shelley termed "my monster." The secrets Coverdale reveals he believes (and he conveys this belief to the reader) to be the essential truth of each character. Coverdale is less interested in penetrating veils than in creating new ones, narratives he designs and therefore controls. His transference imago, the image of the reader he imagines for his manuscript, a figure he unconsciously needs to control, emerges through the secrets he discerns and the secrets he in turn keeps about himself.

Many critical assessments of the novel include the understanding that not one of the four characters Coverdale observes, with the qualified exception of Zenobia, is a fully realized personality. Most critics assume this flaw results from Hawthorne's difficulties with this novel and define the work as "failed utopian satire, failed melodrama, or failed autobiography."[8] Hollingsworth, particularly, "is a dismal failure. He never *does* anything, he seldom displays any emotional fluidity or complexity, he is rarely given one of those saving human touches, which, by their very presence, would make more credible his essential inhumanity."[9] Priscilla, certainly, is little better, defined by her wan, pallid, slender timidity, her asexual tenderness. Even her sibylline powers seem temporary, fleeting reflections of Westervelt's more magnetic but equally stereotypical personality. It is not surprising to learn that Hawthorne extensively rewrote this book and found it difficult to settle on a title, wavering among "Hollingsworth," "Zenobia," "Priscilla," "Miles Coverdale's Three Friends," "The Veiled Lady," "Blithedale," "The Arcadian Summer," and what became his choice by default, *The Blithedale Romance*. What is most striking about Hawthorne's indecisiveness is that all the alternative titles focus the reader away from Coverdale, toward Coverdale's narrative. That is, although Coverdale seems to be modeled on Hawthorne's own personality, Hawthorne's effort was to direct *his* reader's attention away from his mirrored reflection, away from the form of his narration, onto its content. It is not simply that Hawthorne would fear that his reader might mistake the author for Coverdale, but that concealed in the style of Coverdale's narration was a portrait of Hawthorne he himself was loath to unveil.

Throughout Hawthorne's canon images reflected in mirrors abound, usually indicating some reversal or distortion, such as the moments when, in *The Scarlet Letter*, little Pearl is seen doubled by Hester, who stands on the far side of the brook whose shimmering surface reflects her daughter, or when Pearl and Hester both see the scarlet letter magnified disproportionately in the conqueror's armor guarding the entrance to the Massachusett's governor's chamber where Hester's right to keep little Pearl will be decided. These images imply another truth, one bonded to appearance but somehow also tangential, as if another reality existed side-by-side with its mundane version, one made palpable when caught slyly, unaware. Although in medieval inconography mirrors indicate a search for self-knowledge, Hawthorne's concern with reflected images is precisely the reverse. He feared self-revelation, feared catching sight of himself suddenly, accidentally, in a mirror placed to reflect a perspective he has not seen before, one which others, perhaps, have always perceived. What Hawthorne feared was not the truth, but the ugly, determined truth—the intrusion of past into present and future—he assumed must be revealed at last. Furthermore, in what psychoanalytic theory defines as reaction formation—deliberately, although unconsciously, seeking out that which one fears—Hawthorne's fiction raises the specter of his fear in an almost obsessive fashion.

Within the psychoanalytic situation the analyst listens to the analysand's narrative by attending to nonverbal gestures as well as to verbal material. In fact, in order to "catch the drift" of the patient's unconscious within his or her own unconscious, the analyst must suspend ordinary attention and become what Freud called a "burnished mirror,"[10] reflecting back to the patient through the agency of interpretation what the patient does not consciously realize is his or her act of narration. If we extend this model to the literary text, the real reader must also attend to authorial gesture, visible as style, point of view, language, and tone, in order to read past the writer's transference imago, or unconsciously imagined reader.

That writer, then, who like Hawthorne seeks to focus his consciously imagined reader on the subject material of his text and away from its structure seeks also to manipulate the reader he assumes will read the work but fails to scrutinize the reader he unconsciously imagines for the book. Both Hawthorne and Coverdale attempt to control their consciously imagined readers through their subject material, while at the same time, their narratives are fraught with suppressions and gaps unconsciously addressing a reader whose configuration in turn directs textual structure. The secrets Coverdale "discovers" function as the visible conjunction of his conscious and unconsciously imagined readers. As subject, they reveal the "real" reader Coverdale thought would be engaged by melodrama; as structure, they are evidence of suppression rather than revelation, clues to the unconscious image Coverdale possessed of the reader who would ideally gratify his own secret and repressed desires and against whom he simultaneously felt the unconscious need to defend himself.

It is valuable, at this point, to examine the secrets of the other characters which Coverdale attempts to discover. His is not an idle act of voyeurism but the active attempt to dominate other characters through his interpretations. The secrets he reveals are therefore more potent as the symbols of his own desire for and fear of authority than as elucidations of actual mysteries; they are more powerful in revealing *how* he says than *what* he says. The simplest secret Coverdale discovers is that of old Moodie, whose shadowy figure is an almost gratuitous mystery. As Hollingsworth says, at a moment when Coverdale seems intent on obscuring the obvious, "Why do you trouble him with needless questions Coverdale, . . . You must have known, long ago, that it was Priscilla" (79). Coverdale employs Moodie as a means of titillating the reader, exciting a curiosity easily satisfied, with almost none of the loss of narrative authority likely to occur when a large mystery is revealed. Coverdale merely pretends to be mystified by Moodie. Although his reader may be intrigued to discover that Moodie is the father of both Zenobia and Priscilla, that discovery does not shed any direct light on the more significant mystery surrounding the relationships among Hollingsworth, Zenobia, Priscilla, and Westervelt. In a more conventional mystery novel, Moodie would function as the author's red herring, maintaining the reader's interest while diverting the reader from the real solution. Here, however, Moodie's secret functions as the first stage in a hierarchical structure Coverdale builds both consciously and unconsciously. Coverdale is aware that Moodie plays a small role in his melodrama but unaware that Moodie is, perhaps, one of the crucial elements composing his own and Hawthorne's transference imago.

According to Coverdale's conscious understanding, the next secret in ascending order of importance belongs to Hollingsworth. As Coverdale "reveals," Hollingsworth possesses three secrets: the first is his obsession, to the exclusion of human affection, with his philanthropic ideal. He wants to convert Blithedale into a haven for reformed ex-prisoners, a scheme which has been covertly financed by Zenobia. Coverdale, seeking the basis for the connection between Zenobia and

Hollingsworth, determines it is the latter's interest, disguised by purity of intention, in this vibrantly sexual woman's money. Hollingsworth's second secret, implied by the first, is thus the nature of his relationship with Zenobia. Within the conventional melodrama Coverdale creates, Hollingsworth is the hero; but by casting doubt on the integrity of Hollingsworth's interest in Zenobia, Coverdale subtly undermines, for his "real" reader, Hollingsworth's textual position. His ideals are heroic, but the methods he chooses to pursue them are suspect, in a very particular way. It is not just that Hollingsworth is concerned with Zenobia's money but that his concern is out of his own control. Coverdale reveals that Hollingsworth lacks the ability to connect his desires with his actions, a central weakness for the American hero figure modeled on the frontiersmen legendary by 1852, the date of *Blithedale*'s publication. The American hero was valued for his clearheaded, cool appropriation of power, which he accomplished by leading other men using a personal charisma resulting from complete self-control.

Hollingsworth's flaw in self-knowledge, however, leads Coverdale directly to his final secret, his love for, and subsequent dependence upon, Priscilla. Hollingsworth's personal weakness is reflected in his choice of love object, the timid and pliant woman who desires only to bend to masculine desire, whose weakness subtly infects the male—in Hollingsworth's case leading him to lean on her slender arm for a support it demeans him to receive. Through Hollingsworth, therefore, Coverdale intends to manipulate his consciously imagined reader by first inviting the reader to depend on Hollingsworth's heroism and then exposing Hollingsworth's lack of it, making the reader lean on weaker Coverdale, much as Hollingsworth comes to lean on Priscilla. Through this dynamic, Coverdale can be said to act conscientiously, allowing his reader to reexperience an early identification with powerful parents and then move through the process of autonomy which inevitably calls parental authority into question, replacing an idealized parent with a more "real" version and investing a portion of the parent's authority in the self. In effect, Coverdale enables his reader to reject Hollingsworth's authority and replace it with self-command.

The problem which arises in connection with Coverdale's deidealization of Hollingsworth lies in the next series of secrets he uncovers, those about Priscilla, Westervelt, and Zenobia. Theoretically, if Coverdale had written a reconstructed narrative directed to a reader he intended to help attain autonomy and self-reliance, the bulk of his own text, after discovering Hollingsworth's secrets, would be completed by fulfilling sequence, much as the analyst's interpretations aim at restructuring the analysand's narrative by penetrating the resistance demanding suppression. The analyst's efforts are successful, however, to the degree that his interpretations allow the patient to comprehend his or her own place as an active narrator/participant in the reconstructed narrative, and it is his own place in the narrative which Coverdale assiduously avoids. Comparing himself to the "chorus in a classic tragedy" (90), he emphasizes the errors inherent in his mode of observation but evades responsibility for the domination he asserts over his material by virtue of his interpretations. He insists he is the singer, not the song, emphasizing his effacement by physically distancing himself as he discovers the remaining secrets. As the novel progresses, he watches the others interact from the branches of a tree; from behind a tree trunk; from behind curtains and windows; "half an hour late," after the main action; from the audience rather than on the stage. He attempts to efface his voice by cleverly lamenting his ability to do so, thereby focusing his "real" reader on the content of his discoveries, which are marked by suppression and anomaly.

In the ascending order of secrets Coverdale exposes, the next in importance are the intertwined mysteries involving Priscilla, Westervelt, and Zenobia. Although in Coverdale's narrative all three characters are intimately entangled, functioning as aspects of each other, for the purposes of melodrama they can be segregated into the positions of villain, heroine, and female antagonist. Of these, the least important is Westervelt, who balances in the conventionality of his portrayal Hollingsworth's stereotypically heroic characteristics. Westervelt is completely evil, possessing over the two women a power somehow linked with his mesmeric talent. Gradually Coverdale reveals that Westervelt has imprisoned Priscilla, who possesses clairvoyant ability as well, forcing her to perform as the "Veiled Lady" on a Boston stage. This, of course, is also Priscilla's secret. Thus, Westervelt acts as a bridge between the two women, because he is also either Zenobia's former husband or lover.

More important, Westervelt also acts as Coverdale's mirrored image in his interpreted text. Westervelt, like Coverdale, is an observer; he arrives at Blithedale to interpret the relationship between Zenobia, Hollingsworth, and Priscilla and to reclaim both women for his own murky purposes. That is, in Westervelt, Coverdale identifies another mind using its imagination to control other lives through the suppression of narrative sequence. Westervelt deals in secrets; exposed to the light of rational examination, his power appears sordid and incompetent—he loses Priscilla when Hollingsworth exerts over her the equal and opposing force of his own will. By identifying Westervelt as the villain in the melodrama, however, Coverdale diverts his "real" reader from making that same assumption about his own narration. Westervelt functions as Coverdale's surrogate, concealing Coverdale's similar manipulation of character and sequence.

Next in order of conscious importance to Coverdale are the secrets he discovers about Priscilla and Zenobia. Of the two women, Priscilla, whom Coverdale consciously values, is of far less importance to him unconsciously and therefore is the woman whose secrets are most fully revealed. Priscilla can in fact be perceived as not possessing a secret but herself embodying a secret held by each of the other characters. For Moodie, she is the wan symbol of his old age and degeneration; for Hollingsworth, she is the sign and seal of his hidden weakness; for Westervelt, she makes manifest the illusory nature of evil, much as the false teeth he wears belie his appearance of physical perfection; and for Zenobia, she represents the feminine ideal designed by culture to constrain and destroy her own vibrant sexuality and exercise of individual autonomy.

For Coverdale, Priscilla also represents suppression. As a heroine, he offers her to his "real" reader as the sign of secrecy: the disguise culture demands that female sexuality wear in order to suppress female power and autonomy. Priscilla is vital to Coverdale's narrative to the degree that he can manipulate his reader into identifying with her idealized asexuality, thus suppressing what would otherwise be a dangerous attraction to Zenobia. Like Westervelt, Priscilla functions to divert attention from Coverdale's domination of the Blithedale text. She is the ultimate figure of the text itself, endlessly interpreted, allowed to exist only through the interpretive act. Her presence in Coverdale's narrative implies to his reader that, failing interpretive assistance, the text vanishes and that furthermore, in contrast to Westervelt's narrative control, Coverdale's is benign, an effort to release her from Westervelt's prison. By failing to imagine her adequately (her wan, pale slenderness emphasizes her insubstantiality), Coverdale also implies that he protects her from the "debauch" Westervelt visits upon her. Paradoxically, by suppressing her, Coverdale allows her "life." As Keller writes, "By identifying with the father, and disidentifying from the mother, the male child attempts to remove himself from her sphere of influence altogether. Through domination, he learns to transform her omnipotence to impotence."[11] The life Coverdale subtly offers Priscilla is a version of such culturally sanctioned powerlessness.

Yet as Irving Howe says "Zenobia rules the book. 'Passionate, luxurious, lacking simplicity, not deeply refined,' she is the frankest embodiment of sensuality in Hawthorne's work."[12] Accordingly, the secret Coverdale reveals about Zenobia is also the secret he keeps most closely. In his consciously realized address to his reader, Zenobia is the grave danger; in his unconscious address, she is the great prize. If Priscilla is suppression, implying deliberate ignorance, Zenobia is repression, implying unconscious resistance. His interpretation of her narrative is both the most crucial element of his reconstructed text and the one most fraught with secrecy and absence. The mysteries about Zenobia which Coverdale consciously reveals to his reader are, in the end, quite simple: Zenobia loves Hollingsworth, has been either lover or wife to Westervelt, is Moodie's older daughter, and commits suicide after losing Hollingsworth to Priscilla. Consciously, Coverdale offers Zenobia to his reader as a moral lesson, the just operation of culture on the radical manifestation of desire and temptation. Within the content of Coverdale's melodrama, Zenobia's fate is the ground on which all the other characters walk, the inexorable working of culture toward, as Ford Madox Ford wrote, "the preservation of the normal type; for the extinction of proud, resolute, and unusual individuals."[13] In these terms, Zenobia's secrets are most important to Coverdale because in revealing them, he also absolves himself of them. In almost a parody of the analytic situation, it is as if by illuminating Zenobia's concealed narrative, Coverdale releases himself and his personified reader from its power; his interpretation of her certifies both his power over and freedom from her.

Coverdale's narrative is also, like the psychoanalytic situation, itself determined by the repressed, specifically by the transference imago he projects on the figure of his "real" reader. The secrets he reveals about the other characters, and about the reader of a rather conventional melodrama whose configuration can be discerned through them, are belied by the way in which his revelations serve as mirror images of his unconscious desires and fears. More specifically, the authority he attempts to assert over his unconsciously imagined reader conforms to the authority exerted over the analyst by the analysand who uses his or her narrative to make the analyst a character within the tale, thereby subverting the analyst's interpretations of the analysand's act of narration. Coverdale uses interpretation as a weapon, both to dominate and conceal, by giving the appearance of authority to his "real" reader. Implicitly, he invites this "real" reader to complete his gaps using the form and content of conventional melodrama. The reader who accepts this duplicitous authority also will accept Coverdale's final revelation of what he says is his most significant secret: "The reader," Coverdale admits in the closing sentences of his narrative, "since I have disclosed so much, is entitled to this one word more. . . . I—I myself—was in love with PRISCILLA!" (228).

In the light of his transference imago, Coverdale's profession of love for Priscilla is, of course, his final suppression. Philip Rahv has written that "the emotional economy" of the novel "is throughout one of displacement . . . the only genuine relationship is that of Coverdale to Zenobia; the rest is mystification. But the whole point of Coverdale's behavior is to avoid involvement."[14] The material repressed by Coverdale, his inevitable attraction to Zenobia, can be discerned precisely through his hierarchy of secrets; as he reveals them, he leaves behind him a series of gaps and silences composing a subtext addressed to a very different reader than is his consciously delivered narrative. In this alternative version he usurps the reader's place. Here it is the secrets he omits or never reveals which gain significance: What was his relationship with Hollingsworth before their meeting at Blithedale? What is the reason for his apparently long-standing interest in Moodie? Did he know Zenobia would occupy rooms in the particular hotel where he finds her with Priscilla and Westervelt? How does Zenobia lose her money—an important event to which Coverdale devotes half of an elusive sentence? How did he know Hollingsworth would attend Priscilla's final performance as the Veiled Lady? How did he know, in fact, that Priscilla *was* the woman under the veil and Westervelt her hypnotic master? What is the underlying meaning behind Zenobia's "fanciful" tale of the young man who attempts to penetrate the lady's veil— does she allude to an act done by Coverdale and so reveal a historical connection between Coverdale and the other characters that he deliberately conceals?

The most important of Coverdale's suppressions occurs during the scene he claims to come upon "half an hour" too late to hear Zenobia's trial by Hollingsworth, who accuses her of being somehow implicated in Priscilla's psychological imprisonment. The scene is a masterpiece of allusion, as Coverdale weaves together a consistent narrative after the fact, from Zenobia's half-coherent responses to Hollingsworth's now silent accusations. But then the gap between the conclusion of this scene (leaving Coverdale asleep after fantasizing Zenobia's continued presence haunting the glade where she experienced her greatest humiliation) and the first line of the next scene, when Coverdale awakens Hollingsworth to alert him that Zenobia has disappeared and may be drowned, is thoroughly puzzling. Coverdale, he tells his "real" reader, has discovered Zenobia's handkerchief at the end of the riverbank, drawn there by "a nameless presentiment" (213). Accompanied by Hollingsworth and Silas Foster, the commune's legitimate farmer, he then sets out in a punt to drag the river for Zenobia's body. The famous scene which follows is an almost literal transposition of a passage from Hawthorne's Brook Farm notebook after the suicide by drowning of a young woman driven to the act by her emotional and intellectual estrangement from her family and friends. This scene is the juncture between Hawthorne's and Coverdale's mirrored narratives; for both, the suicide functions as the return of the repressed, the grotesque image of their most secret desires and terrifying fears.

For Coverdale, what is most significant about the gap in information between his witnessing Zenobia humiliated and his witnessing her corpse, equally humiliated,[15] is that her death agrees with the secret direction of his desires. Although Coverdale makes it clear to his reader that he apprehends Zenobia's death—he emphasizes that his last kiss on her hand finds it "cold as a veritable piece of snow," provoking him to remark, "It is really deathlike!" and he receives Zenobia's answer, "The extremities die first, they say" (209); then he rises somewhat later from a tumultuous dream just as it is "about to converge on some tragical catastrophe" (210)—he withholds from his reader and from conscious awareness the reason why he knows. Moreover, that reason—understood by Crews to mean that "the story . . . is intricately involved in family matters of a vaguely guilty nature"[16]—leads to a revision of Coverdale's hierarchy of secrets and to a new understanding of the relationship he both desires and fears to establish with his unconsciously imagined reader.

Coverdale has written a version of Freud's family romance, a term Freud used to describe the child's reaction to his or her development of a realistic perspective about parents he or she formerly idealized. In response to disappointment and fear, the child may imagine that he or she is an adopted or a stepchild whose "real" (fantasized) parents are of noble lineage or powerful status. Freud understood that at the center of this fantasy was concealed or repressed despair at the sense of having been abandoned, as well as denial of abandonment.[17] Strung together, all of Coverdale's suppressions serve to focus his unconsciously imagined reader on his interpretations and therefore on his status as an interpreter who is continually losing the subjects of his observation. Zenobia, Hollingsworth, Priscilla, and Westervelt actively engage in movement at, to, and from Blithedale; Coverdale follows in their wake. The act of interpreting their movements permits Coverdale both to deny his sense of loss and to participate vicariously as one of their "family."

Zenobia is the figure most fraught with multiple layers of meaning for Coverdale. Simultaneously, she is temptress (the sexualized mother of the oedipal triangle, whom Coverdale as son both desires and fears) and almost more important, Coverdale's surrogate in his fantasized subtextual narrative. Zenobia literally is the abandoned child Coverdale feels himself to be, for Moodie deserted her after her mother's death, when she was still a young child. Zenobia also experienced, in reality, Coverdale's repressed disillusionment, when she discovered her father to be a degenerated alcoholic and herself his emotional stepchild. Finally, Zenobia's sexual and emotional failure with Hollingsworth makes of Coverdale's similar failure with Priscilla an ironic comedy. Although Coverdale claims that his love for Priscilla is his most secret—and tragic—desire, he is as apparently asexual as she. Zenobia, in contrast, quite clearly desires a union with Hollingsworth which is both physical and spiritual. Hollingsworth, in rejecting Zenobia in favor of Priscilla, certifies the asexual, or "feminine," power in the world. For Coverdale, it is a terrifying vision, which he interprets as the assertion of social authority over desire. To preserve himself from further abandonment by the father, Coverdale must slay the mother by unconsciously repressing her attraction, a psychological dynamic appearing in his text as Zenobia's suicide.

But just as the interpretations offered by the analyst will not illuminate the patient's condition if the analyst omits to scrutinize the transference imago through which the patient delivers the narrative, so a critical interpretation reducing Coverdale to his unconscious desires and fears in his relationship with textual characters will fail to discover the connection between the narrator and author of the text if it focuses exclusively on the content of Coverdale's subtext. Thus, to discern Hawthorne through Coverdale, it is necessary to examine the reader Coverdale unconsciously embeds within the matrix of his "family romance" and whom he addresses as the analysand does the analyst.

In these terms, Coverdale's revealed secrets function as mirrors. He discovers what is precisely suited to conceal that which he unconsciously represses and transfers onto a reader whose existence he both desires and fears. Thus Moodie, a secondary character whose secret Coverdale uses to divert a consciously realized reader, is a primary figure in his unconscious narrative. Moodie is the character Coverdale manipulates most thoroughly, consistently introducing him into the narrative using allusion and inference and finally creating for him a full biography that reduces him to a standard type in nineteenth-century melodrama: the wealthy man who becomes degenerate and abandons his family. In both Coverdale's conscious and unconscious narratives, Moodie is the only literal father figure, one whose abandonment of Zenobia enacted Coverdale's secret fears and induces him to transfer Moodie's guilt onto the more manageable specter of Zenobia's sexuality. If Coverdale can implicate Zenobia in Moodie's desertion, can find her somehow guilty or worthy of being abandoned, he also can keep repressed his terror as well as his yearning for the idealized father who recedes infinitely in time and space.

The reader Coverdale unconsciously addresses, therefore—the figure created out of repressed yearning for an object attainable only in fantasy—is the nostalgic figure of the father who will reject a powerful address but reward with his attention one riven with powerlessness and vulnerability. In this reading, the suppressions marking Coverdale's narrative emerge as the form of his lack of authority. The reader he unconsciously desires is the reader who will complete the gaps, just as in the mirrored image of his overt narrative the woman he consciously desires is the cultural icon designed to "complete" the gap opened by the removal of Adam's rib. Similarly, the reader he unconsciously fears is the reader who will punish him for his assertion of the narrator's authority—the progenitor's position—by abandoning the connection he seeks to create through the text, just as in the overt narrative the woman he most fears is the sexual woman who is punished by abandonment for her attempt to challenge cultural models of authority and power.

On the one hand, then, Coverdale's suppressions form a narrative addressed to a reader on whom he consciously bestows authority, much as the analysand invests the analyst with power. On the other hand, the analyst who bases his or her interpretations on the authority bestowed by this analysand fails to comprehend that together with the investment of power, the analysand also transfers a burden of guilt at its exercise. Coverdale ultimately must love Priscilla because his unconsciously imagined reader is certain not to—a dynamic he has ensured by his insistent derogatory descriptions of her. But the reader who accurately reads Coverdale's subtext and fails to love Priscilla, who perhaps instead loves the vividly attractive figure of Zenobia—an attraction Coverdale conversely engenders by using sensual and intricate language to describe her—also assumes, as penalty for this act of interpretation, the guilt of being seduced by the forbidden object. Thus Coverdale penalizes his unconsciously imagined reader for understanding the text he desires yet fears to have created, penalizes the reader for the power of interpretation he has himself forced this reader to accept, and evades responsibility for his own act of narration.

Coverdale forces his unconsciously imagined reader to usurp his own place as narrator of the Blithedale text, purchasing his innocence at the price of betraying the reader, yet also ensuring his own isolation. Ultimately Coverdale's fear of abandonment leads him to abandon his reader before he can be himself betrayed, just as he abandons sexual interest in Zenobia long before such an interest could draw down upon him her rejection; abandons Hollingsworth before the latter can make explicit his greater loyalty to his philanthropic scheme; and clings instead to Priscilla, whose idealized ethereality makes her a wraith his imagination can control rather than debauch. Finally, the text through which Coverdale hoped to connect with his consciously assumed reader becomes the vehicle of disconnection, the means of preserving an isolating ideality less terrifying than the self-examination necessary to lead him toward community.

The question to consider, then, is Hawthorne's place in Coverdale's narrative. As Coverdale observes Blithedale and its inhabitants, Hawthorne observes Coverdale's act of observation and interpretation. Howe has implied that all the characters in the novel are failed representations because all the relationships among and between them fail.[18] Howe's understanding of failure, though certainly correct, is also a paradoxical sign of Hawthorne's success in realizing an ironic connection with a reader he both consciously and unconsciously imagined for his work; Coverdale is the portrait of Hawthorne's transference imago, a creation possible because in this book Hawthorne becomes both actor and observer, the analysand who observes himself narrating, the writer who is his own reader, the speaker who interprets himself. Through the figure of Coverdale, Hawthorne connects with his consciously realized reader by teaching him or her how *not* to read his work.

Central to a transference reading of *The Blithedale Romance* are Hawthorne's intentions in the novel's last sentence, revealing Coverdale's love for Priscilla. I doubt, given a careful examination of Coverdale's narrative, that Hawthorne believed any "real" reader would have failed to understand the direction of Coverdale's desire long before his final revelation. During the scene describing the last encounter of Zenobia, Hollingsworth, and Priscilla, Coverdale does, after all, nearly make his feelings explicit when he bitterly says, "It suits me not to explain what was the analogy that I saw, or imagined, between Zenobia's situation and mine; nor, I believe, will the reader direct this one secret, hidden beneath many a revelation which perhaps concerned me less. In simple, truth, however, as Zenobia leaned her forehead against the rock, shaken with that tearless agony, it seemed to me that the self-same pang, with hardly mitigated torment, leaped thrilling from her heart-strings to my own" (207).

Instead, Hawthorne seems to offer his "real" reader the last secret kept by a secret-keeper, opening thereby the question of Coverdale's reliability in both conscious and unconscious terms. On the one hand, it is possible to take the attitude that Coverdale's final revelation casts doubt on his entire narrative, making it appear a text of conscious lies designed to conceal a larger, more malignant secret of which Coverdale is fully aware. Such a secret, for example, instead of unrequited love, might involve an act committed by Coverdale in reality as well as in fantasy. Could he, perhaps, really have murdered Zenobia? Hawthorne leaves sufficient clues in the scene detailing the last meeting between Coverdale and Zenobia to invite a suspicious reader to fill in the multiple gaps with an act of violence. Coverdale fantasizes Zenobia "haunting" the glade, after he realizes that "destiny itself, methought, in its kindliest mood, could do no better for Zenobia, in the way of quick relief, than to cause the impending rock to impend a little further, and fall upon her head" (207). After waking with a "nameless presentiment," he is able immediately to locate articles of Zenobia's clothing that convince him she has thrown herself in the river and, by the portentous tone of his voice, to convey this belief to Hollingsworth. The gap Hawthorne leaves between Zenobia's farewell and Coverdale's conviction of her suicide is so deliberate as to suggest that Hawthorne invited such speculation from his consciously realized reader.

On the other hand, the reader who so speculates takes on the role Coverdale has consciously offered *his* reader throughout the novel. This is the reader of conventional melodrama, the reader who smoothes away all the shadowy ambiguities of emotional response in favor of the antipoetic, pragmatic simplicities of good and evil. This is the reader whom Hawthorne knew composed the bulk of the literate public in 1852. As Donald Crowley so rightly observed:

Almost every aspect of Hawthorne's creativity was conditioned by his acute awareness that for over twenty years he had no sympathetic audience . . . [yet] believing that a genuinely democratic literature, by its very nature, demanded a nonelitist audience, he too wished to address that multitude—but on his own terms . . . [he was] faced with the necessity of creating an American audience as well as a genuinely American art. . . . He was often led to begin with a literary convention or stereotype familiar to that audience and then to wrench the cliché—the worn-out form or situation or sentiment—so as to endow it with the force of his originality and thus to transform it into a fresh vision that answered to something deep in the character of the American psyche. [19]

Questioning Coverdale's reliability, then, means also questioning the nature of Hawthorne's conscious and unconscious address to an audience he understood by virtue of his intellectual, emotional, and psychological estrangement from it. Although correct, it is too facile to suggest that Hawthorne's difficulties originated only in his desire to reach a wide public, to create a climate in which writing such as his own could prosper. Herman Melville, writing contemporaneously, provides an antithetical example of the artist who, achieving early popular success, was yet compelled to compose *Moby Dick*, the expression of an artistic force both governed by and governing its author. Instead of composing more sea tales, like *Typee*, *Omoo*, and *White Jacket*, Melville turned to novels focused on metaphysical speculation and psychological complexity. In addition to Hawthorne's obvious and admirable effort to educate American literary taste, the question of his alliance with that uneducated sensibility remains. In watching Coverdale, Hawthorne watched the persona he had created to survive in an unreformed America, a persona designed to protect a secret "real" self by assuming a concealing posture of self-criticism. Unlike Melville, Hawthorne was unable to give up his persona. Coverdale freely admits all the qualities brought to bear against the artist by the American public—that he was effete, useless, foolish, egocentric, parasitic—and, moreover, admits them first, disarming devaluation.

What, then, was the hidden self Hawthorne valued? If he offered Coverdale to a "real" reader as an object lesson in how not to interpret his texts, where did he locate his model of good reading? Who was his good reader? *The Blithedale Romance* offers a critical reader the unique opportunity to scrutinize a writer who is himself scrutinizing the process of narrative and narration. Hawthorne is a mirrored image of Coverdale, which makes him a voyeur who satisfies psychoanalytic comprehension of the act because he is able to observe and to exhibit himself simultaneously.[20] Hawthorne's object, however, is once removed from that of Coverdale, who watched others more closely than he examined himself. Hawthorne desired to halt the process of representation at the moment of distortion. His fear, unlike Ford Madox Ford, who loathed being seen, was the fear of failing to see himself seeing. Ironically, because of this fear, he could then perceive only distortion, depicting Coverdale as the emblem of the myriad ways in which transference operates as tragedy in human communication. Desiring the simplicity of direct connection, Hawthorne's fear provoked him to focus on images of veils and mirrors, to insist on the necessity of distance and structure, on the necessity of the text in which he could stop time long enough to permit the investigation of the power exerted by the past on the creative present.

Hawthorne's problem lies at the heart of the nature of narrative, the human compulsion to convert unformulated experience into causal sequence, dominating and authorizing reality but paradoxically modifying the terror of living by losing life in order to gain control. It is here, of course, that *The Blithedale Romance* finds its most powerful connection with psychoanalytic theory. Transference, the active incorporation of memory into oral and written narrative, is a model for the relationship established between writer and reader because, by definition, transference functions as an implicit dialogue with the past speaking through and to the present. *The Blithedale Romance* is Hawthorne's attempt to connect an interior and an exterior reality through the act of narrative, to understand the distortions made by past desires and needs upon present perception of reality, and to understand the isolation transference implies by ensuring the gap between fantasy and experience. In short, the novel is Hawthorne's attempt to confess and abolish his own secret sense of solitude by entering a covert dialogue with the reader he consciously believed could neither appreciate nor understand him yet whom he unconsciously feared resembled him.

As James Olney says, "Autobiography exercises something very like a fatal attraction for nearly all men and women who would call themselves 'writers.' "[21] The "fatality" of the attraction exerted by the genre on fiction-makers has to do with their desire to assert the reality of the life they ostensibly live only within their imaginations. This desire connects the autobiographical with the psychoanalytic project. The life history which emerges in analysis is distinct from the historical data recording the analysand's factual progress through life in the same way the autobiographer imposes a "fictional" pattern on his or her life history simply by virtue of perceiving it *as* a history. In analysis, transference, like autobiography, is the history of the life lived within the analysand's narrative interpretation.

Moreover, as Olney remarks, the autobiographical project calls into question the same issues on which psychoanalytic concern is focused: "What do we mean by the self, or himself (autos)? What significance do we impute to the act of writing (graphe)—what is the significance of transforming life, or a life, into a text?"[22] Transforming a life into a text makes explicit the distortions made by desire on reality by revealing the ideal reader to whom the text is unconsciously addressed. In the psychoanalytic situation, transforming a life into oral narrative makes visible the transference which unconsciously renders the analyst a specter of past desires and fears effecting present life. As Roy Pascal says, "The autobiographer half discovers, half creates a deeper design and truth than adherence to historical and factual truth could ever make claim to."[23] Similarly, analysands tell their stories in order to construct a bridge between past and present, in order to use present reality to revise the past they possess as narrative by revising the transference distortions disfiguring the analyst/audience. Analogously, creative writers may use the figure of the reader imagined for the work to revise their creative control over it. *The Blithedale Romance* presents an example of a writer attempting to make visible the reader he unconsciously desires and therefore to make visible the unconscious act of interpretation he translates into narrative.

The scenes Hawthorne took from his Brook Farm notebooks are particularly important in this regard because they reveal a striking similarity not only between the exterior lives of the two men but, more significant, in the relationship Hawthorne established between Coverdale and the world of Blithedale. In autobiographical terms, Coverdale was the secret Hawthorne was unable, but desired, to confess. Most pertinent here is Coverdale's observation and interpretation of the scene in which Zenobia's body is pulled from the river. In a sense, it was the memory of this scene which both compelled Hawthorne to compose the novel and remained the unconscious nodal point of the difficulty he experienced composing it. The drowned girl was a young woman from a neighboring farm family who had educated herself beyond the intellectual and emotional parameters of her family's life. According to Hawthorne's report, as well as the report of another Brook Farm member,[24] the girl had taken her own life because of the complete despair engendered by her sense of apparently irremediable isolation and alienation. She could not imagine a version of herself which could allow her to exist with some serenity among the people who composed her entire world. She was unable to create a persona.

For Hawthorne, such a failure would act as both the horrific reflection of his own terrors and an unconscious warning against an existence lived as his narrator in *The Scarlet Letter* advises, one showing "freely to the world, if not your worst, yet some trait whereby the worst may be inferred."[25] Coverdale was the worst of Hawthorne: both the artist who displayed his contempt for his audience by exposing their contempt of him and the artist figure appearing throughout Hawthorne's canon, whose creativity depended on an act of distortion and domination. Yet Hawthorne could not expose him. He needed Coverdale as his own disguise. In the novel Hawthorne translated an acutely desperate young farm girl into a woman of vivid sexuality who had hurled herself against social strictures and been defeated. By transforming the young suicide into Zenobia, whose queenly name reflected her royal personality, Hawthorne elevated a country scandal into classic tragedy, but he also placed between himself and his experience of the event a distance created by a conventional genre structure. In so doing, Hawthorne also made visible the reader he unconsciously needed to salvage his position as observer, and therefore he clung to Coverdale as both his burden and his salvation.

Hawthorne fictionalized the scene describing the aftermath of the suicide—dragging the water for the body, the unsuccessful attempts to straighten the contorted limbs, the unintended yet brutal humiliation of the corpse—because to do so was Hawthorne's only solution to what was for him an experience rather than an act of observation. But his fictional interpretation verges on the banal, for the girl's genuine tragedy lay in her status as an ordinary person confronting impossible ideals in the confines of a mundane existence. Assimilating her, transformed as a queenly figure, into the structures of his unconscious needs, fears, and desires allowed Hawthorne to contain the terror evoked in him by the act she apparently committed because of her failure to solace her sense of isolation, an estrangement mirroring Hawthorne's similar alienation from his own world. Hawthorne, after all, had spent the twelve years after his graduation from Bowdoin secluded in his room, apprenticed to his craft, of course, but also dwelling isolated from a world he could securely contact only through the medium of his art. As he noted in his preface to the third edition of the *Twice-Told Tales,* his writing was his effort to "open an intercourse with the world,"[26] an intercourse possible only because it was the result of mediated experience.

Translating the young suicide into a tragic queen also transmuted the relationship Hawthorne established with his reader. Consciously defining Coverdale as the chorus of a classic play, Hawthorne could return to a memory too terrifying without the metaphorical structures of play, stage, and audience. Through Coverdale, Hawthorne attained the emotional distance he needed to assimilate the event intellectually; by allowing Coverdale to witness a "tragedy," Hawthorne dominated the event by interpreting it in terms of a traditional genre.

At the same time, however, Coverdale was Hawthorne's shame. An important comparison, in this regard, exists in the prefaces Hawthorne wrote to introduce and accompany all his published material. That these prefaces, delivered to Hawthorne's ostensibly "real" audience, spoken in his "real" voice, are fictional, is obvious. In them Hawthorne created the persona through whom he could address in safety the unreformed American public who assumed writing to be the work of an ineffectual, overheated imagination. He did so by becoming, as Coverdale also becomes, precisely the artist figure they despise. The prefaces insist on the "paleness" of the writing they introduce, adding, "Whether from lack of power, or an unconquerable reserve, the Author's touches have often an effect of tameness; . . . the book if you would see anything in it, requires to be read in the clear, brown twilight atmosphere in which it was written; if opened in the sunshine, it is apt to look exceedingly like a volume of blank pages."[27] The prefaces are invariably tame, spoken in tones designed to forfeit the authority of the creator, instead implicitly claiming for their writer the position of witness to his own act of narration. In them Hawthorne, like Coverdale, attempts to efface his narrative authority by making his lack of creative power an explicit dismay, thus concealing that he used this pretense to connect with his reader.

Consciously, Hawthorne addresses a reader more robust, more vivid, more "American" than he; consciously as well, that address is ironic, the persona he discovered would most successfully conceal his intense desire to win an audience, to speak and be heard, to affect the minds and hearts of his countrymen, to be powerful. Unconsciously, however, his desire terrified him because he experienced it as an authority that inherently isolated him from his audience. It was an authority that acknowledged his creativity and admitted his intimate connection with the objects he created. Thus the plaintive voice he developed as a conscious ploy became his unconscious reality. The authority over his texts Hawthorne pretended to give his readers was an authority he became more and more unable to repossess. Interpretation became increasingly confused with narration as a consequence of his unconscious absorption of cultural structures linking the masculine with the interpreting subject and the feminine with the created object. Sadly, observing Coverdale distort the text of Blithedale did not allow Hawthorne to speak more clearly in his other work, neither prefaces nor novels. Coverdale became his reality as the shadowed texts he produced evolved out of the shadowed life he led. Finally, he really was unable to "show freely to the world [his] worst," because he was unable to free his creative act from the gender labels placed on it by his culture.

CHAPTER 4

Jane Austen: Letting Go

I am a Jane Austenite, and therefore slightly imbecile about Jane Austen.
  —E. M. Forster

Miss Austen being, as you say, without "sentiment," without poetry, maybe is sensible, real (more real than true), but she cannot be great.
  —Charlotte Brontë

. . . we confess the greatness of Miss Austen, her marvelous dramatic power, seems more than anything in Scott akin to the greatest quality in Shakespear.
  —Lord Macaulay

. . . there are twenty-five elderly gentlemen living in the neighborhood of London who resent any slight upon her genius as if it were an insult offered to the chastity of their Aunts.
  —Virginia Woolf

Dishwashings.
  —Thomas Carlyle

Jane Austen's books are absent from this library. Just that one omission alone would make a fairly good library out of a library that hadn't a book in it.
  —Mark Twain

I read and re-read, the mouth open and the mind closed.
  —E. M. Forster

THOSE WHO READ Jane Austen's novels either hate them ferociously or love them devotedly. Historically, as Ian Watt writes, reaction to her canon "can be roughly classed according to the general antithesis between the 'heart' and the 'head.' "[1] Some of her contemporaries, such as Scott and Macaulay, derived tremendous pleasure from her classical sense of order and control; others, among them Charlotte Brontë and William Wordsworth, found these same qualities sterile, the unimaginative reconstruction of a banal middle-class world.

133

Thomas Carlyle's vehement epithet prefigured Mark Twain's equally antipathetic reading, both later confounded by E. M. Forster's self-confessed adulation. Forster's devotion, in turn, is echoed by what amounts to a twentieth-century fan club of "Janeites," who seem to use the novels as the key to an exclusive fraternity.

It is an intriguing fact about Austen's novels that they produce the sort of intense reactions usually reserved for real people in the real world. The readers who love or hate her work in effect love or hate the author, consistently conflating Austen's narrative persona with the historical figure of Austen herself. In psychoanalytic terms, Austen's readers are displaying their countertransference to her work, the unconsciously overeactive response an analyst occasionally makes to some patients. Countertransference as a formal concept is limited, in general, to the psychoanalyst's response during the analytic hour. It is considered "eccentric" when the analyst forfeits an enduring emotional distance from the patient and instead responds by satisfying his or her own unconscious life.[2] The analyst "acts out," just as the patient does, a script written during early childhood, directed by responses to early childhood authority figures. Similarly, the vehemence and intensity of Austen readers indicate that, for the majority, the source of their response is unconscious. What moves them lies somehow beneath the text itself, apart from the theme, subject, plot, and characters. Their intensity indicates that it is Austen's use of language, nuance, and structure which circumvents their intellectual and critical faculties. In particular, her use of an overwhelmingly authoritative and didactic narrator evokes the same sort of response originally and unconsciously provoked by authority figures encountered in early childhood.

Austen's narrator is the character most forcefully powerful in her canon, as is implied by her readers, responding to what they think is Austen's personality. Charlotte Brontë, scorning Austen's controlled intellectual point of view, really comments on her narrator's controlling wit and often devasting irony;[4] D. H. Lawrence, who read the novels as the bitter words of a frustrated spinster, [5] hates the narrator's unyielding domination of her world; Carlyle's "dishwashings," coming from a man well known for his misogyny, is surely not a coincidental insult about a narrative voice extremely concerned with the details of female life. On the other hand, the passionate reaction of E. M. Forster and the Janeites is pointedly ironized by Virginia Woolf, although she too was an Austen fan. It is not the "chastity of their Aunts"[6] whom the Janeites devoutly protect but the purity of a nurturing imago, a mother-surrogate all wise and all powerful, whom they leap to defend.

Austen's use of the narrator in *Pride and Prejudice* particularly exemplifies how overwhelming her narrator can be. Time and time again the narrator absorbs character dialogue so that her voice is dominant throughout. For example, after Elizabeth attempts to convince her sister Jane that Mr. Bingley does regard Jane with affection, after the reader has heard Elizabeth's voice and seen Jane's response, the narrator needlessly summarizes: "She represented to her sister as forcibly as possible what she felt on the subject, and had soon the pleasure of seeing its happy effect. Jane's temper was not desponding, and she was gradually led to hope. . . ." More striking, when Charlotte Lucas accepts Mr. Collins's proposal, her shocking action is explained by the narrator; the reader is not permitted an interior view of Charlotte's state of mind: "Charlotte's kindness extended farther than Elizabeth had any conception of;—its object was nothing less, than to secure her from any return of Mr. Collins's addresses, by engaging them towards herself. Such was Miss Lucas's scheme . . . Miss Lucas, who accepted him solely from the pure and disinterested desire of an establishment, cared not how soon that establishment were gained."[7] Charlotte has certainly been depicted before this scene as far too complex a character to deserve the narrator's assertion of a mercenary motivation only.

The narrator especially interposes between Elizabeth and the reader, so that the reader is gradually manipulated to listen to the narrator in order to hear Elizabeth. For example, Elizabeth's reconsideration of Darcy and Wickham after she receives Darcy's letter explaining

Wickham's villainy, is delivered through the narrator. Whereas the reader will later, in *Persuasion*, hear Anne Elliot reflect on her own actions, in *Pride and Prejudice* the reader is told: "She [Elizabeth] perfectly remembered every thing that had passed in conversation between Wickham and herself in their first evening at Mr. Philips's. Many of his expressions were still fresh in her memory. She was *now* struck with the impropriety of such communications to a stranger, and wondered how it had escaped her before." The narrator here is in fact beginning the process of gradually silencing Elizabeth. When Elizabeth first meets Darcy's sister, the narrator explains, conveniently, "Elizabeth soon saw that she was herself closely watched by Miss Bingley, and that she could not speak a word, especially to Miss Darcy, without calling her attention. This observation would not have prevented her from trying to talk to the latter, had they not been seated at an inconvenient distance; but she was not sorry to be spared the necessity of saying much." Later, when Elizabeth realizes she loves Darcy, the narrator seats Elizabeth at "an inconvenient distance" from the reader, so that she may establish her own authority to understand Elizabeth better than either Elizabeth or the reader can presume: "If gratitude and esteem are good foundations of affection, Elizabeth's change of sentiment will be neither improbable nor faulty. But if otherwise, if the regard springing from such sources is unreasonable or unnatural, in comparison of what is so often described as arising on a first interview with its object, and even before two words have been exchanged, nothing can be said in her defence." Even in the love scene itself, the narrator speaks for Elizabeth, who "feeling all the more than common awkwardness and anxiety of his situation, now forced herself to speak; and immediately, though not very fluently, gave him to understand, that her sentiments had undergone so material a change, since the period to which he alluded, as to make her receive with gratitude and pleasure, his present assurances."[8]

The narrator seems almost to act as Elizabeth's duenna, or surrogate mother, because the absorption of Elizabeth's voice is balanced by Elizabeth's consistent silence with Mrs. Bennet. The narrator and

Mrs. Bennet are the two most voluble presences in *Pride and Prejudice,* and when they speak, others fall silent. In response to Mrs. Bennet's chatter, "her daughters listened in silence . . . , sensible that any attempt to reason with or soothe her would only increase the irritation. She talked on, therefore, without interruption from any of them." In fact, there is also an implied connection between the narrator and Mrs. Bennet in the novel's first famous sentence. Although spoken by the narrator, its content is linked with Mrs. Bennet, who devoutly believes that "it is a truth universally acknowledged, that a single man in possession of a good fortune, must be in want of a wife."[3] The presence of mother voices in *Pride and Prejudice* is not accidental. Just as the analyst's eccentric countertransference suggests a concomitant intensity on the part of the patient, the emotional yet intellectually deracinated responses of Austen's readers imply that Austen brought an equally emotional reaction to the reader she imagined for her work. Onto that reader she transferred the configurations of her own unconscious response to authority figures from her early life, particularly her mother. Austen understood her imagined reader as a substitute self for whom she used the female protagonist in her six novels as surrogate and onto whom she projected the conflicts and desires of her own unconscious life.

But in addition to her imagined reader Austen inscribed in her books a "cover reader," apparently the historical reader actually reading her novels. Sandra Gilbert and Susan Gubar, among other critics, have recognized that Austen's novels only appear to affirm dominant eighteenth-century social patterns.[9] While ostensibly addressing her historical contemporaries, Austen was adding a subtext chronicling female life, using the themes of romantic comedy as the same sort of metaphorical disguise she employed quite literally when she was forced to conceal her "unfeminine" writing activity under a desk blotter.[10] Yet, although Gilbert and Gubar certainly are correct in discerning the presence of underlying subversive material in Austen's canon, from a psychoanalytic perspective such material can be considered unconscious inconsistencies distorting the coherence of Austen's narrative. In a text, discontinuities and anomalies signal the presence of unconscious material beyond the writer's aesthetic control. These disruptions are connected to the writer's transference and are usually translated into conflicts between form and subject. To understand the transferred attitudes Austen brought to her imagined reader, then, one must first examine the ruptures in her canon, through which ideas excluded from her conscious awareness are visible. In Austen's novels, three narrative inconsistencies are particularly striking.

First, critical readers have recognized the often abrupt and structurally maladroit quality of the comedic conclusions ending the first five of Austen's novels. Gilbert and Gubar believe that her sudden resolutions, in which the narrator overwhelms and silences character dialogue in favor of conventional social attitudes, conceal the novel's radical subtexts, affirming an autonomy in female life which Austen practiced as an artist but perhaps could not propound forthrightly.[11] Just as her independent and assertive omniscient narrator exercised absolute control over the "happy endings" of her characters, so Austen as a writer escaped, to some degree, the restrictive conditions of eighteenth-century female life. She chose not to marry and selected for herself the position of observer rather than participant in social life. Because of her work, she obtained a freedom from social rules usually given only to much older, wealthier women. After the publication of *Pride and Prejudice*, for example, an anonymous visitor described her as "still a poker—but a poker of whom everybody is afraid . . . a wit, a delineator of character, who does not talk is terrific indeed."[12]

As Gilbert and Gubar realized, in her life and through her narrator, Austen's silent message may be paraphrased "Do what I do, not what I say." Austen's habitual verbal self-concealment may have given her an especially powerful insight into the speech patterns of hypocrisy, displayed through the dialogue spoken by such outrageously hypocritical characters in her books as Mr. Collins, Mrs. Elton, and Isabelle Thorp. But Austen's own hypocrisy, in contrast to her parodies, was a fundamental necessity for her creative survival. It was her defense against patriarchal denial of female authority and female speech. Despite Gilbert and Gubar's important recuperation of the feminist subtext, Austen's conclusions remain, however, problematic. Although her narrator may act as a role model for a covertly addressed reader in her assertion of narrative control, that control is nevertheless used to silence dissent from the novel's female protagonist, and moreover, from the imagined reader addressed by the text, who has been carefully coached to identify with the female protagonist. Nor is it likely that this imagined reader is male. In the traditional Western novel, cultural misogyny has been encoded in the assumption of the male protagonist who acts while the female subprotagonist waits. In a typical college classroom, students of both genders will have no difficulty identifying with the male questor, while only female students will identify with a female character, despite elevation of the character to the status of primary protagonist.

Philip Roth's novel *The Ghostwriter* provides an excellent example of this dynamic in the twentieth century. In his book Roth includes two paired tales, the first told by Nathan Zuckerman, in the first-person voice; the second told about Anne Frank, spoken by Zuckerman using a mixed third- and first-person perspective. The stories demonstrate the similarities between Zuckerman's search for self and the more historically devastated but equally powerful search Anne undertakes. Examining the novel with students reveals that all the students emotionally join Nathan in the first narration, but only female students "act with" Anne. Male students become observers instead, not participating in Anne's self-development but in Nathan's creative act.[13] Analogously, Austen's imagined reader, encouraged to identify variously with Elinor and Marianne Dashwood, Elizabeth Bennet, Catherine Morland, Emma Woodhouse, Fanny Price, and Anne Elliot, is, in reality and within Austen's imagination, female.

Austen's conclusions, therefore, are particularly troubling from a feminist perspective. By the end of her novels, the narrator's point of view, always present, has become didactically overwhelming in its effect on the reader, in an unconscious reflection of eighteenth-century social patterns of domination and subordination. The reader almost is forced by the narrator into the position occupied by an eighteenth-century bride, whose happy marriage signaled the end of her own story, now subsumed by her husband's history and voice. "Narrative outcome is one place where transindividual assumptions and values are most clearly visible, and where the word 'convention' is found resonating between its literary and social meanings."[14] Although the narrator's intention may be to protect her imagined reader and her protagonist, the nature of her protection can easily affect the real reader as unwelcome suffocation. Why, then, would a female writer, who on the one hand seems to support other women in their experience of the realities of female life, on the other hand incorporate patterns of domination placing her reader, through the aegis of her female protagonist, in an identical position of restriction and oppression? Significantly, this pattern is markedly disrupted Austen's final novel, *Persuasion*.

A second anomaly fragmenting the coherence of Austen's canon is her narrator's relationship to a character functioning as a foil for the female protagonist in each novel. This motif is highlighted in an 1816 outline for a novel, a sketch found posthumously among Austen's papers. That the outline was a parody immediately is signaled by its title, "Plan of a Novel, According to Hints from Various Quarters." In it Austen describes a novel focusing on a "heroine, faultless character herself, perfectly good, with much tenderness and sentiment and not the least wit. . . ." Also included is "a young woman in the same neighborhood, of talents and shrewdness . . . having a considerable degree of wit; heroine shall shrink from the acquaintance . . . the good will be unexceptional in every respect, and there will be no foibles or weaknesses, but with the wicked, who will be completely depraved and infamous, hardly a resemblance of humanity left in them."[15] Curiously, although the outline was written at the end of her career as a piece of satire, it accurately describes the female protagonist and her foil in each of Austen's novels, including *Emma*, where characteristics usually lent to the foil are embodied by the protagonist.

According to Lionel Trilling, Emma's "fault is the classic one of hubris, excessive pride, and it yields the classic result of blindness, of an inability to interpret experience to the end of perceiving reality, and we are aware of each false step, each wrong conclusion that she will make."[16] At the end of her life, then, Austen parodied her own aesthetic practices and in so doing she hinted at the presence of an irony undetected by her contemporaries. It is precisely this appreciation of her own subversive irony which emphasizes the discrepancy between the foils' existence and the narrator's use of them.

In creating the foils, or dark female characters, Austen wrote dialogue expressing them as ironic and sophisticated. In fact, their dialogue is suffused with the same wit and irony informing Austen's letters. This resemblance indicates that the foils were created to parody the pleasure Austen derived, but defined as socially malignant, from observing and satirizing the social life of her community. Although the negative evaluation incurred by these characters as a result of their positions in the novels confirms dominant social values, their incorporation also allows Austen the opportunity tacitly to confirm the social realities of female life. These women respond to and discuss the sort of ulterior manipulation of social power employed by all oppressed groups. Through them Austen vividly portrays how living in a subordinate role with only indirect access to social authority and real income warps character and personality. Even the portrait of the unreformed Emma Woodhouse includes this understanding. Emma, rich enough to appreciate the power of wealth, explains, "I shall not be a poor old maid; and it is poverty only which makes celibacy contemptible to a generous public! A single woman, with a very narrow income, must be a ridiculous, disagreeable, old maid! . . . but a single woman, of good fortune, is always respectable, and may be as sensible and pleasant as anybody else."[17] Although Emma's subsequent redemption refutes her early misguided opinions, it is nevertheless clear from the text that they represent an accurate assessment of female life: unmarried women *were* burdens on the community unless they inherited property from husband or father. As Austen wrote in a letter to her niece, "Single women have a dreadful propensity for being poor, which is one very strong argument in favor of matrimony."[18]

Yet, on still another level, even though Austen may sympathize with her foils as understandable products of their environment, the narrator's disapproval and rejection of them is too thorough to be disregarded. They are exiled and silenced by the narrator, usually with a scathing sarcasm verging on verbal brutality.[19] Although it is possible to understand that the narrator, in rejecting these characters, empowers Austen's "cover story," her rejection also denies a part of Austen's own personality and experience in the real world. Such denial coincides with description of the development, because of a failure in the early childhood nurturing relationship, of a "false self," defined as forming "a relationship to external reality which is one of compliance, the world and its details being recognized but only as something to be fitted in with or demanding adaptation. Compliance carries with it a sense of futility for the individual and is associated with the idea that nothing matters and that life is not worth living."[20]

Like her rejected foils, Austen also was silenced and made to comply with the value structure of the community in which she lived. Unlike them, perhaps, she consciously developed a "false self," apparent as the surface plot outlines of her novels, her tales of enlightened compliance with the dominant social order. From the perspective of psychoanalytic transference, however, the textual value systems become less important than the narrative structure rejecting the foils, breeding a striking division and lack of connection among her female characters, both in regard to each other and with the narrator. Ironically, one of Austen's most prominent themes throughout her canon is the need for the individual to exist in community, a social structure she reforms in each book. That she could imagine no alternative manner to deal with her foils other than to banish them from her new utopias indicates that she responded to an emotional process beyond her aesthetic and conscious control. Perhaps life, for her protagonist, was also "not worth living" in these reformed communities, based, as it necessarily must have been, on submission and adaptation. That this motif of rejection is substantially modified in *Persuasion* also suggests its earlier unconscious power. Elizabeth Elliot, the character functioning most like Austen's earlier foils, merely is left, as *Persuasion* concludes, to "feel that to flatter and follow others, without being flattered and followed in turn, is but a state of half-enjoyment."[21]

This rejection of the foils must also be considered in concert with the peculiar absence of natural mothers and Austen's consistent use of the "Cinderella" story as the form of her plots. Essentially the story of a girl's movement from rags to riches because of her innate goodness, the Cinderella story is similar to the later Horatio Alger one, both fables affirming an ultimately just world. It may have been, however, that Austen was less fascinated by Cinderella's "happy ending," although she used it as the conclusion of her own cover story, than by the relationship of mothers and daughters. Cinderella was overmothered. Although her natural, loving mother died the day she was born, she lives with a wicked stepmother and two equally wicked stepsisters who exercise all the mother's authority over her and is rescued by a fairy godmother, whose benevolence is nevertheless limited from the perspective of the tale's narrative structure. The fairy godmother's magic only serves to bring Cinderella to the ball—or into social life—while her warning that Cinderella must leave by midnight, when the magic will lose its potency, emphasizes that Cinderella must learn to mother herself in order to end happily. Carefully read, the tale is an interesting presentation of real female life, describing its oppression in terms of the household drudgery Cinderella performs as well as the poverty and subordination she suffers, while proposing that opportunity, disguised as magic, is a necessity for female success, in the way the Horatio Alger story proposed that individual effort is a necessity for male success. What is important for Austen is that the tale admits the mother's power to save the daughter is limited, the world is more powerful than the mother, and the mother herself may seek to harm the daughter to ensure her own inevitably second-class authority. Cinderella's stepmother finally resorts to locking her in the attic so that one of her natural daughters

143

will have a chance to win the prince. The stepmother seeks social power through a double displacement: she will manipulate the daughter, who will manipulate the throne.

Austen's first three novels all contain depictions of the Cinderella heroine. In *Sense and Sensibility*, Elinor Dashwood is overshadowed by her emotionally melodramatic sister, functions as the household drone, and finds little support from her shallow, highly romantic mother. Although Elizabeth Bennet is not the household slavey of *Pride and Prejudice*, nor does she possess a timid and retiring personality, her marriage to Darcy coupled with the fact that she is her mother's least favorite daughter make her resemble Cinderella as well. Catherine Morland, heroine of *Northanger Abbey*, is another naive innocent who must make her way with only the good wishes of her mother, who has permitted her to leave home under the protection of a mother surrogate much more concerned with the state of Catherine's clothing than her emotional or physical well-being. Much like the original fairy godmother, Mrs. Allen believes that a new dress is the sole item indispensable for Catherine's passage to adulthood.

The first three books also include a mother figure reflecting the wicked stepmother. In *Sense and Sensibility*, Elinor's antagonist is Mrs. Ferrars, who desires to disrupt Elinor's relationship with the male protagonist, ensuring as well that the Dashwood women remain in penury. Lady Catherine de Bourgh is a more full-blown version of the hostile stepmother: autocratic, domineering, egotistically intent on controlling and ruining the lives of all her "dependents" in *Pride and Prejudice*. Only the mother surrogate in *Northanger Abbey* can be considered a benign version, but although Mrs. Allen is not actively malevolent, her complacent self-absorption and complete lack of concern for Catherine's welfare can be construed as passive hostility. Like Cinderella's fairy godmother, Mrs. Allen almost literally abandons Catherine to fend for herself at the ball in Bath.

Each of these first novels contains a nearly explicit fairy godmother figure; the narrator waves the magic wand, providing the heroine with the sort of nurturing denied by the stepmother. The narrator's voice shepherds both the heroine, and that reader sympathetic to her, through all perils, including those created by the heroine's own immaturity. Significantly, saving the heroine from herself frequently means that the narrator must address the reader directly, to explain her heroine's behavior and ask for indulgence for her present or past flaws. About Elinor Dashwood, *Sense and Sensibility*'s preternaturally serious protagonist, the narrator tells us, "Elinor could not be cheerful. Her joy was of a different kind, and led to anything rather than to gaiety. Marianne restored to life, health, friends, and to her doting mother, was an idea to fill her heart with sensations of exquisite comfort, and expand it in fervent gratitude;—but it led to no outward demonstrations of joy, no words, no smiles. All within Elinor's breast was satisfaction, silent and strong."[22] Because the reader, together with the novel's other characters, cannot see or hear Elinor's responses, the narrator must interpret them. Strikingly, the sentence opening *Northanger Abbey* itself is a comic narrative defense of Catherine Morland, whom the reader has not even met before being told, "No one who had ever seen Catherine Morland in her infancy would have supposed her born to be an heroine. Her situation in life, the character of her father and mother, her own person and disposition, were all equally against her."[23] Even though that sentence establishes the satiric posture Austen uses throughout *Northanger Abbey*, this opening nevertheless distances the reader from her protagonist.

In fact Austen only allows her female characters to speak for themselves up until their reformation, the third narrative structure interrupting canonic coherence. Elizabeth Bennet, for example, the most independent and assertive of the three early heroines, is volubly ironic until the climactic scene when she recognizes her pride and prejudice. After that realization, she forfeits her dialogue. In her last conversation with Lady Catherine de Bourgh, Elizabeth resorts to silence as the final indication of her self-development. The reader is told, "In this manner Lady Catherine talked on, till they were at the door of the carriage," whereas "Elizabeth made no answer; and without attempting to persuade her ladyship to return into the house, walked quietly into it herself."[24] That the reader is not given Lady Catherine's dialogue closing this important scene, but instead must accept the narrator's report of it, is consistent with the silencing of both reformed heroines and alternate female foils in each of the novels. Isabelle Thorpe, Catherine Morland's foil, suffers her voice to be muted to the distance of a letter, a device also used to silence Mary Crawford in *Mansfield Park.* In the three early novels the narrative structure indicates that merger with the benevolent "godmothering" narrator is the only solution to female life. This dynamic is demonstrated in reverse form at the conclusion of *Pride and Prejudice* in the narrator's scathing, satiric summation of Mrs. Bennet, a depriving and rejecting antithesis of the narrator—"Happy for all her maternal feelings was the day on which Mrs. Bennet got rid of her most deserving daughters"[25]—while Elizabeth Bennet's inherent reward in marrying Darcy is removal from that mother.[26] In contrast, separation from the narrator is fraught with danger, penalized by complete rejection or exile. While the protagonists merge, the foils, who separate, have in some way betrayed the narrator's value system, have joined the camp of the wicked stepmothers.

In these early books, like the parody "Plan for a Novel," Austen strictly divides the good and the wicked, unconsciously identifying her narrator as all good while rejecting the world beyond the narrator's control as all bad. The narrator is limited in the same way Cinderella's fairy godmother was hampered. The world of external oppression and bad mothering exists despite her desire; the best she can do is insulate her heroine in a supportive community. The only reader, then, Austen could have unconsciously imagined accepting her narrator's protection would be a figure in need of the same sort of rescue as the female protagonist, equally willing to exchange speech in a community which ignored and degraded for her silence in a community that embraced and nurtured her. Real readers, judging from their real responses, react to Austen's strict division with a degree of emotional force implying that they "catch the drift" of Austen's unconscious domination within their own unconscious, experiencing it either as need gratifying or antithetical to self-definition.

That the narrator's statements openly affirm dominant eighteenth-century social attitudes in their content while subtly, in their assertion of authority, providing a feminist model, is less significant in terms of psychoanalytic transference than is the structural position the narrator's address offers Austen's reader. Just as her narrator rescues the female protagonist by overwhelming and merging her voice with the narrator's own, so Austen's reader must accept a relationship with the narrator embodying an identical hierarchy of authority and subordination. The reader who denies narrative authority also denies the text, whereas the reader who submits to narrative domination is rewarded by narrative protection. This hierarchy reflects the dominant patterns of heterosexual relationships during Austen's period. That critics have discerned the presence of Austen's feminist subtext attests to the unconscious condition of Austen's narrative structure. Her covert inscription of the freedom she attained as an artist should have produced an equal, if concealed, freedom for her imagined reader and protagonist. That this hierarchy is progressively modified in Austen's last three novels indicates Austen's own growing comprehension of the nature of her relationship with her imagined reader. In these last novels she gradually came to empower her female protagonist as she qualified the unconditional authority of her narrator.

A good example of such modification is the resolution Austen designed for Mrs. Smith, her personified narrator in *Persuasion;* Mrs. Smith is linked to the third-person narrator through similarities of language. Several times the narrator speaks in extraordinarily bitter tones, far surpassing Austen's former narrative irony. Commenting on the dead son of the Musgrove family, the narrator says, "He had, in fact, though his sisters were now doing all they could for him, by calling him 'poor Richard,' been nothing better than a thick-headed, unfeeling, unprofitable Dick Musgrove, who had never done anything to entitle himself to more than the abbreviation of his name,

147

living or dead." Later, the narrator describes Mrs. Musgrove's grief: "Personal size and mental sorrow have certainly no necessary proportions. . . . But, fair or not fair, there are unbecoming conjunctions, which reason will patronize in vain—which taste cannot tolerate—which ridicule will seize." This extreme language is echoed in Mrs. Smith's response to William Elliot, the man who contributed to the financial ruin of her husband: "Mr. Elliot is a man without heart or conscience; a designing, wary, cold-blood being. . . . He is totally beyond the reach of any sentiment of justice or compassion. Oh! he is black at heart, hollow and black!" Even Anne Elliot finds Mrs. Smith's story does "not perfectly justify the unqualified bitterness."[27] The earlier novels would have us expect that connecting Mrs. Smith with the third-person narrator would result in Anne's merger with her. Instead Anne asserts authority over Mrs. Smith, whose business affairs are assumed by Anne's new husband. Metaphorically, Anne comes to protect and "mother" Mrs. Smith. Simultaneously, Austen empowers her imagined reader, perhaps redefining connection as the fundamental emotional necessity of female life, now distinct from both separation and merger.

In 1900, when Freud treated the eighteen-year-old Dora K., he failed to investigate Dora's relationship with her mother.[28] Contemporary psychoanalysts working with female psychosexual development understand that a daughter's relationship to her mother is centrally important to her self-development, particularly for her lifelong response to authority. Jane Austen was inescapably female. Her novels involve the reader in a world seen from the perspective of a woman living in a patriarchal culture yet responding primarily to the most crucial relationship in female life, that between mother and daughter. In this context it is striking that although daughters abound, mothers are absent in Austen's novels. In both *Emma* and *Persuasion* the heroine's natural mother has died before the novel opens; in Austen's other four books the protagonist's biologic mother is either incompetent or generally absent—in none of these four, with the exception of *Pride and Prejudice,* does the natural mother play an active role in determining plot movement. Nonetheless, Austen identifies each protagonist as a daughter, emphatically placing her in the daughter's role within the context of an extended family. A critical exploration of Austen's relationship with her imagined reader, therefore, must take into consideration Austen's own responses as a daughter in order to understand the authority she asserts over and the autonomy she allows both her imagined and real readers.

Austen's use of the Cinderella story as a fundamental motif is a reflection of her response as a daughter. In her later books, *Mansfield Park, Emma,* and *Persuasion,* the good, natural mother, like Cinderella's biologic mother, is dead or absent before the heroine's story begins. In the early three novels, the natural mother is accepted as "good" only by virtue of a saving incompetence, stupidity, or general absence; for example, excluding the opening and closing scenes of *Northanger Abbey,* Mrs. Morland does not figure in the book, while the alternative good biologic mother, Mrs. Tilney, is important to the plot because of her early death. Instead, the "good" mother is represented by the narrator, who is the externalized voice of the text. The narrator is completely protective in her response to the female protagonists, going so far as to call, fondly, the protagonist of *Mansfield Park* "My Fanny,"[29] indicating that Austen idealized the narrator's persona, a consequence of the repression of ambivalent or hostile feelings of her own toward authority. Austen, in these terms, projects onto her protagonist and imagined reader her own unconscious feelings in regard to female authority, placing the protagonist in the position she herself inhabited as a child. Then she characterizes the bad mother as other than the protagonist's biologic mother, like Cinderella's stepmother, and therefore can portray her as completely wicked with unconscious impunity.

Chodorow's work in female psychology becomes important particularly for an exploration of female transference in her realization that "the infant's experience is a cycle of fusion, separation and refusion with its mother." Because girls identify themselves as like the female mothering parent, they "come to define themselves . . . in relation to

149

others."[30] It is a consequence of Western child-rearing practices that female children find issues of separation and merger, autonomy and control, more confusing than do boys and, furthermore, that girls will locate essential feelings of well-being in situations of community and connection rather than rivalry and competition. The relationship most uncomfortable for the female child, then, is the ambivalent one with her mother, for it paradoxically mandates a sense of competitiveness antithetical to her deepest sense of self.

Austen solved this dilemma, at least in her early novels, with repression. Casting her narrator as an omnipotent fairy godmother enabled her to identify herself with the idealized aspects of her relationship to her own mother, whose bleaker facets she split off and lent to her wicked stepmother figures. Yet because the narrator's omnipotence is limited (she can exclude, not transform), the narrator emerges as both nurturing godmother and destructive stepmother. For the reader she imagines as sympathetic to her protagonist and to her own covertly satiric attitudes about eighteenth-century social conventions, the narrator offers a relationship ideally protective and embracing. To the reader she visualizes as in harmony with dominant social attitudes, she presents the forbidding and formidable personality of her stepmother figures: offensively domineering. In the three novels Austen wrote between 1811 and 1817, however, a developing awareness of the attitudes she habitually transferred onto authority figures is manifested by a change in her narrative structure. In these three books there is a gradual evolution from omniscient overprotectiveness toward a structure in which the protagonist is given an interior monologue previously reserved for the narrator's voice, with concomitant autonomy offered to her imagined reader. To understand how Austen restructured her narrative in *Persuasion,* the final completed novel in the canon, it is first important to examine the connections among narrator, female protagonist, and imagined reader in *Mansfield Park* and *Emma,* Austen's fourth and fifth novels.

Austen wrote all her books between 1796 and 1817. The six novels can be separated into two writing periods divided by nearly ten years of silence during which Austen's father died and the family moved from rural Somerset to Bath, and then back to rural Chawton. The first novels were all composed during the period ending approximately in 1801, before the removal to Bath. The last three, as well as an unfinished fragment of a seventh book, were completed in the latter period, beginning about 1811 and ending with Austen's death in 1817. *Persuasion* was written as Austen became increasingly debilitated, the result of an illness diagnosed posthumously as Addison's disease, which is characterized by emotional depression as well as physical weakness. Thus Austen wrote the first three novels when she was a brilliant young woman in her early twenties with life and all its multifold possibilities before her, the youngest daughter of seven children all devoted to each other and to their parents, living in the countryside she loved, participating in the family's many eventful lives and the social opportunities afforded by "Four and Twenty Families in the Neighborhood."[31] The last three books, in contrast, are the work of a woman in her middle to late thirties, aware of aging,[32] living now in a household composed only of her mother, her older sister, Cassandra, and Martha Lloyd, an old family friend.

Mansfield Park was the favorite book of Cassandra, whom Austen adored and who can be considered one of Austen's triumvirate of literal and emotional mothering figures. Austen, like Cinderella, experienced the curious situation of overmothering. Like many children of her times, for the first eighteen months of her life she was boarded with a wet nurse. Although the wet nurse presumably offered the simplest relationship in practice, it was nonetheless one of the most complex psychologically. In the view of contemporary psychologists, the infant's experience of nursing and weaning form the basis of its choice of cultural symbols.[33] Austen's own mother, according to biographical evidence, was the dominant member of the family, exercising authority of the manipulative but concealed sort over both husband and children. Austen's letters record that her mother was a chronic invalid who used her health to control her family. Mrs. Austen embodied in reality the fairy godmother's limited authority. Powerful in her own family, she was mysteriously limited (from a child's perspective) in power over her own well-being and the larger social structure. She could nurture her children until nurturing became, as inevitably it did, injurious to her health. At that point, her children had necessarily to nurture her. When Austen herself was dying, she still insisted on constructing a mock sofa of two upright chairs placed together so that she could semirecline in the family drawing room. The proper couch she reserved for her mother's comfort.

Cassandra was perhaps the most intriguing member of Austen's constellation of mothers. Although only two-and-one-half years older than Austen, Cassandra exercised parental, and particularly maternal, authority over her younger sister. Generally the more serious sister, with a personality their nephew James Austen-Leigh remembered as grave in contrast to Austen's more frivolous, ironic bent, Cassandra's values, judgment, and general mien elicited both devotion and respect from Austen. She was Austen's "other self,"[34] in character closely resembling Fanny Price, protagonist of *Mansfield Park*, while the novel's foil, Mary Crawford, bears traces of Austen in her lively wit and nearly cynical public perspective. Cassandra can be considered, in fact, the real reader to whom Austen primarily addressed her novels. Cassandra was certainly one of the few members of Austen's family aware of the extent of Austen's creativity, a secret carried forward to exclude Austen's nieces and nephews. Despite Cassandra's real presence in Austen's life, though, Austen's perception of her was, as psychoanalytic transference indicates, formed by a combination of fantasy and reality. Austen perceived her through a screen of both ideality and ambivalence mirroring the split-off unconscious response apparent in the creation of her "dark" foils and wicked stepmother figures in contrast to her Cinderalla protagonists.

The ambiguities between Cassandra and Austen, encompassing Austen's internal conflict between the sister she loved and admired and the authority she resented, are manifested in her creation of Fanny and Mary. Austen demonstrates her ambivalence toward Cassandra through Fanny's character, which is, as so many readers attest, too good to be true. Fanny is so dully self-sacrificial as to provoke in readers the sort of boredom which conceals the more unmanageable emotions of contempt and hostility at her physical timidity and completely submissive personality. As Austen amply displayed in the portraits of Elizabeth Bennet and Emma Woodhouse, she well knew how to create a heroine enchanting as only a human being combining conscience with strength of character can be; yet in creating Fanny, she allowed herself to draw a character whose conscience absorbs all the traits which might make her humanly attractive. And realism in her art was exceedingly important to Austen. In a series of letters written to offer technical advice to a literary niece, each of Austen's kind but firm criticisms was designed to guide the young writer in the direction of authentic representation.[35] In yet another letter to another writing niece, she added "pictures of perfection make me sick and wicked."[36] Still, in the portrait of Fanny Price she committed both errors, creating a heroine Griselda-like in her patient endurance and Cinderella-like in her noble character, combining legend and fairy tale to form a "perfect picture."

Fanny receives her exaggerated qualities as a consequence of Austen's unconscious failure to control aesthetic technique because of her conscious address to the figure she understood as the real Fanny. Transferring the split-off and unconsciously repressed negative attitudes toward her sister into the text in the creation of Fanny, Cassandra's fictional surrogate, resulted in a character both more perfect than her life model and more timid, weak, and submissive. Austen's unconsciousness about the ambivalence informing her relationship with Cassandra exacts a peculiar revenge: Fanny is repulsive precisely because she is idealized. Moreover, in a replication of the unconscious irony undermining Fanny's portrait, although the narrator rejects Mary Crawford, Fanny's foil, the text as a whole validates Mary's characterization. Mary has all the lines, dialogue making her entrancing to her audience both within and without the text. Even Edmund Bertram, the voice of good sense in the book, is enchanted. Not coincidentally, in life Austen herself was the sister with "all the lines." Her letters are marked by satiric wit and verve, making her sound much like Mary Crawford.

The narrator's rejection of Mary is significant also for what it implies about Austen's assumptions about her imagined reader. Imagining her reader as Cassandra/Fanny, Austen created the narrator to rescue Fanny from her hostile environment, of which Mary is a central representative. To effect this rescue, the narrator needed to exercise complete control over the textual world, clearly defining value systems, repudiating characters alien to those values, and affirming the characters in harmony with them. Critics have noted that one of the most scathing wicked stepmother portraits is that of Fanny's Aunt Norris,[37] whose thoroughly malign, egocentric personality is not softened by the stupidity or general incompetence Austen used to modify similar characters in other books. As a villain, Aunt Norris structurally balances Fanny's position as heroine, the former entirely wicked, the latter completely good.

The narrator, in direct address to the reader, consistently reinforces the evil of Aunt Norris's behavior, both before and after a demonstration of her character in action and dialogue. For example, after Mrs. Norris has manipulated the Bertrams into retaining Fanny as a permanent resident at Mansfield Park, the narrator reinforces their dialogue by stating, "Mrs. Norris had not the smallest intention of taking her. It had never occurred to her, on the present, but as a thing to be carefully avoided." Earlier, after Mrs. Norris has proposed aiding their penurious sister by adopting one of her children, the narrator makes clear that "Mrs. Norris had not the least intention of being at any expense whatever in her maintenance . . . nobody knew better how to dictate liberality to others." The reader is given no opportunity to scrutinize Aunt Norris without narrative direction, a dynamic equally in force for Fanny, as the narrator explains away her weaknesses and reveals hidden strengths. After Fanny refuses romantic overtures from Henry Crawford, the narrator explains that "Fanny knew her own meaning, but was no judge of her own manner. Her manner was incurably gentle, and she was not aware of how much it concealed the sternness of her purpose. Her diffidence, gratitude, and softness, made every expression of indifference seem almost an effort of self-denial; seem, at least, to be giving nearly as much pain to herself as to him."[38]

Each of the other characters also is surrounded by narrative explanation and description. The text as a whole in fact is curiously opaque, offering the real reader the smooth surface of narrative opinion while prohibiting direct access unmediated by the narrator. The only point falling outside this opacity is Mary Crawford's dialogue which disputes, by virtue of vibrant satire, Fanny's moralisms about Mary's character. Mary remains attractive despite all efforts to devalue her. The reader is able to meet her directly, particularly in the novel's early stages, and it is only when Mary's attraction could be too seductive to the reader (as she attracts Edmund despite his best efforts to remain judgmental and detached) that the narrator directly confirms Fanny's perception, silencing Mary in order to banish her from the textual Eden. Mary's irony is finally reduced to sarcasm in her last letters, echoing the dialogue in Austen's first novel, *Lady Susan*, unpublished at her death.

Lady Susan was the sort of reversed protagonist Austen later created more successfully in the antiheroic figure of Emma Woodhouse. In this context, however, that Lady Susan possessed the foil's characteristics is less important than the form in which her character is delivered to the reader. The manuscript was written in epistolary style, so all the characters write; but Lady Susan's letters provide the dominant voice of the book, a voice unmediated by narrative authority. The fact that Austen abandoned this novel—and also revised the original version of *Pride and Prejudice,* substituting the omniscient narrator for its initial epistolary form—indicates her discomfort with a form that permitted characters to speak for themselves. When they did so, Austen must have appreciated her own satiric perspective voicing moral attitudes antithetical to her self-acknowledged identification of obedient daughter. These were the attitudes she herself learned to silence in social groups, not simply because they challenged cultural assumptions, but also because they challenged the authority structures in her own family and made suspect the idealism she consciously brought to bear in the creation of her female protagonist, an ideality necessary to render the protagonist worthy of the narrator's nurturance and protection. In protecting her protagonist, and her imagined reader, Austen's narrator also protected Austen herself from the split-off and terrifying bad-mother imago. This imago remained unconscious because in that state it could be contained within the text, yet in *Mansfield Park* it escaped through the fissures opening in the dialogue Austen wrote for Mary Crawford.

Transferring her own complicated, primarily unconscious attitudes toward authority into the text of *Mansfield Park*, then, led Austen to create a protagonist ideally worthy and in need of the material protection and rescue an omniscient narrator in control of characters and plot could provide. The reader is imagined as the protagonist's counterpart and offered equal narrative protection at the price of equal submission. All subversive tendencies are lent to the protagonist's foil, who is narratively disparaged and finally exiled. That the protagonist's virtue can be experienced by a real reader as repulsively sanctimonious while the foil's "tainted" words provide moments of textual brightness,[39] indicates, however, that Austen was unconsciously conflicted about both the wholly ideal nature of the protagonist and the narrator's act of rescue.

The novel's abrupt conclusion, manufactured through two acts of sudden plot reversal, indicates the intensity of that conflict. The narrator, in what amounts to a fiat, shuts off the reader's relationship with Mary Crawford, banishes Mary, heightens omniscient narrative authority, and ties together plot strands with a suddenness that emphasizes the distance between Fanny and the real reader. As Kingsley Amis notes, "To invite Mr. and Mrs. Edmund Bertram round for the evening would not be lightly undertaken";[40] perhaps it would have been as formidable an event for their author as for the reader. Fanny's rescue is purchased at the price of her autonomy as she merges with Edmund's voice, while the narrator speaks for them both. Ironically, although Mary's voice is thoroughly rejected, she, unlike Fanny, is allowed access to the reader to the end, for her last letter, labeled as "all wrong,"[41] nonetheless retains her own voice. In contrast, the imagined reader, like Fanny, forfeits independent speech and is forced to merge with the narrator.

Thus the consequence of imagining a protagonist and a reader in need of rescue of *Mansfield Park* is an overwhelmingly dominant narrative voice, rigidly defined textual values enforced by a narrative opacity that closely directs the reader's experience of the reading event, and a severely marked separation of good and bad characters. Ironically, perhaps the reason so many of Austen's contemporaries selected *Mansfield Park* as their favorite among her novels was this sharp division.[42] The reader choosing "wrong" was well punished. Austen's contemporaries, who experienced a similar sharply defined division in the social sanctions directing their lives, could with perhaps less discomfort than a modern reader accept and delight in the same hierarchical structure mirrored in *Mansfield Park*.

Emma, the novel most disliked by Austen's contemporaries, is the book most appreciated by modern readers and contains Austen's own favorite protagonist. *Emma*, begun in January 1814, was completed by the end of March 1815, more quickly than any of the novels preceding it, indicating an ease of composition that makes its subject matter significant for psychoanalytic transferrence. *Emma* begins a development in Austen's narrative structure that is more fully realized in *Persuasion*. Although Emma's character clearly is descended from Elizabeth Bennet, she also can be understood as a figure of Mary Crawford in the process of redemption. With Emma, Austen translated the foil of *Mansfield Park* into the new novel's protagonist, signaling a new awareness of the strengths as well as the weaknesses of that character. As Trilling points out, Emma "believes she is clever, she insists that she is right, but she never says she is good. . . . She believes in her own distinction and vividness and she wants all around her to be distinguished and vivid."[43] This reversal indicates Austen's growing acceptance of her felt experience in the real world, which she could now partially accept in her protagonist, and a concomitant transformation in the relationship she permits her narrator to form with this protagonist and with her imagined reader.

Fanny Price also appears in translated form in *Emma*, in the character of Jane Fairfax, Emma's Cinderella foil. On the one hand, in the context of Austen's canon, the reader Austen imagined for *Emma* should be found in Jane Fairfax, who both embodies all the narrator's values and is in need of rescue from the larger social world. On the other hand, it could be assumed that the imagined reader is Emma's surrogate, in need of rescue from her own delusions; but in contrast to the position offered to the imagined reader in *Mansfield Park*, where the reader and Fanny were merged, the imagined reader in *Emma* is situated somewhere between the two female characters. Until the novel's denouement, nearly its conclusion, neither girl is complete; each complements the other. Emma's strength of will and imagination are balanced by Jane's strong moral sensibility and rational ideals. Although this duality is a familiar Austen motif, appearing with particular clarity in the paired sisters of *Sense and Sensibility* and *Pride and Prejudice*, in *Emma*, Austen includes a special twist. In addition to being a version of Emma's *Pilgrim's Progress*, as a novel, *Emma* is about the writing of fiction. Jane's character and situation, as it is delivered to the real reader, is a function of Emma's creativity; the reader must see through Emma to see Jane. The imagined reader can be located neither in Emma nor in Jane because the necessity of separating Emma's fictions about Jane from Jane's real circumstances gains the reader's attention for both characters. Emma's fiction making, then, is centrally important to the novel's approach to its reader. Through Emma as a fiction maker Austen tests her own narrative structures. Scrutinizing the imagined reader Austen provides for Emma's fictions should illuminate the imagined reader she visualized for her own.

Emma writes two major (and several minor) narratives. The first, although lesser, is her fairy tale romanticizing Harriet Smith as an orphan of noble birth, destined for a second-rank prince. Although this narrative is directed ostensibly to Harriet, as Emma unfolds it to her in serial form, its plot is motivated by Emma's willful misreading of Harriet's character and circumstances. Harriet, as she really is, cannot be the audience Emma imagines for her story because Harriet as she is could neither appreciate nor participate in it. The second, more important narrative involves Emma's creation of a melodramatic gothic romance modeled on the bare outlines of Jane Fairfax's life. Here too the fiction Emma creates depends on a willful misunderstanding of Jane's character, but the immediate audience is Frank Churchill, not Jane. Frank is revealed as the most inappropriate audience Emma could select for a story that links Jane romantically with the husband of her benefactor, when in fact Jane and Frank have entered a secret engagement. In constructing Jane's story, then, Emma doubly deceives herself, in the nature of both her protagonist and her audience.

These two major narratives function on at least two important levels. First, each reveals Emma's character initially to the reader and later to herself. Second, Emma functions in the narratives as the sort of dominant narrator Austen uses in the third-person mode in all her earlier books. Yet in *Emma* the reader is permitted far more direct access to Emma: "We come close to Emma because, in a strange way, she permits us to—even invites us to—by being close to herself."[44] Almost without narrative mediation Emma is allowed to make errors of judgment for which Elizabeth Bennet, for example, was provided narrative justification. Meeting Emma directly means that Austen was willing here to provide her imagined reader with a parody of her own narrative act.

Emma's egocentric misidentification of her audience and misreading of her characters indicates that she suffers from a failure of empathic response. She mistakes her sympathy for Harriet, born of her desire for a malleable companion, for a genuine appreciation of the nature and conditions of Harriet's life. Her failure to recognize Jane Fairfax's real virtues originates in her profound inability to suspend her own identity in order temporarily to assume Jane's perspective. Emma suffers from the converse of Fanny Price's disorder: rather than submitting too completely to the other, Emma is irrevocably separate. Defined psychoanalytically, the terms sympathy and empathy are somewhat at variance with their colloquial use.[45] Sympathy as a felt emotion is connected to the psychoanalytic concept of identification, an immature response fundamental to human development. As the child gradually develops an autonomous existence, it also must develop an autonomous ego and know itself as similar to but distinct from the parent figures. Relationships motivated by identification generate sympathy as their fundamental emotion, fueled by an apprehension of the other as like the self. Relationships motivated by empathy are defined as a temporary and partial merger of self and other. Ironically, only one in possession of a secure sense of self can participate in an empathic relationship, by moving beyond the anxiety of self-loss to authentically recreate the other's experience. Emma, as demonstrated through her misprision of both her protagonists and her audience, is incapable of empathic response and therefore misunderstands the limits of her ability to control the world. Identifying others as like herself, she is an omnipotent creator.

Emma herself, therefore, is the best audience for her own fictions. Because the imagined reader is subject to unconscious as well as conscious manipulation by the writer, the writer who like Emma identifies her imagined reader as like herself mistakes her sympathetic desire to defend the reader against her own unconscious conflicts for an empathic appreciation of the imagined reader as other. Such a writer will incorporate a large proportion of subjective unconscious material into the narrative. Imagining the audience as like herself, she will structure her narrative unconsciously to satisfy her own needs and to defend against fears of which she is consciously unaware. For example, as Emma creates the story of Harriet's reformed life, she fleshes out the plot line with aristocratic parents and an appropriate suitor, meanwhile sinking Harriet's real but plebian love interest. Later, assessing the success of her narrative, Emma decides that there were "no alarming symptoms of love. The young man had been the first admirer, but she trusted there was no other hold, and that there would be no serious difficulty on Harriet's side to oppose any friendly arrangement of her own."[46] She directs her story to an audience who will applaud a narrator acting with such magnanimity toward her protagonist; as narrator, she supplies a nurturing environment which ignores the protagonist's autonomous needs. Emma thus congratulates herself for what amounts to affirming her own distorted perception of reality, derived from her own status as a motherless daughter nurtured primarily by a governess subordinate to her in public power.

Issues of public power and domination also direct her narrative about Jane Fairfax. There, she intends to affect her audience with her penetrating perception of a reality ignored by less sophisticated eyes. Ironically, she chooses her ostensible audiences with precision: Harriet, a seventeen-year-old naif, receives the fairy tale; Frank Churchill, a spoiled young sophisticate, receives the gothic romance. Harriet, far more pliable than Frank, accepts her role, giving up her own desires to secure Emma's protection. In both narratives the real reader has no place unless he or she is willing to accept the writer's direction. The real Harriet Smith, who does not fit anywhere in Emma's story about her, can hear it only by virtue of meshing with Emma's distorted perception, motivated by her own unconscious needs and desires. As Harriet acknowledges, "I do not mean to set up my opinion against yours."[47] Frank Churchill, in contrast, understands quite well the discrepancy between his identity and Emma's fiction and rejects her narrative.

The writer who is able to bring an empathic rather than a sympathetic response to her imagined reader will also be able to exercise a greater degree of aesthetic and technical control over her material. That in this book Austen understood Emma as a storyteller unconsciously identifying her audience and characters with herself indicates that Austen had herself begun to imagine an audience distinct from herself. Diagnosing Emma, she examined her own creative practice and was able to bring an empathic response to her conception of the imagined reader precisely because she identified that reader as neither Emma nor Jane.

Until the denouement on Box Hill, Emma and Jane are carefully balanced, forcing the real reader to attempt an impossible choice between the egocentric creativity of one and the sacrificial refinement of the other. That the real reader can choose neither indicates that Austen made her final choice unwillingly as well. Empathetically understanding her imagined reader as like both characters enabled her aesthetically to balance the reader's perspective but also indicates that Austen's final decision in favor of Jane Fairfax was perhaps directed by historical necessity, as revealed by the sudden resumption of dominant narrative address after the denouement. As Rachel Blau DuPlessis notes, Emma's "proper negotiation with class and gender makes the heroine from an improper hero." As a consequence of this choice, Austen is forced to silence Emma even more completely than Elizabeth Bennet, who is left with at least a remnant of her former wit. Emma's marriage to Mr. Knightley presumes a reformation of Emma's character based on submerging her personality in his. Emma's silencing also places the imagined reader in a position subordinate to that of the narrator. It is the narrator who creates the reformed community, who decides that "the wishes, the hopes, the confidence, the predictions of the small band of true Friends who witnessed the ceremony, were fully answered in the perfect happiness of the union,"[48] rejecting dissent in the same way Emma earlier rejected Harriet's yeoman connections.

It seems that what began in this novel as Austen's empathic understanding of the separation between herself and her imagined reader, gained through a heightened consciousness about her narrator's link to the textual world, still ends with her identification with the cultural authority system reflected by an omniscient and didactic narrator. Perhaps because Austen could imagine no resolution for Emma other than the traditional "happy ending," neither could she create, at this point in her writing career, any connection between her narrator and imagined reader other than merger, echoing the structure of eighteenth-century marriage. In so doing, Austen retained her narrator as an idealized "good" mother figure, equally idealizing Emma's re-formed character to force the imagined reader beyond the choice be-tween Emma and Jane. By the end of the novel Emma and Jane are one character, Mr. Knightley and the narrator are one voice. The bad mother, located initially within Emma's flawed character, is forced outward, figuratively and literally banished from the textual "brave new world."

Eradicating the bad-mother figure, as well as excluding all dissident elements from the new community, indicates that issues of separation and merger were particularly important for Austen when she wrote *Emma*. Initially placing the bad mother within Emma's character opened a new relationship between her narrator and imagined reader. The narrator, in loving Emma, also loved the bad mother, an emotion which modified narrative authority over the reader. Because, in con-trast to earlier novels, Austen was able to suspend the narrator's rigor-ous moral evaluation of the bad mother, she was able also to allow the bad mother to speak, through Emma, directly to the reader. Direct access to the imagined reader modified the terror inherent in the bad mother. Instead of evil authority, she appears as narcissistically self-indulgent, while the narrator responds with the sort of parental affec-tion offered to a spoiled but well-loved child. The real reader responds to the relationship between the narrator and Emma, almost function-ing as mediator between the two, acknowledging Emma's trespasses on the one hand, experiencing her as delightful on the other. Until the denouement, the narrator, Emma, Jane Fairfax, and the imagined reader participate in a relationship marked by a fluctuation between separation, merger, reseparation, remerger, and so on. The narrator encourages the reader to respond positively, now to Emma as she entrances Harriet by recreating Cinderella's story with Harriet at its center; now to Jane as she, in turn, displays her real affection and makes real sacrifices for her Aunt Bates; now negatively to Emma as she tramples on the separate lives of Harriet and Robert Martin; now negatively to Jane for her "repulsive reserve." After the denouement, however, separation, for the narrator and the imagined reader, is impossible; all voices are merged in one idealized cultural icon, the image of the Emma/Knightley marriage.

Although the idea is current in contemporary psychology that women to fail to separate emotionally from their mothers until they are well into the fourth decade of life, some research, including Chodorow's, indicates that such separation is never possible, nor necessarily desirable.[49] Instead, female life may be lived most fruitfully in emotional connection with others. But connection in this context is distinctly different from merger. The latter term inherently assumes a loss of individual autonomy D. W. Winnicott understood as prohibiting a creative life and resulting instead in a life experienced as worthless and in action that adapts to the larger environment rather than uses the world to enhance life.[50] *Connection* can be understood as the dynamic satisfying both female psychological necessity and the demands of reality. Connection is, in fact, the same quality of conscious awareness as empathy. One can only connect to the other if one possesses an autonomous sense of self; just as the empathic response is temporary, so is connection, always potential rather than fixed. Austen would seem to have come to a conscious appreciation of her desire for connection; perceived it as distinct from merger; understood the necessity of separation; redefined it as autonomy; and demonstrated this new comprehension in the narrative structure of her final completed novel, *Persuasion.*

Each of Austen's novels focuses on the desire for daughters to marry and, moreover, to marry well. In keeping with historical convention, marriage in the novels is the business of the mothers or their surrogates. Mrs. Bennet is consumed by the question; Mrs. Dashwood's flights of fancy fuel Marianne's misguided romance; Mrs. Norris schemes for her nieces; and Lady Russell supervises Anne Elliot's choice of husband. Even Mrs. Weston, Emma's more wise than usual ex-governess, admits to a secret fantasy concerning Emma and her stepson. What is more, none of Austen's fictional mothers is more interested in the question of her daughter's marriage than is the narrator. The rescue of the female protagonist is always accomplished by marriage and through the narrator's manipulation of plot material and with the narrator's final applause. Yet although this motif is emphatically asserted in *Persuasion*, where the pivot of the plot depends on a virtual duel between Anne Elliot's suitors, the narrator's position on marriage seems confused. The novel's final paragraph implies that Anne will suffer grief as well as "suffer" happiness as the price of marriage to a naval officer: "His profession was all that could ever make her friends wish that tenderness less; the dread of a future war all that could dim her sunshine. She gloried in being a sailor's wife, but she must pay the tax of quick alarm for belonging to that profession which is, if possible, more distinguished in its domestic virtues than in its national importance."[51] In this book, what seems as well made a marriage as all its fictional antecedents is colored by narrative ambiguity. Although it appears to be more to Anne's benefit to marry than remain single (her bloom is related to her sexual renascence), the novel's conclusion is less naively "happy" and more ambivalently realistic.

Although Austen died only one year after completing *Persuasion*, its narrative structure indicates she had begun to grapple with the inconsistencies between the life she lived and the model of cultural femininity she inherited. As Alice Munro notes with wry irony about some women near Austen's age, "They were all in their early thirties. An age at which it is sometimes hard to admit that what you are living *is* your life."[52] Austen's struggle, central to feminist philosophy, has been replicated by the female writers succeeding her. Just as her narrator served as an overmother for her protagonists and imagined reader, so Austen herself often serves as a professional mother figure for modern female writers who perceive in her work the conflicts fragmenting their own professional autonomy. For example, Virginia Woolf, whose respect for Austen's work led her to include Austen's fictions within her own fiction,[53] speculated that at the age of sixty Austen would have produced fiction structured with reflective interior monologues replacing the exterior control exercised by her narrator.[54] In short, Austen would have written fiction much like Woolf's. To do so, of course, would have required that Austen leap nearly one hundred years to embrace a species of infant modernism, by definition breaking with historical continuity and received tradition.

The structural development to which Woolf alluded is highlighted by reference to Austen's transference to her imagined reader. In psychoanalytic terms, Austen "worked through" a conflict about mothers and daughters that informed her fiction. Defined by Hans Loewald, *working through* "seems to be the work of the ego to repeat 'actively' what was experienced 'passively,' to repeat on a higher level—a level of more dimensions and further differentiated and integrated experience and functioning. Working through has decidedly to do with redoing, not with undoing, the past. The repetition involved here is not duplication or reiteration, but recreation, to be distinguished from reproduction."[55] In ways discussed below, Anne Elliot is more completely an autobiographical figure than Austen's earlier protagonists. With Anne, Austen blurred the boundaries between fiction and autobiography, actively "recreating" a life she had to some degree experienced passively according to the law of her culture—according to the word of her mother covertly relaying patriarchal sanctions.

Critical comment about Austen's novels frequently derides the narrowly domestic focus of her work. Located primarily in drawing rooms of country houses, Austen's novels polish and repolish the "little bit (two inches wide) of ivory" on which she worked.[56] Yet from the perspective of female autobiography, Austen's is not the restricted point of view of an apolitical mind but, rather, the historical viewpoint of a life lived anterior to the larger world of public affairs. Hers is the story of the life most gentlewomen lived. Female autobiographers, unlike their male counterparts, labor under a peculiar handicap. Like most women, they often experience the realities of their lives as fictional, as someone else's story. Their autobiographies frequently are written as journals or diaries, segmented into their socially determined roles of mother, wife, daughter, sister, and so forth.[57] Female autobiographers do not seem to ask "Who am I? but

instead conflate identity with function in a social context. Male autobiographers often exclude the details of their domestic lives from their
histories and focus on their public careers, making domestic life seem
merely an adjunct to public power. Marriage is what female autobiographers write about, in the process frequently confusing the personal
with the intimate; their marriage is equivalent to their life. Ironically,
marriage can also be a professional woman's best defense. When
female professionals want to conceal or defuse anxiety generated by
their public power, they talk about their children. It is understandable
that Austen, with her anxieties about authorship and authority,[58]
would focus almost exclusively on domestic life.

Biographical evidence indicates that she certainly was aware of
world events,[59] that she chose her subject and consciously excluded
the "larger" world from her fiction. What she wrote about instead was
her own life, a subject particularly evident in *Persuasion*, a novel about
women in a world where men often seem no more than appendages,
"necessary adjuncts" to the real story. The real story, in contrast, is
Anne Elliot's emancipation from her inherited designation as perpetual daughter. It was, perhaps, a story Austen could attempt only at
this point in her real life, when in her late thirties it had become clear
that the life she was living *was* her life. It is well documented that
chronic stress can produce physical disease, in particular can effect
illnesses such as Addison's disease. Perhaps Austen, in recognizing
her narrator's role as creator of a world, also recognized her own
responsibility for her life; perhaps she realized that to tell her story
she would have to admit her power in the world, the very realization
from which she would suffer most.

To recapitulate, the imagined reader Austen addressed in *Mansfield
Park* was a duplicated figure of Fanny Price, also the fictional portrait of
Austen's sister Cassandra. Fanny, suffering in silence the malignities
of an uncaring world, is protected by the mothering narrator, who
finally rescues her by reforming the world, removing from it at the
same time all the elements of wit and irony informing both the
narrative voice and the foil character. As the narrator concludes, "Let

other pens dwell on guilt and misery, I quit such odious subjects as soon as I can, impatient to restore everybody, not greatly in fault themselves, to tolerable comfort, and to have done with all the rest."[60] In *Emma*, the imagined reader was a figure combining the best traits of Emma and Jane Fairfax, on the one hand sensitive to Emma's character flaws, and on the other hand, possessing some of Emma's own imagination and spirit. Rescue in this novel involved reformation both of the world and of Emma's overly authoritative personality, after which both female characters, and the imagined reader, are deprived of their voices; harmony and silence correlate in *Emma*. Ironically, the last spoken words in the novel are given to Mrs. Elton, who has been excluded from the reformed community surrounding Emma. Mrs. Elton, the soul of dissension, concludes with the thought that Emma's wedding was "extremely shabby, and very inferior to her own—'Very little white satin, very few lace veils; a most pitiful business!' "[61] In both books, then, Austen marries her daughters well and yet indicates her psychological discomfort through the "bride price." The protagonists, like their historical counterparts, speak now through their husbands and, moreover, through their mother, the narrator. With this dynamic, the narrator is subtly transformed from fairy godmother to wicked stepmother, whose power is once removed, operating through her daughters. She becomes a mother-in-law, with "the best intentions," giving the daughter a future through the son. The imagined reader is equally ensnared. She must either submit to narrative authority or suffer exile; she too is deprived of an autonomous voice within the text.

In *Persuasion*, Austen proceeds to incorporate what was for her a radical difference in plot and structure. Instead of focusing on the progress toward a happy marriage, *Persuasion* begins after the happy marriage no longer appears possible. Even though Anne eventually will marry "well," she does so only after separating from her surrogate mother, Lady Russell. Her marriage is a subsidiary concern; her real struggle is finding her own voice, and once found, it is never relinquished. *Persuasion*'s imagined reader is Anne herself, in a motif reminiscent of *Mansfield Park*. But whereas Fanny Price serves as the vehicle with whom the real reader must identify in order to accept the textual world, Anne functions as an experience for the real reader, with whom the reader must journey because her progress carries her beyond fictional and conventional boundaries into the realities of Austen's life. In writing *Persuasion*, Austen moved beyond unconscious transference to address a consciously realized reader for whom she could no longer provide conventional answers; happy marriage in this book is not enough. It is this ambivalence that indicates her answers had become inadequate, her questions paramount. Here Austen seems most modern. Because of its ambivalence *Persuasion* is an uncomfortable book for a real reader; perhaps it was uncomfortable for Austen as well. But its very dis-ease indicates that Austen was engaged now in a struggle with her life and art she could not resolve, either for herself or for her reader, a struggle that finally engendered collaboration with, rather than domination over, her reader and involved a radical restructuring of her narrative voice.

Excluding Anne and the narrator, there are six central female characters in *Persuasion*; they are used either to illuminate Anne's character; or, more important, to develop it through the relationship they share with her; or both. To understand who Anne is, the reader must first understand who she is not, as Austen compares her with the Musgrove sisters and with her own sisters, Elizabeth Elliot and Mary (Elliot) Musgrove. Louisa and Henrietta Musgrove exist primarily to move the plot. Daughters of a large, good-natured family, they allow Austen to explore the distinction between biting sarcasm and wry irony. Together they occupy the position of ingenue: young, marriageable girls whose very marriageability provides their sole interest. In particular, the younger sister, Louisa, illustrates first, the dangers of stubborn assertion of individual will and, second, the delusive nature of will without character. Louisa's headstrong personality causes her to fall and hurt her head in the famous scene on the Cobb at Lyme Regis, then to recover tremulous and timid, the alternative to her former thoughtless self-assertion. Yet the Musgrove girls do exemplify the relationship of sisters: They care more for each other than for any human being; they help each other write the stories of their lives through mutual participation and interest. Each is the other's avid reader. If they lead predictable lives, they nevertheless are motivated by a loyalty and family solidarity completely absent among Anne and her sisters.

Mary and Elizabeth Elliot serve to reveal the barren ground from which Anne must blossom. Aggressively egocentric, they both consider Anne's altruism and moral principles generally incomprehensible, always insignificant. Their presence emphasizes Anne's isolation, apparently intact since the death of her mother fourteen years before the novel begins, when Anne was fourteen. "Lady Elliot had been an excellent woman, sensible and amiable; whose judgment and conduct, if they might be pardoned the youthful infatuation which made her Lady Elliot, had never required indulgence afterwards." Anne, it seems, closely resembles this mother, possessing all the qualities of heart and mind designed to make her "nobody with either father or sister; her word had no weight,"[62] a significant combination for Anne. Quite literally, when the novel opens there is no other with whom she can speak. Although she has a protector and mother surrogate in Lady Russell, even their relationship is limited by Lady Russell's egocentric world perspective. In fact it is this very Lady Russell who earlier, when Anne was nineteen, mistakenly persuaded her to break off her engagement to a young sailor yet to make his fortune. Beginning with this initial breaking of her "word," Anne now finds herself, at the age of twenty-seven, in the position of possessing no words. Finally, her identity has become so effaced that she is deprived even of the word *no*, as those with whom she lives, both Musgroves and Elliots, expect her assistance without also acknowledging her existence. In the early stages of the novel, Anne is in the unique position of being a character who is remarkable because she is metaphorically absent from the world she inhabits.

Whereas Fanny Price's silence was suffused by a timid virginity that made her a potential ingenue, Anne's lends her a special power. Because it is the silence of death, the silence achieved after the bloom of

first youth has died, it is a silence of knowledge rather than of innocence. Anne, unlike Austen's earlier heroines, is on the other side of
love and sexuality; although she will blossom, it will be a renascence
rather than a birth. She is, therefore, able to understand the life her
silence permits her to observe; her perception is trustworthy because it
is based on experience. Unlike Emma, whose fictions were marred by
her inability to imagine a life she had not lived, Anne's experience
places her in the odd position of being a writer without tools, without
either the words or the audience for her narrative.

Anne's awakening actually has less to do with her renewed sexuality than with a finding of words, the discovery of a voice she recognizes as her own and with which she can write an autobiography
instead of remaining a living chronicle of the other lives she encounters. Fraught with the dangers usually associated with sexual awakening, Anne's progress is perhaps even more dramatically vital. She
must negotiate the distance between the safety of self-abnegation and
the terrors of self-articulation, and she must do it from within her
community. With this novel, Austen apparently understood the illusory nature of her reformed communities created by shutting her
characters up in her narrator's attic. Madwoman no longer, with
Anne Elliot, Austen acknowledges that "happy endings" are delusive
to the degree that they *are* endings. Allying Anne with a sailor is very
different from marrying Emma to Mr. Knightly and sending them
both to the safe haven of Hartfield or from locating Fanny Price with
Edmund in Mansfield Park. Rather than a self-enclosed fantasy island
represented by a landed manor estate, a species of Cinderella's castle,
Anne is left with the wide world, its vagaries admittedly beyond the
scope of the narrator's manipulation.

Anne develops her voice through a progress from country to city
that mirrors an emotional movement from an understanding of herself as everyone's daughter to a recognition of her ability to guide
herself. This progress is accomplished through three central female
relationships: with Lady Russell, with Mrs. Smith, and with the narrator. By the novel's conclusion, what began as Anne's odyssey also

becomes the narrator's journey toward a creative identity unrealized in the earlier novels. Each of the three female characters functions as a voice with whom Anne must establish a dialogue, a voice she must assimilate, and a voice from which she must distinguish herself. That such distinction will be a struggle for her is made clear by her emphatic definition, early in the novel, as an "attentive listener" (29). She is given the position also occupied by the reader: listener to all the voices surrounding her.[63] Yet Anne is not completely speechless. Her speech is interior, like Emma's; but where Emma tended to speak her fantasies either out loud to herself, to Harriet, or to Frank Churchill, Anne is given a genuine interior monologue. She reflects and meditates rather than fantasizes. As Woolf realized, Austen created in Anne a character engaged in perceiving the world by apprehending its effects on herself. She is a self-acknowledged filter, whose firmly established moral character serves to illuminate the world surrounding her.

Although Anne's character is defined initially by the narrator, in this novel the narrator's own voice is less firmly established. Beginning with a scathing portrait of Sir Walter and Elizabeth Elliot, the narrator wavers among tones of bitter antipathy toward the Elliot family, irony verging on sarcasm toward the Musgroves, and near adulation of Anne. Instead of Austen's usual mode, in which the narrator functions as the bridge between disparate characters, it is Anne's interior monologue which serves to stitch the novel's warring elements into a whole cloth, her own empathy which allows her to be regarded as general intermediary. For example, when Anne visits the Musgroves, her role there is defined for the reader by Anne herself: "How was Anne to set all these matters to right? She could do little more than listen patiently, soften every grievance, and excuse each to the other; give them all hints of forbearance necessary between such near neighbours, and make those hints broadest which were meant for her sister's benefit" (46). Later, after observing Captain Wentworth with the Musgrove sisters, she, rather than the narrator, indicates the possible impropriety of his behavior: "As to Captain

Wentworth's views, she deemed it of more consequence that he should know his own mind, early enough not to be endangering the happiness of either sister, or impeaching his own honour" (77). Even more pointedly Anne, and *not* the narrator, is permitted in this novel to understand herself, as is evidenced after she realizes Captain Wentworth may still possess some tender feelings for her: "But neither Charles Hayter's feelings, nor anybody's feelings, could interest her, till she had a little better arranged her own. She was ashamed of herself, quite ashamed of being so nervous, so overcome by such a trifle; and it required a long application of solitude and reflection to recover her" (81).

Some of the narrator's traditional function is thus absorbed by the female protagonist, so that Anne becomes as necessary to the reader as is the narrator. Given only the narrator's perspective on the Elliots, the reader would find the family rendered as little more than stereotyped figures of incompetent egocentricity and Sir Walter reduced to his conceit and vanities: "Vanity was the beginning and the end of Sir Walter Elliot's character; vanity of person and of situation. . . . He considered the blessing of beauty as inferior only to the blessing of a baronetcy, and the Sir Walter Elliot who united these gifts, was the constant object of his warmest respect and devotion" (4). Through Anne, on the other hand, the Elliot characterizations are made more humanly authentic, and Sir Walter, rather than a simple figure of malicious stupidity, becomes a father and husband whose character flaws are also failures of relationship. After hearing her father described as a fool in a letter written by William Elliot, "Anne could not immediately get over the shock and mortification of finding such words applied to her father" (204). Similarly, Elizabeth Elliot is "cold and repulsive" (181), not merely to fill that role in a drawing room comedy, but to the degree that she humiliates and denies the sister she cannot appreciate. Mary Musgrove also gains authenticity through Anne's perspective. Instead of a younger version of Mrs. Bennet, she becomes less characterologically stupid and more maliciously egocentric as she fails to acknowledge Anne's presence in any way other than to make increased demands on her time and attention. Anne almost immediately becomes a collaborator of the novel and, as surrogate for Austen's imagined reader, offers the reader the invitation to expand the world of the text, also to become a cocreator.

Anne's developing autonomy, therefore, is of vital concern to the reader. If the narrator were to marry off and so silence this protagonist, she would also silence the textual voice operating to gain authenticity for the narrative. Austen's concern with realism is significant in this context. Her books were real to her, delineating real people, real places, real situations. To silence Anne at this point in Austen's career would violate an aesthetic tenet as crucial to her as the unconscious conflict leading her to rescue her protagonist by assuming, through her narrator, the dominating voice of her social system. Her alternative, then, was to recognize Anne's collaboration and to allow Anne to develop some understanding of it herself. To do this, Austen needed to give Anne a voice, a perspective of her own, that is possible only because she separates from her mother, from her culture, and finally from the narrator herself.

Loewald emphasizes, in his definition of psychoanalytic repetition, that although a person's life is to a large degree determined by the experiences she or he meets in early childhood, the manner in which these are reexperienced greatly affects the individual sense of self:

Everything depends on . . . to what extent they are repeated passively—suffered again even if "arranged" by the individual that undergoes them—and to what extent they can be taken over in the ego's organizing activity and made over into something new—a re-creation of something old as against a duplication of it. In such re-creation the old is mastered, where mastery does not mean elimination of it but dissolution, and reconstruction out of the elements of destruction. We may thus distinguish between repetition as reproduction and repetition as re-creation, the passive and the active form.[64]

Anne's life, until the opening scenes of *Persuasion*, has been a passive reexperience of her early encounters with her family, in which she was generally dominated and disregarded. Absorbing the identity of a self worthless to others, she tended to re-create the same situation in each new adult encounter.

With her father and sister, for example, she assumed her advice would go unheeded and therefore gave advice which, although well founded, was of a type certain to be ignored. With her sister Mary she assumed she would be devalued and unappreciated and so tended to nurture Mary in a way designed to make her own demands invisible and to heighten Mary's already importunate selfishness. With the large and noisy Musgrove family, she assumed she would be over-looked and so usually chose to play the piano in order to allow the others to dance, suffering the obvious fate of the piano player who is a vehicle to some other pleasure. Even with Lady Russell, whom she knew loved her, she assumed her point of view would go unheard and therefore generally did not bring forward differences in their opinions; was silent about her dislike of Bath, a city Lady Russell relished; and was silent about her sorrow at her broken engagement, an action Lady Russell applauded. Finding her own voice meant, for Anne, that she would re-create actively the situations forming the context of her life. In Loewald's terms, a passive acceptance of a fate somehow outside herself had to be transformed into an active partici-pation in a life she perhaps could not control but for which she could bear some responsibility.

For Anne to accomplish this transformation, Austen also had to transform her narrator by infusing the sense of choice and self-control into a narrative voice previously experienced by her characters and by her reader as an overwhelming domination, the converse of the sub-mission she demanded from her characters. The narrator, too, would need to re-create actively the relationship she shared with the textual world in order to allow Anne and the reader to infuse what had become a bitterly sarcastic perspective with the sense of free play necessary for the growth of an empathic apprehension of her culture. Just as Anne was Austen's creation, so the narrator, in this novel, becomes Anne's creature—benefiting from the autonomous perspective Austen was forced to bestow on Anne in order to maintain authenticity in her narrative.

Paradoxically, in granting Anne autonomy, the narrator, along with Anne, gains respite from the burden of self-consciousness isolating them both from the wider community. In the early stages of the novel, Anne's primary emotion is an autumnal sadness, a feeling based on a sense of alienation from her environment. The narrator's early sarcasm about the Elliots is the tangential emotional mode to Anne's sadness and is also engendered out of emotional isolation. Yet the concluding fates of the minor characters indicate that with Anne's self-discovered voice, the narrator also discovered an empathy unexperienced in Austen's earlier novels. The Elliots, for example, are neither banished nor rejected; instead they are relegated to lives naturally lived by people of their character: "They [Sir Walter and Elizabeth] had their great cousins, to be sure, to resort to for comfort; but they must long feel that to flatter and follow others without being flattered and followed in turn, is but a state of half-enjoyment (251). Mary Musgrove is permitted to console herself with the knowledge that "Anne had no Uppercross Hall before her, no landed estate, no headship of a family; and if they could but keep Captain Wentworth from being made a baronet she would not change situations with Anne" (250). Even William Elliot, the proper villain of *Persuasion*, suffers an exceptionally gentle conclusion. Failing to win Anne, he settles in London with the strongly implied possibility of marriage to Mrs. Clay, Elizabeth's devious companion. Here the narrator displays a sly irony: William Elliot and Mrs. Clay are perfectly suited to each other, both with characters marked by clever circumspection, their compatibility indicating a "happy" match. These characters, then, are allowed to remain in the world; people of perhaps less moral value than Anne, they are not subjected to the exile practiced on Austen's earlier secondary figures. In *Persuasion*, the world is not reformed so much as acknowledged. Life for Anne will be a process of creative adaptation going beyond Austen's earlier need to feel life possible only within a utopian ideal.

Austen's portrait of Lady Russell coincides with her developing perception of reality as an ambivalent ground. Unlike Austen's earlier surrogate mother figures, Lady Russell is attractive because she is what W. D. Fairbairn has termed a "good-enough" mother,[65] one who provides adequate nurturing, neither overly hostile nor overly solicitous: "She was a woman rather of sound than of quick abilities . . . a benevolent, charitable, good woman, and capable of strong attachments; most correct in her conduct, strict in her notions of decorum, and with manners that were held a standard of good breeding" (16). In addition, she favors Anne above the other members of the Elliot family, and it is this prejudice, immediately established by the narrator, which gains the reader's affection for Lady Russell so that shortly thereafter, when the narrator clarifies Lady Russell's shortcomings, they are easily overlooked. "She had prejudices on the side of ancestry; she had a value for rank and consequence, which blinded her a little to the faults of those who possessed them" (16). That this failing is a central sin in Austen's ethical universe becomes less important for the reader than are Lady Russell's "good intentions." Loving Anne, she desires for Anne only the best she understands her culture to offer—the best, that is, she would accept for herself. The reader who accepts Lady Russell's conception of the "best" is guided by the narrator into the same trap which ensnared Anne: at the age of nineteen, she rejected Frederick Wentworth because Lady Russell could not bear to see her throw herself away on a young man yet to make his fortune when, as a baronet's daughter, she might choose among the nobility. Anne had allowed Lady Russell's world view to misguide her, although the narrator is careful to absolve Anne of the major burden of responsibility for the broken engagement. It was morally correct that Anne, at nineteen, follow the advice of the woman who stood in her mother's emotional place; rather, it is Lady Russell who failed Anne by failing to distinguish her own needs and desires from Anne's separate welfare.

The first step toward independence Anne must take, then, involves understanding the difference between herself and Lady Russell, an understanding she gains by recognizing her own competence. After the scene at Lyme Regis, when Anne's is the only cool head capable of dealing with the aftermath of Louisa Musgrove's disastrous fall, Anne steadily gains an appreciation for her ability to direct the behavior of others and, therefore, to guide herself. Although telling Lady Russell about her renewed romance with Frederick remains a concern until the novel's last chapter, this confrontation scene between the two women, so frequently mentioned, is never written. By the time Anne tells Lady Russell about Frederick, Lady Russell's response is no longer a matter of great anxiety for Anne because she has come to understand her initial misjudgment and her present decision in terms of her own identity. Understanding why she was correct in accepting her mentor's earlier advice, she also understands why now, at the age of twenty-seven, she can pursue her own life without feeling that to do so is a betrayal. Speaking to Frederick, Anne says, "I have been thinking over the past and trying impartially to judge of the right and wrong, I mean with regard to myself; and I must believe that I was right, much as I suffered from it, that I was perfectly right in being guided by the friend whom you will love better than you do now. To me, she was in the place of a parent" (246). Moreover, because Anne recognizes the distinction between her needs and those of her mother, Lady Russell is guided by her. Anne has, by the end of the novel, become the stronger personality; with an irony characteristic of Austen, Lady Russell's character is in a subtle way used against her. Always valuing rank above character, Lady Russell is manipulated toward an implicit recognition of Anne's newly discovered emotional rank and, as has been her style, accedes to the dominant point of view.

But although this emotional manipulation resembles Austen's more devastating earlier ironies, it is far more gentle than exiling Mrs. Norris and Maria Bertram from Mansfield Park to live together and torture each other for the rest of their lives. Anne's domination of Lady

Russell is of the sort practiced inevitably by the more self-conscious over the less self-aware. Her love for Lady Russell remains intact, and because she has gained a comprehension of her own character, she can offer Lady Russell genuine empathy. She can understand Lady Russell because she understands herself. Lady Russell is offered her own world back, because Anne has transformed what might have been a rebellion into a connection. She invites Lady Russell to rejoice in her happiness; she does not attempt to shut Lady Russell out of her life. Lady Russell can respond only by accepting Anne's invitation, coming to appreciate Frederick almost as much as Anne does, although perhaps failing to understand that her new perception is Anne's view of the world rather than her own freely chosen perspective. Finally, Anne, in a sense, becomes Lady Russell's mother—or at least Anne, now able to mother herself, no longer needs Lady Russell's protection against the specter of the bad mother.

In Austen's earlier novels, the bad mother was represented by her procession of wicked "stepmother" characters, such as Mrs. Bennet, Mrs. Ferrars, Lady Catherine de Bourgh, Mrs. Norris, aspects of Emma herself. Unconsciously the bad mother also was located in the narrator's implicit control over the protagonist's life. Functioning as the protagonist's final voice, the narrator represented the text's internalized nightmare. Loosely translated, Austen's unconscious equation implied that if the narrator spoke for the protagonist, she would not speak against her. That her power silenced the protagonist and made of her the narrator's creature was less important, perhaps less terrifying, than permitting such power autonomy in the external world. Austen, therefore, withdrew her protagonists from the world. In her reformed communities, the bad mother could be contained and restrained, controlled by externalization. But for Anne to become a speaking subject, it was necessary that Austen grapple with the bad mother, not in the form of a character easily punished through plot devices, but as embodied by the narrator. With Woolf, I believe that Austen, in the novels she might have written, would have developed this struggle fully; as it stands, *Persuasion* is the book in which she opens her negotiation, specifically through the relationship between Anne and her old school friend, Mrs. Smith.

It is, of course, no coincidence that Mrs. Smith is named, in a sense, after Harriet Smith, *Emma's* passive young friend for whom she created a fictional past and future. The surname of anonymity, Smith conceals both Harriet's illegitimate birth and the suspicious origins of Mrs. Smith's husband. In each case the name signals cultural disharmony, certifying an absence in the dominant social structure, a gap in public authority. As Sir Walter notes with disgust, "A widow Mrs. Smith—and who was her husband? One of the five thousand Mr. Smiths whose names are to be met with everywhere" (150).

But unlike Harriet, Mrs. Smith possesses intelligence, and instead of acting as a docile protégé, she was a nurturing figure for the younger Anne during their joint stay at boarding school. Mrs. Smith is, in fact, motherly; kind, interested, devoted to Anne, concerned for her welfare; in her motherliness, she absorbs the role in Anne's life played by Lady Russell earlier in the novel. By the time Anne begins to visit Mrs. Smith in her unfashionable lodgings in Bath, Lady Russell has vanished as a vital character from the novel. Although the narrator mentions her occasionally and the reader is told Anne participates in social events with her, Lady Russell has no further dialogue with Anne or dramatic scenes which would make her a real presence in Anne's unfolding story. Instead, this position is marked out for Mrs. Smith, and in a particularly intriguing way.

Mrs. Smith cannot walk. She is forced to stay in her rooms at all times other than when she is conveyed by her nurse to the mineral baths for which the city is famous. Yet although her body is imprisoned, her mind is not. "Call it gossip if you will" (147), she explains to Anne. Mrs. Smith employs the best of all possible spies, Nurse Rooke, "A shrewd, intelligent, sensible woman. Hers is a line for seeing human nature; and she has a fund of good sense and observation which, as a companion, make her infinitely superior to the thousands of those who, having only received 'the best education in the world,' know nothing worth attending to" (148). As a visiting nurse, Nurse Rooke has access everywhere, and because she ministers to people weakened in body and spirit, access to their most private secrets as well. Like Anne, she is a very good listener. Together she and Mrs. Smith weave a narrative of Bath, entangling from a variety of separate strands a tale of the city's social underside, and enjoy themselves by comparing the disparities between the city's public and private faces.

Thus Mrs. Smith, who is defined by the narrator as genuinely worthwhile, who clearly loves Anne, is also a specter of the bad-mother imago. Although she loves Anne, she also loves the stories she creates, and as is clear from the way she attempts to manipulate Anne, the younger woman is simply another, although the best loved, of her characters. As I earlier noted, Mrs. Smith is the narrator's surrogate in the text; as the narrator is the internalized voice of the text, so Mrs. Smith is the internal voice of Bath. Both are talking heads, able to participate actively in the world only through their imaginative reconstructions of apparently insipid social circumstances, yet thereby controlling those circumstances by virtue of their narrative act. It is the re-presentation not the reality which permits plot design to emerge; it is the storyteller who directs and makes sense of the action. Both Mrs. Smith and the narrator are motivated by the "best of intentions," concealing their sharp teeth by always directing their bite against those characters who seem to deserve punishment. But they penalize their favorites nevertheless by their close manipulation of the world in which the favorites act and live. Mrs. Smith, for example, is willing to accept and work to accomplish Anne's marriage to the man who financially ruined her own husband, as well as indirectly caused his death, because she believes she can manipulate his power through Anne. Like all of Austen's wicked stepmother figures, she accepts the fundamental rule of double displacement, gaining power to the throne through power over the daughter married to the throne.

Still more important, in addition to representing an internalized bad-mother imago, Mrs. Smith's characterization signals Austen's realization that cultural sanctions are transmitted to daughters by their mothers rather than their fathers, in the sense that an oppressed class within a hierarchical social structure tends to replicate its own subordination. Thus Mrs. Smith as metaphor unifies the internal and external worlds of Austen's novels. As personified narrator, she symbolizes the narrator's internalized creative power; as Anne's final surrogate mother in the text, the story she creates for Anne absorbs dominant social perspectives. It is "right" that Anne marry William Elliot, "right" that Mrs. Smith use all her rhetorical creativity to bring that marriage about, just as ten years earlier it was "right" for Lady Russell to interfere with Anne's engagement to Frederick Wentworth. Mrs. Smith is, therefore, the point of conjunction at which Austen's interpersonal and cultural transference is made visible. For Austen, Mrs. Smith was the device she used to separate from her own mother and from a social structure defining her as a perpetual daughter.

The crucial moment in the development of Anne's relationships with the narrator, Lady Russell, and Mrs. Smith occurs in the last third of the novel when Lady Russell encourages Anne to marry William Elliot, the heir to Kellynch Hall, the man who ruined Mrs. Smith's husband. This would not be merely an appropriate marriage, Lady Russell emphasizes, but would permit Anne to resurrect her dead mother: "I own that to be able to regard you as the future mistress of Kellynch, the future Lady Elliot—to look forward and see you occupying your dear mother's place, succeeding to all her rights, and all her popularity, as well as to all her virtues, would be the highest possible gratification to me" (152).

For Anne, such a temptation is equal in force to Eve's seduction of Adam, but converse in effect. If Anne agrees to the marriage, she reestablishes Eden, making of Kellynch a utopian ideal similar to all of Austen's earlier reformed communities. In addition, she affirms a triple mothering: gratifying Lady Russell, memorializing her own mother, and accepting the narrator and Mrs. Smith as overmothers. In keeping with the earlier books, this decision would result in Anne's silencing. Her life thereafter would be shrouded by the "glass shade" Forster describes as drawn between a married couple and the world,[66] her voice absorbed by her husband, her story told by the narrator.

At this point, Austen signals a radical change in her world view. Not only does Anne reject William Elliot, she does so twice, first to Lady Russell, second to Mrs. Smith; and through Mrs. Smith, she stands against the narrator. Furthermore, within the textual world Lady Russell, Mrs. Smith, and the narrator all seem to offer Anne wise counsel: Frederick apparently is ready to marry Louisa Musgrove; William Elliot is both wealthy and devoted to Anne. "Natural law" seems to encourage the marriage. Anne's trial thus demands that she make an "unnatural" decision, against the mothers, for her own perspective, in her own voice. According to scanty biographical evidence, Austen seems to have made the same choice in her own life, deliberately selecting the unmarried state and a household of women but, significantly, one in which she could continue to use her own voice in her novels. Two letters Austen wrote to her niece Fanny, when the latter was considering marriage to an eminently suitable young man, illustrate her growing independence from cultural assumptions about marriage: "Anything is to be preferred or endured rather than marrying without affection. . . . It is very true that you may never attach another man his equal altogether; but if that other man has the power of attaching you more, he will be in your eyes the more perfect."[67]

In making the decision to reject William Elliot, then, Anne stands against her triumvirate of mothers, as Austen stood against all conventional opinion in choosing a single life. Just as Anne is on trial, so is Austen's contemporary reader, who is asked implicitly to applaud Anne's autonomy. This constitutes a radical shift in narrative address. The reader is asked to resolve the plot by permitting Anne to exercise rather than to submerge her will; unlike Emma Woodhouse, Anne retains the status of a "hero." Like the three mother figures, Austen's contemporary reader— and by extension the modern reader who has entered the text correctly—still clinging to opinions held by the dominant social structure, must now face a character defined by her individual point of view.

It is important here to recall that psychoanalytic identification also functions for the reader who naively but necessarily identifies with a textual character. In Austen's utopian communities, empathy is unavailable. Her narrator, authoritative and commanding, identifies the protagonist as like herself. A correct reading of these novels occurrs when the reader identifies with the protagonist, meshing with the narrator's unconscious need to rescue at the price of denying the protagonist's autonomy. Why should a modern reader, after Freud and the feminist movement, identify with Emma Woodhouse or believe that she could be satisfied with the repression of her creative fancy surely necessary for her "proper" marriage to Mr. Knightley? Why should we now, in the late twentieth century, believe that Fanny Price is rewarded when she marries the man who molded her character toward sacrifice and submission? It is, perhaps, easier to accept Elizabeth Bennet's happiness with Darcy, but only because her marriage removes her from a depriving and rejecting mother. Darcy, like all of Austen's male protagonists, with the possible exception of Henry Tilney, seems curiously asexual, possessing a rigidity which could only be experienced as oppressive by her lively, vibrant heroines.

Marianne Dashwood ultimately stands as the exemplar of Austen's dominating conclusions. The narrator of *Sense and Sensibility* tells us:

Marianne Dashwood was born to an extraordinary fate. She was born to discover the falsehood of her own opinions, and to counteract, by her conduct, her most favourite maxims. She was born to overcome an affection formed so late in life as at seventeen, and with no sentiment superior to strong esteem and lively friendship, voluntarily to give her hand to another!—and *that* other, a man who had suffered no less than herself under the event of a former attachment, whom, two years before, she had considered too old to be married,—and who still sought the constitutional safeguard of a flannel waistcoat.[68]

Although this passage can easily be understood as satiric, Marianne's fate is nonetheless a harsh one. Couched within the passage is the narrator's admission that Marianne, a girl of high-spirited and romantic character, marries a man for whom she possesses "no sentiment superior to strong esteem and lively friendship." Through Marianne, Austen demonstrates her real comprehension of cultural suppression of women. Marianne, whose romantic illusions were the socially sanctioned articulation of a more profound and human desire for freedom of expression, suffers the penalty patriarchal culture imposes on young girls who seek self-definition. When her first lover betrays and abandons her, she "realizes" her error, which she articulates as youthful foolishness. We understand that her culture has directed her to experience the desire for autonomy in a way inevitably punished by degradation. Her reward for new "self-knowledge," then, is marriage to a man twice her age and completely antithetical to her character. Here Austen, *not* her narrator, seems to suggest that female automony is suppressed by transforming "bad" girls into "good" wives.

In *Persuasion,* Austen offers the reader the radically different opportunity to experience an initial identification with Anne and then to separate from her when the narrator, through Mrs. Smith, discovers that Anne will not marry William Elliot and resurrect her mother. This reader is forced to develop some definition of self because Anne's development acts as a model. Losing control of Anne, the narrator also loses control of the reader, who can feel with, rather than for, Anne. Austen has finally separated from her narrator. Many of the narrator's functions in Austen's earlier novels are given to Anne, as when Frederick seems to be equally attached to Louisa and Henrietta Musgrove, and Anne, not the narrator, guides the reader in a crucial plot understanding: "Other opportunities of making her observations could not fail to occur. Anne had soon been in company with all the four together often enough to have an opinion . . . she considered Louisa to be rather the favourite" (82). Later, instead of the narrator describing Captain Benwick, a secondary figure, Anne offers him direct advice, thus outlining his character for the reader: "She ventured to hope he did not always read only poetry . . . that the strong feelings which alone could estimate it truly were the very feelings which ought to taste it but sparingly" (100–101). Anne occupies the still center of this novel, dominating the other characters where earlier the narrator has been domineering: "Anne, attending with all the strength and zeal, and thought, which instinct supplied, to Henrietta, still tried, at intervals, to suggest comfort to the others, tried to quiet Mary, to animate Charles, to assuage the feelings of Captain Wentworth. Both seemed to look to her for directions" (111).

The reader also gradually comes to depend on Anne for direction. When Louisa Musgrove and Captain Benwick become engaged, the surprise of their disparate match is explained by Anne, not the narrator: "Where could have been the attraction? The answer soon presented itself [to Anne]. It had been in the situation. They had been thrown together several weeks; they had been living in the same small family party, and Louisa, just recovering from illness, had been in an interesting state, and Captain Benwick was not inconsolable" (166–167). Anne thus demonstrates an ability (formerly reserved for Austen's narrator) to penetrate the surfaces of reality. Finally, Anne understands even her *own* disguises, indicating she does not need, as the reader now does not, the narrator's assistance toward self-recognition: "She now felt a great inclination to go to the outer door; she wanted to see if it rained. Why was she to suspect herself of another motive? Captain Wentworth must be out of sight. She left her seat, she would go, one half of her should not be always so much wiser than the other half, or always suspecting the other of being worse than it was" (175).

Thus, in the wider social context from which Austen wrote, Anne's progress demonstrates Austen's conscious appreciation of the structures of dominance and subordination she had unconsciously transferred into her earlier work. *Persuasion*, unlike her other books, has a distinctly modern feel to it, a sense of unanswered questions and the ambivalence of a twentieth-century perception of reality. This uncertainty permits the reader to enter a creative collaboration with the

186

narrator and Anne. *Persuasion* can be concluded, "post-novel," in a variety of ways by the reader: tragically—Frederick is killed in the next war; happily—Frederick returns safely from the next war to be reunited with Anne and their fine (and numerous) children; melodramatically—Anne dies in childbirth; or comically, which this reader, given Austen's far superior proclivity, does not dare to imagine. In contrast, there is no possible ending for any of the female protagonists ensnared by the conventional conclusions of the earlier novels other than that they "lived happily ever after." In granting Anne Elliot a voice, Austen moved beyond Emma Woodhouse's creative lies designed to dominate and to end in the merger of writer and reader, toward the construction of a fiction based on dialogue and autonomy.

By allowing Anne to make a marriage marked by uncertainty, Austen signaled a break with patriarchal tradition that was later to be developed more fully by contemporary female writers. Offering her reader a creative collaboration in *Persuasion,* she articulated a female strength traditionally invisible. Many of the domestic activities performed daily by women are described by mental health experts and social critics as "nurturing," "caretaking," and so forth. These terms possess a history of cultural disparagement and are often loosely translated to mean indirect manipulation. In psychoanalyst Jean Baker Miller's view, however, "Another way to describe this activity is to say that women try to use their powers, that is their intellectual and emotional abilities, to empower others, to build other people's strength, resources, effectiveness, and well-being."[69]

Culture and Transference

The ideal described here requires an exquisite balancing act. It presupposes that the fears of merging, of loss of boundaries, on the one hand, and the fears of loneliness and disconnection, on the other, can be balanced. It also presupposes the compatibility of one's contrasting desires for intimacy and for independence.

—Evelyn Keller, *Reflections on Gender and Science*

T RANSFERENCE GUIDES the relationship between the analysand and analyst, as the former perceives the latter through a screen of unconscious conflicts and desires originally experienced with important figures in early childhood. In brief, transference means unconsciously fictionalizing the present according to a narrative created in the past. In addition, this fiction reflects social structures in the wider culture which organize the family unit during any particular historical period. Similarly, writers imagine, consciously and unconsciously, readers for their work. The consciously addressed reader functions as the figure to whom the writer directs narrative material, whereas the reader imagined unconsciously—the transference imago—affects narrative structures in the same way the analysand "acts out" the transference. In a literary work, the writer's unconsciously imagined reader particularly affects such textual elements as style, genre, narrative design, language, and point of view. Also, just as the analysand transfers attitudes, the writer unconsciously encodes larger social patterns into his or her address to the imagined reader. Just as the analyst detects repressed material by discerning breaks in the coherence of the analysand's narrative, so the writer's unconsciously imagined reader is visible at points of narrative fracture. The four writers in this book diversely represent such disjuncture.

Jean Rhys's unconsciously imagined reader can be discerned through the disjuncture between the content of her novels and her exercise of narrative authority. Her five books are all focused on a victimized female protagonist. Yet the effaced third-person narrator Rhys uses throughout her canon develops a relationship of victimizer to victim, both with this protagonist and with the reader who is encouraged to identify with the protagonist. That is, Rhys's narrator unconsciously addresses Rhys's reader so as to keep the reader in the victim's position and invest the narrator's position with the very authority consciously disparaged in the text.

Ford Madox Ford, though his work is marked by variations in genre, narrative perspective, and content, maintained a fixed connection with his unconsciously imagined reader over a fifty-year writing career. An explicitly forthright and frank narrative address coexists with an implicitly complex and fragmented narrative structure so that the reader who accepts the invitation to exercise authority over the confused text and narrator finds him or herself snared in maze designed to empower the narrator and writer. Ford's work brings out issues of power and authority linked both to gender and to aesthetic production in Western culture.

Because the transference imago originates in very early childhood, stories of authority and submission, dominance and subordination, hierarchy and power are prominent in the narratives analysands deliver to analysts. Accordingly, the position the analysand grants to the analyst—one that is more or less powerful than the analysand himself or herself occupies in the role of narrating subject—effects the strategies through which the narrative is developed. It is in this concern with authority and creative power that the transference phenomenon conforms to issues asserted during the act of composition when the writer confronts, both consciously and unconsciously, questions about his or her authority in the text and over the creative process. As the analysand's transference imago is projected on the analyst, so the writer's unconscious conception of the reader affects the meaning of and aesthetic techniques used in the text.

Nathaniel Hawthorne's *The Blithedale Romance* provides an example of a writer consciously troubled by the nature of narrative, its power to interpret, and therefore necessarily to distort, reality. Through Miles Coverdale, the novel's first-person narrator, Hawthorne observes his own act of fiction, explicitly inviting his consciously addressed reader to do the same. Simultaneously, however, Hawthorne makes Coverdale the content of a larger narrative designed to conceal, both from Hawthorne's unconsciously imagined reader and from Hawthorne himself, the use of narrative to protect the writer from the experience of unmediated memory. Hawthorne's work thus represents the tragedy the transference phenomenon indicates about the patriarchal community: the inevitable and determined repression at the core of desire.

Jane Austen's canon is marked by the presence of an overwhelming and didactic narrator whose comedic world is designed to protect the female protagonist. Yet this narrator accomplishes her goal through "happy endings" which effectively silence and absorb the protagonists' voices, unconsciously reflecting the very eighteenth-century structures of authority and submission the texts attempt to subvert. Closer examination, however, reveals a progressive movement culminating in *Persuasion* that indicates Austen gradually understood this anomaly by becoming more conscious of the reader to whom she directed her work. She was able to grant to her last protagonist an autonomy unavailable in the earlier, more authoritarian books. In particular, the final paragraph of *Persuasion* offers an example of the way narrative can be used to avoid an address that either dominates or submits to the reader: "Anne was tenderness itself, and she had the full worth of it in Captain Wentworth's affection. His profession was all that could ever make her friends wish that tenderness less; the dread of a future war all that could dim her sunshine. She gloried in being a sailor's wife, but she must pay the tax of quick alarm for belonging to that profession which is, if possible, more distinguished in its domestic virtues than in its national importance."

Although emphasizing the "happy ending" of Anne's marriage to Frederick, the paragraph nevertheless internally resists its own facile comforts. This marriage, unlike those concluding Austen's earlier novels, contains danger, "the dread of a future war." Uncertainty therefore is primary, and happiness is clearly a transitional quality extending moment by moment into a future constantly denied by the lack of closure which is the central consequence of Frederick's profession. The reader of this paragraph is invited to understand Anne's conclusion as existing within Anne's ability to create present-time narrative, to make her life happy as she experiences it rather than as it is consonant with traditional, closed structures of happiness. Thus, the reader, like Anne and like the narrator (who in this book is not given narrative power to authorize the pattern necessary for traditional satisfaction), paradoxically gains autonomy by accepting narrative uncertainty. All—narrator, protagonist, and reader—must rely on the creative acts of the other to achieve satisfaction from the conclusion of this novel.

Lillian Smith wrote, "Freud said once that woman is not well acculturated; she is, he stressed, retarded as a civilized person. I think what he mistook for her lack of civilization is woman's lack of *loyalty* to civilization."[1] Freud's definition of transference was affected, to some degree, by this misunderstanding. In developing his theory he did so from an insider's perspective, from inside a culture which invested his gender and his race with authority and power. Thus he failed to imagine and narrate adequately transference between social positions, focusing instead on transference among positions he thought inhabited a cohesive whole. It is the lack of cohesion, the real distinctions among gender, race, and classes in Western culture, on which feminist theorists are now focusing attention.

Naomi Schor, like other feminist literary theorists, asserts that revision of critical and psychoanalytic theory, especially the theories of Jacques Lacan, requires a revalorization of the imaginary—or maternal—mode in contrast to the symbolic, or paternal.[2] Such revision also emphasizes literary structures which lack traditional forms of closure, relying instead on ambiguity, indeterminacy, and transitional (rather than fixed) images and details. Such texts address a reader whose creativity is called upon to complete unfinished, unplotted narratives describing life late in the twentieth century, after the failure of the patriarchal romantic fantasy. These writers, including Grace Paley, Alice Munro, Peter Taylor, Doris Lessing, and others, define this fantasy in their texts as, in content, expressing a nostalgic yearning for idealized emotional and sexual union and, in form, reinforcing the devaluation of the feminine that is necessary to contain the unconscious terror the idea of such union provokes. In the final paragraph of *Persuasion*, Jane Austen also invites the reader she imagined for this novel to examine traditional fantasies of romance, instead offering her real reader the solution embedded in the act of imagining a life responsive to but not restricted by cultural patterns. Keller defines such complex structures as

dynamic autonomy which is a product at least as much of relatedness as it is of delineation: neither is prior. Dynamic autonomy reflects a sense of self (Winnicott calls it the "true self") as both differentiated from and related to others, and a sense of others as subjects with whom one shares enough to allow for a recognition of their independent interests and feelings—in short for a recognition of them as other subjects. . . . This ideal—for most of us only occasionally realized—enables the very real indeterminacy in the distinction between subject and object to function as a resource rather than as a source of confusion and threat. In particular, it permits the use of that indeterminacy in the interests of a clearer perception . . . of the other in his or her own right. Accordingly, it gives rise to a sense of agency in a world of interacting and interpersonal agents with whom and with which one feels an essential kinship, while still recognizing and accepting, their independent integrity.[3]

In what follows, I offer, as transitional conclusion, brief transference readings of work done by Alice Munro and Grace Paley that explore a relationship with the reader founded on collaboration, locating authority within the connection between writer, narrator, and reader as independent subjects whose autonomy is based on mutual relatedness. I selected the two writers because each is an example of a writer in the process of making conscious both cultural and individually transferred needs and desires; each moves, with less or greater speed, toward the ideal of mutual recognition.

Of particular interest in this sort of reading is Alice Munro's short story "Labor Day Dinner," from her collection *The Moons of Jupiter*.[4] Like most of Munro's work, "Labor Day Dinner" is located in contemporary society and has a female protagonist for whom the Western romantic fantasy has failed. Munro's protagonists, like those of Jean Rhys, are women who have sought their autonomous identity in heterosexual love relationships and who have discovered that the submissive behavior demanded by such connections is the reason for their failure.

I have seen her change," Roberta's seventeen-year-old daughter writes in her journal, "from a person I deeply respected into a person on the verge of being a nervous wreck. If this is love I want no part of it. He wants to enslave her and us all and she walks a tightrope trying to keep him from getting mad. She doesn't enjoy anything and if you gave her the choice she would like best to lie down in a dark room with a cloth over her eyes and not see anybody or do anything. This is an intelligent woman who used to believe in freedom. (147)

Despite the hyperbole coloring her adolescent voice, Roberta's daughter accurately summarizes her mother's dilemma. Having left her husband in order to "find" herself, she has discovered the cultural prison into which autonomous women are placed, and placed, moreover, by their own desires. For Roberta, the great irony is that her active exercise of desire has denied her the assertion of subjective will; instead, she finds her desire objectified and her self-identity voided because to desire as a Western female is to become a desirable object.

But unlike Rhys's protagonists, who never recover from what Freud understood at the individual psychological level as a wound to secondary narcissism and what at the cultural level can be understood as sexual oppression, Munro's protagonists seek amelioration by articulating their positions. They consciously scrutinize the distorted relationships which are destroying them, consciously attempt to understand how their exercise of will has become a form of self-abasement and humiliation. For Roberta, as for several female protagonists in this collection, this conscious articulation is a form of what Freud defined as the "repetition compulsion." Insistently reiterating the conditions of their misery, they are lost in a maze of self-condemnation. Ironically, having *once* exercised desire, albeit the negative version experienced as the desire to leave, they locate their current paralysis in a self-willed failure of desire, omitting from conscious scrutiny the cultural mythos suppressing female action.

Roberta comes to define her predicament as a personal failure, which she solves by a further extension of negative desire: "She is polite. She yawns, and there is a private sound to her yawn. This isn't tactics, though she knows indifference is attractive. The real thing is. He can spot an imitation; he can always withstand tactics. She has to go all the way, to where she doesn't care. Then he feels how light and distant she is and his love revives. She has power" (158).

In other words, by willing herself to be desireless, Roberta is able, she thinks, to retrieve the power she possessed when George courted her. In so doing, however, she ignores the motif governing courtship, that of a subject in pursuit of an object, and so, ironically, purchases her authority by furthering her objectification. Munro offers her reader an identification with this protagonist that connects passivity to power, simultaneously valorizing the reading activity as another gesture of passivity, one which brings to the text a lack of active desire that mirrors Roberta's distorted autonomy. The reader joins Roberta in the denial of pleasure that is also the denial of textual (and masculine) authority. If this were the limit of Munro's connection with her reader, her work would take its place among the bleak representations of contemporary culture found in stories of the minimalist school: stories focused on life in a culture so rigidly structured that imagination is devalued, stories the unfinished quality of which merely disguises their sense of being "finished off." Fortunately Munro subverts such a culturally consonant reading by engaging her reader on another level as well.

Like Jane Austen, Munro and other contemporary female writers such as Grace Paley write with didactic purpose. Whereas Austen, writing with the authority of the eighteenth-century omniscient narrative voice, could express herself with a straightforward address to her reader that unconsciously reflected authority structures she intended to subvert, Munro and Paley are fully cognizant of the authority inherent in the narrative act and deliberately seek to engage their readers by subverting narration itself. Their didacticism is couched in images and patterns that generate connections among and between the stories in their collections, so that although their narrators are generally third person, the stories each writer creates somehow escape the narrator's power. Their narrators are, in a sense, deauthorized. Their most significant mode is implication; they imply rather than relate the larger narrations encompassed by the entire volume. In Munro's collection, each story points toward absence, implicitly recognizing cultural suppression of female desire by acknowledging that the story that might be told is culturally unavailable. In "Labor Day Dinner" this second level of engaging the reader, in a creative collaboration, emerges in several ways.

Munro chooses to conclude her story with a scene denying conclusion. Roberta, George (her lover), and Roberta's two daughters are returning to their own farm after the dinner of the story's title. It is late evening; they are physically and emotionally worn; they drive, with a peculiar static quality, back to a reiteration of their apparently endless disharmony. Suddenly,

the big car flashes before them, a huge, dark flash, without lights, seemingly without sound. It comes out of the dark corn and fills the air right in front of them the way a big flat fish will glide into view suddenly in an aquarium tank. It seems to be no more than a yard in front of their headlights. Then it's gone—it has disappeared into the corn on the other side of the road. They drive on . . . they feel as strange, as flattened out and borne aloft, as unconnected with previous and future events as the ghost car was, the black fish. The shaggy branches of the pine trees are moving overhead, and under those branches the moonlight comes clear on the hesitant grass of their new lawn. (159)

In a traditional narrative, Roberta, George, and the girls would certainly die, creating a tragedy that in its consonance with the romantic despair fundamental to Western fantasy, is culturally satisfying and reinforces structures suppressing female activity. (Roberta's despair would thus be cosmically punished though the deaths of her lover and children.) Munro's conclusion, because it resists traditional mythos, invites the reader to focus on the reader's dissatisfaction, which mirrors Roberta's disconnection "with previous and future events." This new narrative, Munro implies, has not yet been imagined; yet it is only through imagination that Roberta can proceed. Like the "hesitant grass," she has a chance now to grow and, although apprehensively and uncertainly, to recuperate herself as a desiring subject creating her own narrative.

Munro has laid the foundation for Roberta's recuperation in a series of images representing the other female characters in the story. In a way, Munro is teaching her reader to grasp her story through a critical interpretation made available by the school of New Criticism. Despite the New Critic's focus on the image and their theoretical valorization of ambiguity, however, they valued most those texts exercising traditional authority over their readers. Insisting on obscurity and denying paraphrase, they became surrogate creators, standing in for writers before whose creative act the reader was expected to submit. Munro's effort, in contrast, extends the use of imagery to offer the reader an autonomy located in ambivalence, to engage the reader in, rather than deny access to, the creative act.

"Labor Day Dinner" contains three other important female characters in addition to Roberta. Two are her daughters, aged twelve and seventeen. As daughters, they are Roberta's extensions into the future, yet through two important images Munro makes clear that they will not recapitulate their mother's cultural position. Neither dresses for the dinner; instead, each costumes herself. The costumes are significant images for Munro. "Angela [the older girl] wears an emerald-green damask with long sun-faded stripes, draped so as to leave one golden shoulder bare. She has cut vine leaves out of the same damask, pasted them on cardboard, and arranged them in her hair" (135). Although Angela's costume seems to be a traditional version of a Greek goddess, it resists the traditional mythos in two ways. First, because it is the costume of a goddess, it implies Angela's active self-creation. Second, it is contrived from a box of old curtains, fabric used to cover a window. The window connotes a space both interior and exterior; it defines a potential space like the neutral area of experience Winnicott describes as permitting that temporary suspension of boundaries between "me" and "not-me" required for all empathic experience. This is "experience that allows for the creative leap between knower and known. It acknowledges the ebb and flow between subject and object as the prerequisite for both love and knowledge."[5]

Eva (the younger girl) also wears a costume put together from curtain material, and hers further emphasizes the potential space both girls inhabit.

Eva is wearing several fragile, yellowed lace curtains draped and bunched up, and held together with pins, ribbons, and nosegays of wild phlox already drooping and scattering. One of the curtains is pinned across her forehead and flows behind her, like a nineteen-twenties bridal veil. She has put her shorts on underneath, in case anybody should glimpse underpants through the veiling. Eva is puritanical, outrageous—an acrobat, a parodist, an optimist, a disturber. Her face, under the pinned veil, is lewdly painted with green eyeshadow and dark lipstick and rouge and mascara. (135)

Eva, then, is veiled, reinforcing the potentiality of her position, while her shorts and garish makeup refute the traditional mythos of both the submissive bride and the mystery of the veil. Behind her veil is another veil, the force and power of her imaginative self-creation, as she employs the "recklessness and valor" (135) of her female childhood to revise the image of female adulthood she parodies.

Munro emphasizes the suspension of boundaries implied by the costumes of the two girls with a second powerful image: Valerie, the woman who hosts the dinner. Valerie functions as an exemplum for Roberta, a woman who has decided not to participate in the romantic fantasy but who nevertheless exudes sexuality, for she has created herself as a desiring subject.

You could never say that Valerie is looking to be courted or admired. She is a tall, flat-chested woman, whose long plain face seems to be crackling with welcome, eager understanding, with humor and intelligence and appreciation. Her hair is thick, gray-black, and curly. This summer she recklessly cut it off, so that all that is left is a curly crewcut, revealing her long, corded neck and the creases at the edge of her cheeks, and her large, flat ears. "I think it makes me look like a goat," she has said. "I like goats. I love their eyes. Wouldn't it be wonderful to have those horizontal pupils. Bizarre!" (138)

Not an object to be possessed, but a subject—specifically a goat, symbol of patriarchal hypersexuality—Valerie parodies traditional mythology even as she denies its authority. Recognizing herself, she recognizes as well her cultural position, authorizing her sexual desire although its object is still unknown.

In an ironic revision of the gothic tradition of using the house—the castle or manor—to represent the suppression of female desire, Munro extends Valerie's self-affirmation to the image of her house, which she has worked on for fifteen years to make of it the expression of her own self-satisfaction. The house is both finished and unfinished. This summer, for example, has seen the addition of "a little brick-walled, brick-paved area that Valerie . . . does not like to call a patio. She says you can't have a patio on a farmhouse. She hasn't decided yet what she does like to call it" (142). Like the image of the absent window implied by the curtain material covering Angela and Eva, Valerie's nonpatio exists in a space both internal and external. Neither a complete room, nor an unconstructed outdoor area, it exists between the house and the garden. It is a space denying enclosure, implying the absence of restriction coupled with the presence of possibility. Having no name, it possesses any name, representing Valerie's creative authority precisely in her refusal to name it, as she herself refuses to be named by cultural conventions. She offers Roberta, and through her Munro's reader, a model of affirmation which deliberately refuses to define the thing it will not name. Were Roberta able to recognize Valerie—a dangerous move because Valerie represents the potential and unknown in contrast to the inherited and secure—Roberta could also recognize herself as potential, the as yet unwritten subject in a narrative she creates, she authorizes, she empowers.

By making conscious through implication the power of potential female action, by insisting on uncertainty, by denying closure, Munro addresses her reader by making the reader uncomfortable in the face of her narrative. Given the insistent affirmation infusing the images of Valerie and of Roberta's two daughters, the reader cannot rest with ease within Roberta's malaise. Her failure becomes less tragically destined and complete, and more transitional. Understood as representing projections of Roberta, the other female characters imply the presence of what in Roberta's character is experienced as absence: the subjective and affirmative assertion of desire. To enter Munro's text, her reader must recognize the creative potential located in the denial of narrative authority. Like Valerie, the reader must resist the easy act of naming which substitutes nostalgia—the valorization of inherited mythos—for personal autonomy. Finally, Munro requests her reader to resist conclusion, to rest instead in the uneasy area of process which, because it *is* process, invites the reader's collaboration in a continually unplotted narrative.

Alice Munro's work can be located loosely within a culture experienced by women who grew to maturity under the influence of traditional patriarchal social forms and discovered, as they entered their forties, that the feminist movement had illuminated cultural structures heretofore invisible. But although Munro's major characters can make visible certain of the ideological elements suppressing them, they remain in despair in the absence of a new narrative. Grace Paley, although also describing female life in contemporary Western culture, has developed a different response in her characters which itself offers her reader an alternative to traditional mythos. Where Munro's work may be described as static transition, Paley's is dynamic, emphasizing the current period as a process of regeneration. Although Paley, like Munro, works with narrative structures denying closure and emphasizing ambiguity, she includes technical changes which explicitly function to deauthorize the narrator and almost demand the reader's collaboration in constructing the textual world. That is, Paley, in contrast to Munro, explicitly defines life as the art of fiction, finding in that conjunction the affirmation of continuous creation.

Paley has published three collections of short stories, each of which functions in some way as a unified text. I chose for critical interpretation her most recent collection, *Later The Same Day*[6] (although, as its title implies, this last group of stories is connected through character and narrative design to both of the earlier books). It is extraordinarily difficult to summarize the plot structures of any of the stories in Paley's work. This difficulty is itself evidence of Paley's emphatic lack of closure. For example, the first story in the collection is titled "Love." Only five pages long, it moves from the interior meditation of an unnamed female narrator; through exterior dialogue, not defined by quotation marks, between the narrator and her husband; back into interior reflection; through a limited third-person perspective; and concludes with a sentence spoken by the narrator's husband.

The plot, then, is not a movement from event to event but a movement among and between narrating perspectives that wander freely in past, present, future, and "fictional" time, the latter as the narrator and her husband create stories to represent their emotional reality. Although "Love" focuses on the female narrative voice, her perspective is one among several, constantly undermined by her own willingness to suspend narrative authority, freely conceding that her "plot" is dialogue. The reader addressed by this story is given no formal place to lodge; the reader, like the narrator, finds a traditionally fixed position made fluid, transformed into the process of recognition. For example, returning home after a brief shopping trip, the narrator describes her encounter with an old friend, more recently a new enemy. Her husband responds: "Well of course, he said. Don't you know? The smile was for Margaret but really you do miss Louise a lot and the kiss was for Louise. We both said, 'Ah!' Then we talked over the way the SALT treaty looked more like a floor than a ceiling, read a poem written by one of his daughters, looked at a TV show telling the destruction of the European textile industry, and then made love" (7). In this short paragraph the reader is located at the conjunction between the fluid conversation and the moment of emotional revelation—"Ah!"—invited both to participate in epiphany and to rest in the mundane events of "real" time that are always the aftermath of illumination, the real life which supports and is supported by revelation. The paragraph enables the reader to participate in art *and* in life.

"Love" is a love story because it describes the way a loving relationship is lived. With its title, it also acts as an implied corrective to cultural fantasies which define love stories as tales of romance. Because "Love" is so unromantic, it permits its reader both to make visible cultural structures that authorize literary traditions of the romantic and to draw an interesting analogy between cultural suppression of women and narrative suppression of the reader. In both suppressions, free use of the imagination to create alternative fictions representing an experiential reality is severely curtailed. In seeking to restore and revalue female imagination, Paley's work offers her reader an opportunity for creative free play, for her text can be unified only with the addition of the reader who will respond to textual strategies that subvert traditional literary patterns; Paley's reader must grapple with the real, rather than the ideal, object.

Although two of Paley's subversive techniques are relatively facile—the absence of quotation marks to separate speaking characters and the use of titles that refer the reader forward and back in the collection—in Paley's work these devices are used as first-level teaching codes for her reader. Paley does not use an experimental technique to defamiliarize the reader; instead, her effort is to give the reader creative confidence which she will, at another textual level, call upon as a resource for a larger, more significant collaboration between reader and writer.

The absence of quotation marks is general throughout her volume. By omitting textual signifiers noting separation, Paley emphasizes fluid boundaries between characters, and that fluidity requires the reader to pay close attention to the text at its simplest level. Who said what becomes a process of reader collaboration, reflecting the collaborative quality of the conversations in which no particular speaker is empowered, where each statement is vital only because it engenders response. With this technique, of course, Paley alludes to the structure of a cooperative female culture existing subversively within the larger patriarchal social order. The fluid conversations reflect Chodorow's work on the psychodynamic development of the female ego; because of gender coincidence, the little girl's ego structures never entirely separate from the mother identification. Thus women find most comfortable relationships that emphasize connection and cooperation, whereas men, whose ego development depends on separation, are generally more at ease in relationships structured to emphasize hierarchy and distance.

If Paley's work merely valorized the feminine against the masculine model, however, it would retain didactic importance but lose psychological significance for the reader, who would be requested to accept another sort of subordinate position, that of the student of an ideology enforced in an old authoritarian way. Such an assertion of feminist ideas would deny its own effort. Instead, Paley undermines ideology by scrutinizing the act of interpretation, which she implies is the act of distorting fiction according to personal and cultural needs and desires: "In this simple way the lifelong past is invented, which, as we know, thickens the present and gives all kinds of advice to the future" (121). That is, "in this simple way," Paley ironically comments on the reader's effort to interpret the text, to make a fiction out of another fiction. Defining the act of reading as an act of fiction making makes visible, and therefore simultaneously undermines as it affirms, both the writer's and the reader's unconscious transference. Given that transference *is* the unconscious act of making fictions, explicitly defining interpretation as fiction denies the content of transference while paradoxically validating its process. Moreover, Paley almost demands that her readers interpret her elusive stories—two of which are titled "The Story Hearer" and "Listening," titles literally directing the reader's activity—but emphasizes that the reader's interpretations must be as fluid as the conversations shared by her characters. In particular, the story titled "Somewhere Else" makes this effort to explore the rigid content of unconscious transference by insisting that it is a distorting lens. At the same time, the story affirms the continuous necessity for the process of fiction by juxtaposing two central images.

Like several of her other stories, "Somewhere Else" is a two-part story, designed so that each section comments on the other. In the first section, twenty-two Americans are touring China. They all are devoted to Chinese culture and politics, all in their forties and fifties, all experiencing the trip as the culmination of a life-long fantasy. Their intention is to love the Chinese people, on whom they have transferred all their aspirations, ideals, and desires for radical change in their own country. Paley, of course, is well aware of the fiction-making process her Americans bring to China, a realization she signals to the reader when the tourists find they have violated a crucial Chinese precept: "We took too many photographs. We had learned how to say hello, goodbye, may I take your photograph? Frequently the people did not wish to be photographed" (47). Taking photographs, as both the Chinese and the Americans understand, is an act of interpretation. The frozen images will be used in a larger process of making political interpretations, just as their memories, frozen internal portraits, will be used to construct the fiction of China they will bring back to America when the trip concludes.

The Chinese tour guide and political counselor accuses the group of taking, without permission, the picture of a "lower middle peasant lugging a two wheel cart full of country produce into the city. A boy had been sleeping on top" (49). According to Paley's American narrator: "Ah, what a picture! China! The heavy cart, the toiling man, the narrow street. . . . In the foreground the photographed man labored—probably bringing early spring vegetables to some distant neighborhood in order to carry back to his commune honey buckets of the city's stinking gold" (49). By juxtaposing the Chinese guide's straightforward language with the narrator's ironically romantic interpretation of the picture, Paley subtly undermines the content of the photograph, implying that the camera lens inevitably distorts because omitted from the photograph is the context of its taking. Where is the photographer? What were his or her intentions when the picture was snapped? What is the nature of the relationship between photographer and subject? The fixed photograph transforms the subject of the picture into an object represented *by* the picture, and in so doing, it denies dialogue. The peasant has become an object of interpretation, an object of fictional transference.

In the second section of the story, however, Paley affirms the process of making fiction, which she here translates into the process of taking photographs. Although unconsciously transferred needs, desires, and conflicts inevitably distort connections between and among human subjects, transference as an emotional metaphor signals the human desire for connection and community. Seeking to enter the world as a human subject, the self uses transference needs to make the world like itself. Ironically, the content of transferred fantasies, like the finished photograph, omits to scrutinize the relationship. Acting on the content of transference inevitably transforms the other into an object to be interpreted according to individually transferred needs. But just as the desire to take the picture of another subject—to transfer fantasies—is the desire for connection, so the process of making fiction, for Paley, becomes the desire—inevitably distorted—to make connection, to return the other to the status of human subject relating to the self as another human subject. In this effort Paley alludes to what Keller has defined as dynamic objectivity, "a form of knowledge that grants to the world around us its independent integrity but does so in a way that remains cognizant of, indeed relies on, our connectivity with that world. In this, dynamic objectivity is not unlike empathy, a form of knowledge of other persons that draws explicitly on the commonality of feelings and experience in order to enrich one's understanding of another in his or her own right."[7]

In the second section of the story, Paley uses the image of a photograph *not* taken to illuminate dynamic objectivity. Joe Larson, one of the group of former tourists, now all returned to America, is on his way to a reunion at which the Chinese photographs will be shown. Joe has been working with a youth group, reclaiming devastated buildings in the South Bronx ghetto. He has also been filming the work—"Maybe just to keep a record" (56). Walking back to the subway, a detail indicating that he is just as much a foreign presence in the South Bronx as he was in China, Joe pauses for one last long pan shot of the building he and his group have spent the day reconstructing. The shot unintentionally takes in "a group of guys on one of the stoops" (57). Joe feels uncomfortable enough about including human subjects in the photograph to move with increased speed toward his subway entrance. Suddenly, he hears a running thud. "A human form flew past me, ripping the musette bag [with the film inside] off my shoulder" (57).

Unable to accept the loss of his film, but perhaps even more unable to leave the area without attempting to explain and apologize, Joe approaches the group of Puerto Rican men to which the thief has retreated. There, he sees the film taken out of the camera, unraveled, and destroyed. At this point, the thieves demonstrate that their action was a political gesture. They return the empty camera. Joe protests: "Here, you take the camera. No, no, said the leader. Take it, I said. No, no—you crazy, man? Listen, take it, use it. We'll come over and help you out. You can make a movie. . . . I shoved the camera into their hands. I walked away fast. And here I am—that's all there is. What do you think?" (57).

Although Joe's final question is delivered to his friends, the former

Chinese tourists, it also functions as a direct address to Paley's reader. "What do you think?" invites her reader to project an interpretation, a photograph, onto an image inviting such projection precisely because Joe's photograph has been destroyed. In its absence, the photograph Joe attempted to take provides the open creative arena for character and reader to converse, to create together a visibly fictional conclusion to Joe's adventure. Juxtaposed to the earlier photograph of the Chinese laborer and coupled with the latter's ironic interpretation by Paley's narrator, Joe's absent photograph affirms the process of fiction making in contrast to the interpreted story. In so doing, the two images affirm the desire for human connection inherent in the transference phenomenon; the interpreted photograph of the Chinese laborer bears witness to the distorted uses fantasy makes of reality, while the absent photograph denies distortion by insisting on dialogue. As with her technical decision to abandon quotation marks, the two images emphasize Paley's determination to collaborate with her reader. Implying that the point of her text is its function as a ground upon which she and her real reader can meet, Paley also implies that such a meeting is possible only when interpretation is understood to close off the process of fiction, a process which, finally, grants to both reader and writer the possibility of empathy, the potential to recognize the other as other because the self, by denying the interpreted photograph, has become visible to itself by making transference conscious.

Notes

INTRODUCTION

1. Sigmund Freud, *Dora: An Analysis of a Case of Hysteria*, Vol. 3 of *The Standard Edition of the Complete Psychological Works of Sigmund Freud*, ed. James Strachey and Alix Strachey (London: Hogarth, 1925), 139.

2. Rachael Blau DuPlessis, *Writing beyond the Ending: Narrative Strategies of Twentieth-Century Women* (Bloomington: Indiana Univ. Press, 1985), 3.

3. Examination of transference issues in the Dora case by psychoanalysts and literary theorists has been extensive. Among the many articles, of particular interest is Stephen Marcus, "Freud and Dora: Story, History, Case History," *Representations: Essays on Literature and Society* (New York: Random House, 1975), 247–311.

4. J. L. Austin, *How to Do Things with Words* (Cambridge, Mass.: Harvard Univ. Press, 1962), 14–15.

5. David Gordon, *Literary Art and the Unconscious* (Baton Rouge: Louisiana State Univ. Press, 1976), xiii, xiv.

6. Sigmund Freud, *The Unconscious*, Vol. 16 of *the Standard Edition* (1925), 161–215.

7. Philip Rieff, *Freud: The Mind of the Moralist* (Chicago: Univ. of Chicago Press, 1959), 38.

8. Annie Reich, "On Counter-Transference," *International Journal of Psychoanalysis* 32 (Spring 1958): 26.

9. Ibid., 25.

10. Warren Poland, "On Empathy in Analytic Practice," *Journal of the Philadelphia Association for Psychoanalysis* 1 (1976): 284.

11. Georges Poulet, "Criticism and Interiority: Discussion," in *The Languages of Criticism and the Sciences of Man: The Structuralist Controversy*, ed. Richard Macksey and Eugenio Donato (Baltimore: Johns Hopkins Univ. Press, 1970), 85.

12. Sigmund Freud, "Two Encyclopedia Articles," in *The Standard Edition* 18:239.

13. Ralph Greenson, "Empathy and Its Vicissitudes," *International Journal of Psychoanalysis* 41 (1970): 418–424.

14. Stanley Olinick, *The Psychotherapeutic Instrument* (New York: Aronson, 1980), 6, 9.

15. Poland, "On Empathy in Analytic Practice," 286.

16. Herman Nunberg, "Character and Neurosis," *International Journal of Psychoanalysis* 37 (1956): 38.

17. Stephen Black, "A Psychoanalytic Theory of the Literary Process," typescript, 1975, 20.

18. Jean Paul Sartre, *What Is Literature?* (New York: Harper & Row, 1965).

19. Olinick, *Psychotherapeutic Instrument*, 54.

20. Sandra M. Gilbert and Susan Gubar, *The Madwoman in the Attic: The Woman Writer and the Nineteenth-Century Literary Imagination* (New Haven, Conn.: Yale Univ. Press, 1979), particularly pt. 1, "Toward a Feminist Poetics," 3–93.

21. Charlotte Brontë, *Jane Eyre* (New York: Norton, 1971), 382–386.

22. W. K. Wimsatt and Monroe Beardsley, "The Intentional Fallacy," in *The Verbal Icon: Studies in the Meaning of Poetry* (Lexington: Univ. of Kentucky Press, 1954), 3–21.

23. E. D. Hirsch, Jr., *Validity in Interpretation* (New Haven, Conn.: Yale Univ. Press, 1967), 8.

24. Ibid., 23.

25. Ibid.

26. Wolfgang Iser, *The Implied Reader: Patterns of Communications in Prose Fiction from Bunyan to Becket* (Princeton, N.J.: Princeton Univ. Press, 1979), 169–170.

27. Jane Tompkins, "An Introduction to Reader-Response Criticism," in *Reader-Response Criticism: From Formalism to Post-Structuralism*, ed. Jane Tompkins (Baltimore: Johns Hopkins Univ. Press, 1980), xv.

28. Norman Holland, *Five Readers Reading* (New Haven, Conn.: Yale Univ. Press, 1975).

29. David Bleich, *Subjective Criticism* (Baltimore: Johns Hopkins Univ. Press, 1978).

30. Gordon, *Literary Art and the Unconscious*, xvi.

31. J. L. Austin, *How to Do Things with Words*, 109.

32. William Stengeman, *The Forms of Autobiography: Episodes in the History of a Literary Genre* (New Haven, Conn.: Yale Univ. Press, 1980), xii.

33. Roy Pascal, *Design and Truth in Autobiography* (Cambridge, Mass.: Harvard Univ. Press, 1960).

34. James Olney, "Autobiography and the Cultural Moment: A Thematic, Historical, and Bibliographical Introduction," in *Autobiography: Essays Theo-*

retical and Critical, ed. James Olney (Princeton, N.J.: Princeton Univ. Press, 1980), 20.

35. Ibid., 22.

36. D. W. Winnicott, *Playing and Reality* (London: Tavistock, 1971), 65.

37. Ibid., 94.

38. Meredith Skura, *The Literary Use of the Psychoanalytic Process* (New Haven, Conn.: Yale Univ. Press, 1981), 63, 64.

39. Ibid., 65.

40. Evelyn Keller, *Reflections on Gender and Science* (New Haven, Conn.: Yale Univ. Press, 1985), 99.

1. JEAN RHYS

1. Mary Mason, "The Other Voice: Autobiographies of Women Writers," in *Autobiography: Essays Theoretical and Critical*, ed. James Olney (Princeton, N.J.: Princeton Univ. Press, 1980), 210.

2. Estelle C. Jelinek, "Introduction," in *Women's Autobiography: Essays in Criticism*, ed. Estelle C. Jelinck, (Bloomington: Indiana Univ. Press, 1980), 210.

3. Diana Athill, "Introduction," Jean Rhys, *Smile Please: An Unfinished Autogiography* (New York: Harper & Row, 1979), 5.

4. Cynthia S. Pomerleau, "The Emergence of Women's Autobiography in England," in *Women's Autobiography*, ed. Jelinek.

5. Jelinek, "Introduction," 37.

6. A. Alvarez, "The Best Living English Novelist," *New York Times Book Review*, 17 March 1974, 6–8.

7. Thomas F. Staley, *Jean Rhys: A Critical Study* (Austin: Univ. of Texas Press, 1979), 1.

8. Jean Rhys, *Quartet* (1929; reprint New York: Harper & Row, 1957), epigraph by R. C. Dunning.

9. Jean Rhys, *After Leaving Mr. Mackenzie* (1930; reprint, Harmondsworth: Penguin, 1971), 37.

10. Jean Rhys, *Good Morning, Midnight* (1938; 1st Perennial Library Edition, New York: Harper & Row, 1982), 33–34, 38.

11. Athill, "Introduction," 3.

12. Rhys, *Smile Please*, 104.

13. Athill, "Introduction," 3.

14. Ibid., 4.

15. Staley, *Jean Rhys*, 35.

16. Rhys, *Smile Please*, 20, 40.

17. Ibid., 20.

18. Ibid., 85, 124–125.

19. Rhys, *Quartet*, 184–185.

20. Rhys, *After Leaving Mr. Mackenzie*, 137.

21. Jean Rhys, *Voyage in the Dark* (1934; reprint, London: Penguin, 1980), 159.

22. Rhys, *Good Morning, Midnight*, 189.

23. Staley, *Jean Rhys*, 37.

24. Rhys, *Quartet* 29, 59.

25. David Plante, *Difficult Women: A Memoir of Three* (New York: Dutton, 1979), 40 (both quotations).

26. Natalie Shainness, *Sweet Suffering: Women as Victim* (New York: Bobbs-Merrill, 1984), 20.

27. Erik Erikson, *Childhood and Society* (New York: Norton, 1950), 247.

28. Plante, *Difficult Women*, 42.

29. Rhys, *Good Morning, Midnight*, 19.

30. Shainness, *Sweet Suffering*, 47–48, 64.

31. Rhys, *After Leaving Mr. Mackenzie*, 44.

32. Staley, *Jean Rhys*, 37.

33. Rhys, *Quartet*, 98.

34. Rhys, *After Leaving Mr. Mackenzie*, 94.

35. Jean Rhys, *Voyage in the Dark*, 35, 140.

36. Rhys, *Good Morning, Midnight*, 72.

37. Staley, *Jean Rhys*, 98.

38. Rhys, *Good Morning, Midnight*, 185.

39. Jean Rhys, *Smile Please*, 140.

40. Rhys, *Good Morning, Midnight*, 184, 190.

41. Shainness, *Sweet Suffering*, 101.

42. See, for example, Dennis Porter, "Of Heroines and Victims: Jean Rhys and *Jane Eyre*," *Massachusetts Review* 17 (Autumn 1976): 540–552.

43. Evelyn Keller, *Reflections on Gender and Science* (New Haven, Conn.: Yale University Press, 1985), 111.

44. Doryann Lebe, "Individuation of Women," *Psychoanalytic Review* 69 (Spring 1982): 65.

45. Nancy Chodrow, *The Reproduction of Mothering: Psychoanalysis and the Sociology of Gender* (Berkeley and Los Angeles: Univ. of California Press, 1978).

46. Ibid., 42.

47. Edward Said, "A Meditation on Beginnings," *Salmagundi* 1 (1978): 44.

48. Jean Rhys, *Wide Sargasso Sea* (1966; reprint, New York: Norton, 1982), 170.

49. Ibid., 20, 23, 22.

50. Ibid., 107.

51. Rhys, *Smile Please*, 133.

52. Rhys, *After Leaving Mr. MacKenzie*, 98.

53. Shainness, *Sweet Suffering*, 159, 41.

2. FORD MADOX FORD'S *THE GOOD SOLDIER* AND THE TIETJENS TETRALOGY

1. Ford Madox Ford, *The Good Soldier* (New York: Knopf, 1951), xviii.

2. Michael Killigrew, "Introduction" to *Memories and Impressions* by Ford Madox Ford (Harmondsworth: Penguin, 1979), 11.

3. Ford Madox Hueffer, "On Impressionism," *Poetry and Drama* 2 (June–December 1914): 323–334.

4. Ibid.

5. Ford wrote, in an essay recalling a conversation he held with Thomas Hardy just after he had submitted his first manuscript to a publishing house, that in talking to Hardy, "I made the discovery that I—but tremendously!—wished that the book should succeed," in *Memories and Impressions*, 93.

6. Ford Madox Ford, *Parade's End* (New York: Random House, 1979), 629. Originally published as *Some Do Not* (London: Seltzer, 1924); *No More Parades* (London: Boni, 1925); *A Man Could Stand Up* (London: Boni, 1926) and *The Last Post* (London: Boni, 1928).

7. In addition to Ford's affirmation of the value of privacy, the motif appears thematically in his novels—particularly *The Good Soldier* and *Parade's End*, where privacy is considered synonymous with good breeding—Arthur Mizener documents Ford's horror at the publicity Ford's wife Elsie sought during their divorce proceedings. See *The Saddest Story: A Biography of Ford Madox Ford* (New York: World Publishing, 1971).

8. Hueffer, "On Impressionism," 328.

9. Charles Brenner, *An Elementary Textbook of Psychoanalysis* (New York: International Universities Press, 1955), 105.

10. Ibid., 113, 112.

11. Evelyn Keller, *Reflections on Gender and Science* (New Haven, Conn.: Yale University Press, 1985), 109.

12. Ibid., particularly pt. 2, "The Inner World of Subjects and Objects," 67–127.

13. Sondra Stang, *Ford Madox Ford* (New York: Unger, 1977), 6.

14. Ford Madox Ford, "Collaborating with Conrad," *Memories and Impressions*, 260.

15. Ford Madox Ford, *Between St. Dennis and St. George* (London: Hodder & Stoughton, 1915), 7.

16. Ford, "Collaborating with Conrad," 261.

17. Fred Chappelle, "The Storytellers," *I Am One of You Forever* (Baton Rouge: Louisiana State Univ. Press, 1985), 98.

18. Ford, "Collaborating with Conrad," 261.

19. Mizener, *Saddest Story*, 341–342.

20. Ford, "Collaborating with Conrad," 261.

21. Joseph Conrad, "Preface," *The Nigger of the 'Narcissus,'* 1897.

22. Stang, *Ford Madox Ford*, 6.

23. Ford Madox Ford, "The King of Hearts," *Memories and Impressions*, 99, 38, 40.

24. Ford, *Parade's End*, 231.

25. Olive Garnett, quoted in Thomas Moser, *Ford Madox Ford: The Life in the Fiction* (Princeton, N.J.: Princeton Univ. Press, 1980), 35.

26. Stephen Crane, quoted in ibid.

27. W. Ronald D. Fairbairn, *An Object Relations Theory of the Personality* (New York: Basic Books, 1954), 88.

28. Ford Madox Ford, "Mixing Up Names," *Memories and Impressions*, 60.

29. Stang, *Ford Madox Ford*, 41. Nine of the thirty-one novels Ford considered historical; he did not include *Parade's End* in that group.

30. Brenner, *Elementary Textbook of Psychoanalysis*, 204.

31. Ford Madox Ford, "My Father," *Memories and Impressions*, 66.

32. Ibid., 61–62.

33. Ibid., 40.

34. Ibid., 69, 67.

35. Ibid., 63.

36. Ibid., 66–67.

37. Moser, *Ford Madox Ford: The Life*, 24.

38. Ford Madox Ford, *The Good Soldier* (New York: Vintage, 1955), 225.

39. Denis de Rougemont, *Love in the Western World* (New York: Pantheon, 1956), 15.

40. Ford Madox Ford, "The Writer to His Children," *Memories and Impressions*, 28.

41. Keller, *Reflections on Gender and Science*, 111.

42. Susan Lanser, *The Narrative Act: Point of View in Prose Fiction* (Princeton, N.J.: Princeton Univ. Press, 1981), 78.

43. Ford, *Good Soldier* (1955), 12, 3.

44. Ford Madox Ford, *Joseph Conrad: A Personal Remembrance* (London: Duckworth, 1924), 204–208.

45. Ford, *Good Soldier* (1955), 3.

46. Mark Schorer, "An Interpretation," *The Good Soldier*, v–xv.

47. See the summary of the critical debate on the novel by Lawrence Thornton, "Escaping the Impasse: Criticism and the Mitosis of *The Good Soldier*," *Modern Fiction Studies* 21 (1975): 237.

48. Ford, *Good Soldier* (1955), 236–237.

49. Ibid., 245, 253, 256.

50. Stella Bowen, *Drawn from Life* (London: Collier, 1940), 62.

51. Stang, *Ford Madox Ford*, 93.

52. Hueffer, "On Impressionism," 325.

53. Stang, *Ford Madox Ford*, 108.

54. Ibid., 44.

55. A crucial scene in the first volume of the tetralogy, *Some Do Not . . . ,* couples Sylvia Tietjens with the black magic practiced in German legends of the Black Forest.

56. Ford, *Parade's End*, 187.

3. NATHANIEL HAWTHORNE'S *THE BLITHEDALE ROMANCE*

1. Frank Kermode, "Secrets and Narrative Sequence," *Essays on Fiction* (London: Routledge & Kegan Paul, 1983), 136.

2. Evelyn Keller, *Reflections on Gender and Science* (New Haven, Conn.: Yale Univ. Press, 1985), 106.

3. Among the many such critics Irving Howe, Frederick Crews, and Philip Rahv.

4. Frederick Crews, "Turning the Affair into a Ballad: *The Blithedale Romance*," in *Nathaniel Hawthorne: A Collection of Criticism*, ed. J. Donald Crowley (New York: McGraw–Hill, 1975), 88–89.

5. Nathaniel Hawthorne, *The Blithedale Romance* (1852; reprinted New York: Norton, 1978), 196. All quotations from this edition.

6. Crews, "Turning the Affair into a Ballad," 89.

7. Kermode, "Secrets and Narrative Sequence," 136.

8. Crews, "Turning the Affair into a Ballad," 88.

9. Irving Howe, "Hawthorne: Pastoral and Politics," in *The Blithedale Romance,* eds. Seymour Gross and Rosalie Murphy (New York: Norton, 1978), 295.

10. Sigmund Freud, "Recommendations to Physicians Practicing Psychoanalysis," in *The Standard Edition of the Complete Psychological Works of Sigmund Freud,* ed. James Strachey and Alix Strachey (London: Hogarth, 1958), 12:118.

11. Keller, *Reflections on Gender and Science,* 111.

12. Howe, "Hawthorne," 293.

13. Ford Madox Ford, *The Good Soldier* (New York: Knopf, 1951), 238.

14. Howe, "Hawthorne," 296.

15. Coverdale rather slyly notes, "Being the woman that she was, could Zenobia have foreseen all these ugly circumstances of death, how ill it became her, the altogether unseemly aspect which she must put on, and especially, old Silas Foster's efforts to improve the matter, she would no more have committed the dreadful act, than have exhibited herself to a public assembly in a badly-fitting garment" (218).

16. Crews, "Turning the Affair into a Ballad," 92.

17. Sigmund Freud, "Family Romances," in *The Sexual Enlightenment of Children,* ed. Philip Rieff (New York: Macmillan, Collier Books, 1974), 41–45.

18. Howe, "Hawthorne," 288–297.

19. J. Donald Crowley, "Introduction," Hawthorne, *Blithedale Romance,* 6–7.

20. Otto Fenichel, *The Psychoanalytic Theory of Neurosis* (New York: Norton, 1945), 71.

21. James Olney, "Autobiography and the Cultural Moment," in *Autobiography: Essays Theoretical and Critical,* ed. James Olney (Princeton, N.J.: Princeton Univ. Press, 1980), 4.

22. Ibid., 6.

23. Roy Pascal, *Design and Truth in Authobiography* (Cambridge, Mass.: Harvard Univ. Press, 1960).

24. Georgiana Bruce Kirby, *Years of Experience: An Autobiographical Narrative* (1887; reprint, New York: AMS Press, 1971), 173.

25. Nathaniel Hawthorne, *The Scarlet Letter* (New York: W. W. Norton, 1962), 183.

26. Nathaniel Hawthorne, "Preface," *Twice-Told Tales* (New York: Lancer Books, 1968), 9.

27. Hawthorne, *Twice-Told Tales,* 586.

4. JANE AUSTIN

1. Ian Watt, "Introduction," *Jane Austen: A Collection of Critical Essays*, ed. Ian Watt (Englewood Cliffs, N.J.: Prentice-Hall, 1963), 4.

2. See, among other psychoanalysts who have considered the issue, Stanley Olinick, *The Psychotherapeutic Instrument* (New York: Aronson, 1980), and Annie Reich, "On Counter-Transference," *International Journal of Psychoanalysis* 32 (Spring 1958): 25–31.

3. Jane Austen, *Pride and Prejudice* (1813; reprinted London: Oxford Univ. Press, 1932), 79, 3.

4. In a letter to George Henry Lewes, 1848, Brontë described Austen as "shrewd and observant, without 'sentiment,' without poetry . . . (more real than true) . . . she cannot be great" (Quoted in Watt, "Introduction," 4.

5. D. H. Lawrence, "A Propos of Lady Chatterley's Lover," *A Selection from Phoenix* (Harmondsworth: Penguin, 1930), 359.

6. Virginia Woolf, "Jane Austin," *The Common Reader* (New York: Harcourt Brace, 1925); reprinted in Watt, *Jane Austen*, 15.

7. Austen, *Pride and Prejudice*, 120, 121.

8. Ibid., 207, 268, 279, 366.

9. Sandra M. Gilbert and Susan Gubar, *The Madwoman in the Attic: The Woman Writer and the Nineteenth-Century Literary Imagination* (New Haven, Conn.: Yale Univ. Press, 1979), 146–187.

10. William Austen-Leigh and Richard Arthur Austen-Leigh, *Jane Austen: Her Life and Letters, A Family Record* (New York: Russell & Russell, 1965), 241.

11. Gilbert and Gubar, *Madwoman in the Attic*, 146–187.

12. Quoted by Virginia Woolf in "Jane Austen," 16.

13. Philip Roth, *The Ghostwriter* (New York: Ballantine, 1979).

14. Rachael Blau DuPlessis, *Writing beyond the Ending: Narrative Strategies of Twentieth-Century Women* (Bloomington: Indiana Univ. Press, 1985), 3.

15. Jane Austen, "Outline for Plan of a Novel," in Austen-Leigh and Austin-Leigh, *Jane Austen: Her Life*, 338–339.

16. Lionel Trilling, "Introduction" to *Emma* (Boston: Houghton Mifflin, 1957), xv.

17. Jane Austen, *Emma* (1816; reprinted London: Oxford Univ. Press, 1933), 85.

18. Austen-Leigh and Austen-Leigh, *Jane Austen: Her Life*, 351.

19. D. W. Harding, "Regulated Hatred: An Aspect of the Work of Jane Austen," reprinted in Watt, *Jane Austen*, 166–179.

20. D. W. Winnicott, *Playing and Reality* (London: Tavistock, 1971), 51.

21. Jane Austen, *Persuasion* (1818; reprinted London: Oxford Univ. Press, 1933), 251.

22. Jane Austen, *Sense and Sensibility* (1811; reprinted London: Oxford Univ. Press, 1933), 315.

23. Jane Austen, *Northanger Abbey* (1818; reprinted London: Oxford Univ. Press, 1933), 13.

24. Jane Austen, *Pride and Prejudice*, 358.

25. Jane Austen, *Northanger Abbey*, 252.

26. Jane Austen, *Pride and Prejudice*, 385.

27. Jane Austen, *Persuasion*, 51. 68, 199, 208.

28. Sigmund Freud, *Dora: An Analysis of a Case of Hysteria* (New York: Macmillan, 1963).

29. Jane Austen, *Mansfield Park* (1814; reprinted London: Oxford Univ. Press, 1934), 461.

30. Nancy Chodorow, *The Reproduction of Mothering: Psychoanalysis and the Sociology of Gender* (Berkeley and Los Angeles: Univ. of California Press, 1978), 73.

31. Jane Austen, *Pride and Prejudice*, 29.

32. In a letter addressed to Cassandra, dated November 6, 1813, Austen wrote, ironically, "By-the-bye, as I must leave off being young, I find many douceurs in being a sort of chaperon, for I am put on the sofa near the fire, and can drink as much wine as I like." Quoted by Austen-Leigh and Austen-Leigh, *Jane Austen: Her Life*, 288.

33. Winnicott, *Playing and Reality*, 1–26.

34. Austen-Leigh and Austen-Leigh, *Jane Austen: Her Life*, 235.

35. In a letter dated May or June 1814, Austen wrote her niece Anna: "I do not like a lover speaking in the 3rd person; it is too much like the formal part of Lord Orville, and, I think, is not natural." Quoted by Austen-Leigh and Austen-Leigh, *Jane Austen: Her Life*, 354. In a subsequent letter to Anna, commenting on the same manuscript, Austen wrote, "For, though I find your papa did walk out immediately after *his* arm was set, I think it can be so little usual as to appear unnatural in a book" (355), adding in a subsequent letter, "You will be in danger of giving false representations" (356).

36. Ibid., 354.

37. Prominently noted by Harding, "Regulated Hatred," 177.

38. Jane Austen, *Mansfield Park*, 24, 8, 254.

39. Lionel Trilling, "Mansfield Park," in Watt, *Jane Austen*, 128–129.

40. Kingsley Amis, "What Became of Jane Austen?" in ibid., 142.

41. Jane Austen, *Mansfield Park*, 344.

42. Austen-Leigh and Austen-Leigh, *Jane Austen: Her Life*, 296, 303.

43. Trilling, "Introduction," *Emma*, xv.

44. Ibid.

45. Olinick, *Psychotherapeutic Instrument*, 75.

46. Jane Austen, *Emma*, 31.

47. Ibid., 54.

48. DuPlessis, *Writing beyond the Ending*, 7, 484.

49. Doryann Lebe, "Individuation of Women," *Psychoanalytic Review* 69 (Spring 1982): 65–66; Chodorow, *Reproduction of Mothering*.

50. Winnicott, *Playing and Reality*, 51.

51. Jane Austen, *Persuasion*, 278.

52. Alice Munro, *The Moons of Jupiter* (Harmondsworth: Penguin, 1977), 82.

53. Virginia Woolf, *The Voyage Out* (1915; reprinted New York: Harcourt & Jovanovich, 1920), 62. Mrs. Dalloway, a minor character affirmatively placed in the narrative structure, reads *Persuasion* to her husband.

54. Virginia Woolf, "Jane Austen," in Watt, *Jane Austen*, 15–25.

55. Hans Loewald, *Papers on Psychoanalysis* (New Haven, Conn.: Yale Univ. Press, 1980), 68.

56. In a letter to her brother Edward, dated December 16, 1816, Austen wrote, "How could I possibly join them on the little bit (two inches wide) of ivory on which I work with so fine a brush, as produces little effect after much labour?" Quoted by Austen-Leigh and Austen-Leigh, *Jane Austen: Her Life*, 378.

57. Estelle C. Jelinek, "Introduction," in *Women's Autobiographies: Essays in Criticism*, ed. Estelle C. Jelinek (Bloomington: Indiana Univ. Press, 1980), 17.

58. Gilbert and Gubar, *Madwoman in the Attic*, 146.

59. For example, according to material collected by Austen-Leigh and Austen-Leigh, the Austen family included among its members Eliza Hancock, who married the Comte de Feuillide, subsequently guillotined during the Reign of Terror. Austen would have been made indirectly aware of news coming from France by the comtesse, who was living in England at the time of her husband's death.

60. Jane Austen, *Mansfield Park*, 461.

61. Jane Austen, *Emma*, 484.

62. Jane Austen, *Persuasion*, 10, 11.

63. At various moments in the novel, Anne is so placed to overhear conversations by each of the other characters; the primary example of this motif occurs when Anne, seated in a concealing hedgerow, overhears a conversation about herself spoken by Frederick Wentworth and Louisa Musgrove (84–86).

64. Loewald, *Papers on Psychoanalysis*, 69–90.

65. W. Ronald D. Fairbairn, *An Object-Relations Theory of the Personality* (New York: Basic Books, 1954), 88.

66. E. M. Forster, *Howard's End* (New York: Vintage, 1921), 258.

67. Austen-Leigh and Austen-Leigh relate Austen family anecdotes to the effect that Austen received two or three proposals of marriage, finally accepting and then quickly rejecting one received when she and her sister were visiting their brother James in 1802. *Jane Austen: Her Life*, 84–95. Austen's shadowy romances are also discussed by most of her biographers, including, most recently, John Halperin, *The Life of Jane Austen* (Baltimore: Johns Hopkins Univ. Press, 1984).

68. Jane Austen, *Sense and Sensibility*, 378.

69. Jean Baker Miller, *Toward a New Psychology of Women* (Boston: Beacon, 1986), xx.

CONCLUSION

1. Lillian Smith, *The Winner Names the Age: A Collection of Writings* (New York: Norton, 1978), 191.

2. Naomi Schor, *Breaking the Chain: Women, Theory, and French Fiction* (New York: Columbia Univ. Press, 1985), 149–185.

3. Evelyn Keller, *Reflections on Gender and Science* (New Haven, Conn.: Yale Univ. Press, 1985), 111.

4. Alice Munro, *The Moons of Jupiter* (London: Penguin, 1984) 134.

5. Keller, *Reflections on Gender and Science*, 99.

6. Grace Paley, *Later the Same Day* (New York: Farrar, Straus & Giroux, 1985).

7. Keller, *Reflections on Gender and Science*, 117.

Select Bibliography

Austin, J. L. *How to Do Things with Words*. Cambridge, Mass.: Harvard Univ. Press, 1962.

Black, Stephen. "A Psychoanalytic Theory of the Literary Process." Typescript. 1970.

Bleich, David. *Subjective Criticism*. Baltimore: Johns Hopkins Univ. Press, 1978.

Bolesky, Dale. "Resistance and Character Theory: A Reconsideration of the Concept of Character Resistance." *Journal of the American Psychoanalytic Association* 31, supplement (1983).

Brenner, Charles. *An Elementary Textbook of Psychoanalysis*. Rev. ed. New York: Doubleday, 1974.

Brontë, Charlotte. *Jane Eyre*. New York: Norton, 1971.

Chodorow, Nancy. *The Reproduction of Mothering: Psychoanalysis and the Sociology of Gender*. Berkeley and Los Angeles: Univ. of California Press, 1978.

Erikson, Erik. *Childhood and Society*. New York: Norton, 1950.

Freud, Sigmund. *Dora: An Analysis of a Case of Hysteria*. Vol. 3, *The Standard Edition of the Complete Psychological Works of Sigmund Freud*, ed. James Strachey and Alix Strachey. London: Hogarth, 1925.

———. "Two Encyclopedia Articles." In Vol. 18, *The Standard Edition*. 1923, 192y.

———. *The Unconscious*. Vol. 16, *The Standard Edition*. 1925.

Gilbert, Sandra M., and Susan Gubar. *The Madwoman in the Attic: The Woman Writer and the Nineteenth-Century Literary Imagination*. New Haven, Conn.: Yale Univ. Press, 1979.

Gordon, David. *Literary Art and the Unconscious*. Baton Rouge: Louisiana State Univ. Press, 1976.

Greenson, Ralph. "Empathy and Its Vicissitudes." *International Journal of Psychoanalysis* 41 (1970).

Hirsch, E. D., Jr. *Validity in Interpretation*. New Haven, Conn.: Yale Univ. Press, 1967.

Holland, Norman. *Five Readers Reading*. New Haven, Conn.: Yale Univ. Press, 1975.

Iser, Wolfgang. *The Implied Reader: Patterns of Communication in Prose Fiction from Bunyan to Becket*. Princeton, N.J.: Princeton Univ. Press, 1979.

James, Henry. *Hawthorne.* Ithaca, N.Y.: Cornell Univ. Press, 1956.

Jelinek, Estelle, C., ed. *Women's Autobiography: Essays in Criticism.* Blooming-ton: Indiana Univ. Press, 1980.

Keller, Evelyn. *Reflections on Gender and Science.* New Haven, Conn.: Yale Univ. Press, 1985.

Kirby, Georgiana Bruce. *Years of Experience: An Autobiographical Narrative.* 1887. Reprint. New York: AMS Press, 1971.

Lichtenstein, Heinz. *The Dilemma of Human Identity.* New York: Aronson, 1977.

Loewald, Hans. *Papers on Psychoanalysis.* New Haven, Conn.: Yale Univ. Press, 1980.

Miller, Jean Baker. *Toward a New Psychology of Women.* Boston: Beacon, 1986.

Nunberg, Herman. "Character and Neurosis." *International Journal of Psycho-analysis* 37 (1956).

Olinick, Stanley. *The Psychotherapeutic Instrument.* New York: Aronson, 1980.

Olney, James, ed. *Autobiography: Essays Theoretical and Critical.* Princeton, N.J.: Princeton Univ. Press, 1980.

Pascal, Roy. *Design and Truth in Autobiography.* Cambridge, Mass.: Harvard Univ. Press, 1960.

Plante, David. *Difficult Women: A Memoir of Three.* New York: Dutton, 1979.

Poland, Warren. "On Empathy in Analytic Practice." *Journal of the Philadelphia Association for Psychoanalysis* 1 (1976).

Poulet, Georges. "Criticism and Interiority: Discussion." In *The Languages of Criticism and the Sciences of Man: The Structuralist Controversy,* ed. Richard Macksey and Eugenio Donato. Baltimore: Johns Hopkins Univ. Press, 1970.

Reich, Annie. "On Counter-Transference." *International Journal of Psychoanaly-sis* 32 (Spring 1958).

Rhys, Jean. *Smile Please.* New York: Harper & Row, 1979.

Rieff, Philip. *Freud: The Mind of the Moralist.* Chicago: Univ. of Chicago Press, 1959.

Sartre, Jean Paul. *What Is Literature?* New York: Harper & Row, 1965.

Shainness, Natalie. *Sweet Suffering: Woman as Victim.* New York: Bobbs-Merrill, 1984.

Skura, Meredith. *The Literary Use of the Psychoanalytic Process.* New Haven, Conn.: Yale Univ. Press, 1981.

Staley, Thomas F.. *Jean Rhys: A Critical Study.* Austin: Univ. of Texas Press, 1979.

Stang, Sondra. *Ford Madox Ford.* New York: Unger 1977.

Stengeman, William. *The Forms of Autobiography: Episodes in the History of a Literary Genre.* New Haven, Conn.: Yale Univ. Press, 1980.

Tompkins, Jane, ed. *Reader-Response Criticism: From Formalism to Post-Structuralism.* Baltimore: Johns Hopkins Univ. Press, 1980.

Wimsatt, W. K., and Monroe Beardsley. *The Verbal Icon: Studies in the Meaning of Poetry.* Lexington: Univ. of Kentucky Press, 1954.

Winnicott, D. W. *Playing and Reality.* London: Tavistock, 1971.

———. *Through Paediatrics to Psycho-Analysis.* New York: Basic Books, 1975.

Withim, Philip. "The Psychodynamics of Literature." *Psychoanalytic Review* 56 (1970).

Wollheim, Richard. *Sigmund Freud.* Cambridge: Cambrige Univ. Press, 1971.

Index